"This book offers a thoroughly researched, field-tested approach to design for sustainability in grassroots maker enterprises. With its practical framework, design examples and focus on renewable materials, it challenges our current unsustainable trajectory of unbridled growth and waste. It is an important, eminently useful and much-needed contribution to the field."

—*Stuart Walker, Chair of Design for Sustainability, Lancaster University, UK and author of Design Realities: creativity, nature and the human spirit*

"This book provides useful insight into sustainable product design practice especially for developing economies. It advocates for a sustainable design system that balances social, economic and cultural factors in production to consumption systems. The recommendations in the book by Dr Reubens, are backed by research and several years of experience in creating quality bamboo products which are sustainable."

—*Lilac Osanjo, Director, School of The Arts and Design, University of Nairobi, Kenya*

"Design practitioner Rebecca Reubens succeeds in bringing systematic design to crafts people that employ renewable, abundant materials. Her reflections in this book result in a practical framework for holistic sustainability to protect the environment and grow the economy, and also sustain and nurture the culture, skills and communities of craftsmen. Its application paves the way to craft out of poverty, with valuable and sought-after products, that sustain the planet and the culture and traditions of its people."

—*René Van Berkel, PhD, United Nations Industrial Development Organization (UNIDO), Project Manager Greening Handicrafts Value Chains in Vietnam*

"The design fraternity talks a lot about design for inclusive sustainability, however, this is rarely put into real practice. Rebecca's tremendous work creates a truly inclusive approach for design for sustainability, by including cultural elements next to the ecological, economical and social. Her book and approach offer a new way of design thinking, and simultaneously a very hands-on approach to apply holistic sustainable design in daily design practice. This is definitely the way forward to walk the talk and tackle the wide range of the societal challenges we encounter nowadays!"

—*Jan Carel Diehl, Associate Professor, Design for Sustainability at the Faculty of Industrial Design Engineering, Delft University of Technology, Netherlands*

T0382833

"The book is an insightful outcome of an exciting interplay between research and practice. Insights that can only emerge from someone who has deeply engaged with issues of sustainability both practically and critically. In challenging the typically narrow perspectives on sustainability, the work has much to offer to both practitioners and researchers interested in social enterprises and sustainability. The shout out for recognizing the critical role for craftspeople and indigenous knowledge in challenging complex problems is a call that needs to be heard across disciplines."

—*Ankur Sarin, Assistant Professor in the Public Systems Group and Ravi J Mathai Center for Innovation in Education at the Indian Institute of Management, Ahmedabad*

"This book is an invitation to designers for imagining and developing alternative models of engaging with society, environment, and people that address sustainability holistically. While craft-based livelihood development models have been widely experimented with over the past 40 years in developing countries, this book does an excellent job of examining how designers are responding to current anthropogenic pressures in increasingly fragile ecologies."

—*Tanishka Kachru, Associate Senior Faculty and Head, NID Publications, National Institute of Design*

"This book not only explores the differences and interactions between sentimental value and aesthetic value, but it also offers practical approaches for implementation of a sustainable product design process. As climate change looms ever closer, the author provides well-written and inspiring research on how, as designers and consumers, we can take responsibility for creating a sustainable future. The writer has conveyed an in-depth knowledge of the subject so that it can be easily absorbed by a wide audience."

—*Patrick Gilabert, United Nations Industrial Development Organization (UNIDO), Director Brussels Office and Representative to the European Union, European Investment Bank, Secretariat of the ACP Group of States*

"Rebecca Reubens has written an inspiring book which introduces a holistic sustainability design approach. The book clearly illustrates how collaboration of craft and design can contribute economic growth in developing countries with renewable materials. I suggest this book can open up new perspectives for researchers, practitioners and strategists who study sustainability."

—*Gülay Hasdogan, Professor of Industrial Design, Middle East Technical University, Turkey*

"This book is a result of Dr Reubens' devotion to not only researching sustainable materials, but to her hands-on practical experience and those of her students. Her discipline and natural design-sense combine to provide her with the keen perspective of the relationship between the environmental impact of how a society creates products, and how that impact can be minimized. Her dedication to bamboo has been well-recognized by her peers and this book contains the best information on bamboo available in print."

—Susanne Lucas, Executive Director of the World Bamboo Organization

"Some years ago, a group of us came together under an IUCN umbrella to try and understand what sustainability actually was, or could be. We concluded, after much ground investigation on several continents, that sustainability was a mountain wrapped in mist. We may not know precisely what it is, but we all want to get there. Mapping the journey with intelligence may be more important than predictions or arrivals. That is the value of Rebecca Reubens' effort. Her experience reminds us that sustainability will ultimately need to be demonstrated by ordinary folk within the marketplace, through livelihoods, products and services that enhance the wellbeing of communities as well as of the environment that shelters us all. Although this book focuses on handcraft and on bamboo, its lessons extend well beyond the handmade or any one material. I hope this book will receive the serious attention which it so richly deserves, and most particularly among the generation now coping with the havoc my generation has inflicted upon them."

—Ashoke Chatterjee, former Director, National Institute of Design,
and former President, Crafts Council of India

Holistic Sustainability Through Craft-Design Collaboration

This book explores the intersection of craft, design and sustainability in the developing world. It argues that most sustainable design approaches and efforts fall short of implementing holistic sustainability, and that, in order to reach this goal, design must be underpinned by alternatives to the mainstream, technology-intensive, industrial design paradigm.

Renewable materials such as bamboo, cork and hemp – which are abundantly available in the developing world – have the potential to be a viable resource base for sustainable development. Current sustainable design initiatives and approaches already recontextualize these materials using industrial techniques and technologies. However, these efforts fall short of impacting holistic sustainability and tend to focus on the ecological aspect. This book offers the development of one alternative to design for holistic sustainability, called the Rhizome Approach, which draws on existing sustainability praxis and craft. *Holistic Sustainability Through Craft-Design Collaboration* includes customizable tools which aim to empower designers to guide and evaluate their own designs. Through these tools, and the Rhizome Approach in general, the book aims to enable designers, and students of design, to move beyond green and sustainable design, to holistic sustainability design.

Rebecca Reubens did her Ph.D. on the intersection between craft, design and sustainability at Delft University, the Netherlands. She practices in the same domain through her sustainability design firm Rhizome, and is an ambassador for the World Bamboo Organization.

Routledge Studies in Sustainability

https://www.routledge.com/Routledge-Studies-in-Sustainability/book-series/RSSTY

Holistic Sustainability Through Craft-Design Collaboration

Rebecca Reubens

Routledge
Taylor & Francis Group
LONDON AND NEW YORK

earthscan
from Routledge

First published 2019 by Routledge

2 Park Square, Milton Park, Abingdon, Oxon, OX14 4RN
711 Third Avenue, New York, NY 10017

Routledge is an imprint of the Taylor & Francis Group, an informa business

First issued in paperback 2020

British Library Cataloguing-in-Publication Data
A catalogue record for this book is available from the British Library

Library of Congress Cataloging-in-Publication Data
Names: Reubens, Rebecca, author.
Title: Holistic sustainability through craft-design collaboration / Rebecca
 Reubens.
Description: Abingdon, Oxon ; New York, NY : Routledge, 2019. | Series:
 Routledge studies in sustainability | Includes bibliographical references
 and index.
Identifiers: LCCN 2018061584 (print) | LCCN 2019017770 (ebook) |
 ISBN 9781351065665 (eBook) | ISBN 9781138479470 (hbk) |
 ISBN 9781351065665 (ebk)
Subjects: LCSH: Sustainable design. | Product design. | Handicraft industries.
Classification: LCC TS171.4 (ebook) | LCC TS171.4 .R48 2019 (print) |
 DDC 658.5/752—dc23
LC record available at https://lccn.loc.gov/2018061584

ISBN: 978-1-138-47947-0 (hbk)
ISBN: 978-0-367-72966-0 (pbk)

Typeset in Goudy
by Apex CoVantage, LLC

To Errol Reubens, for everything, always.

Contents

Figures

Author profile

Dr. Rebecca Reubens practices at the intersection of sustainability, design and craft through her sustainability design consultancy, Rhizome. A large part of her work has been in the development sector, with institutions, governments, NGOs, MSMEs and communities in Europe, Asia and Africa. Recently, her work has included mainstreaming sustainability, including through Rhizome's work for Indian conglomerates such as the Godrej group.

She believes that design can make sustainability desirable and commercially viable, and that renewable materials processed by craft producers are among the viable routes to holistic sustainability.

Rebecca is an alumna of the National Institute of Fashion Technology, and the National Institute of Design, India and Delft University of Technology, the Netherlands. She remains connected to academia by teaching at design institutions in India, including the Faculty of Design, CEPT University, Ahmedabad, where she is an adjunct professor.

She is passionate about bamboo, and this remains the material of choice for much of her work. She is a world bamboo ambassador for the World Bamboo Organization. Her publications include the book *Bamboo: From Green Design to Sustainable Design*.

Acknowledgments

A lot of individuals and institutions serendipitously lined up across the span of many years and three continents for this book to be possible. While I can list but a few of them here, I thank them all from the bottom of my heart.

Han Brezet, Henri Christiaans and JC: You were the holy trinity for my Ph.D., on which this book draws. You gave me the space to find my own path, and let me learn at my own pace. You mercilessly played the devil's advocate with brilliant flashes of constructive criticism to refine my arguments. And you were also the calm amid the storm who took the many colored, tangled ideas I had and put them in order.

Marcel Crul: Thank you for the wonderful opportunity to work with the SPIN project in Vietnam and supporting my research there. This book would be missing a whole chapter or two had it not been for you.

Rene van Berkel: Thank you for the opportunity to work on the labeling project for UNIDO, which was the last missing bit of the jigsaw for me.

M.P. Ranjan: I wish you were here to see this book coming to fruition. Thank you for pushing me into the world of development and believing I would somehow fit there.

Nikheel Aphale: You gave form to my thoughts and made them communicable through the wonderful diagrams in this book.

Kathleen Reubens: You instilled in me the need to try to leave them better than I found them. For this, and for so many other things that are too numerous to list here, I am grateful.

Errol Reubens: You have always been my inspiration for holistic thinking, only you do it so organically, it looks uncomplex. Thank you for always supporting me and believing in me.

Errol Reubens Jr.: For so many little things that made the big things possible – thank you.

Rohit, Nirbhay and Varya: You make it all worth it and possible.

Jeanette and Suren Tyagi: Thank you for your unconditional support always.

All the craftspeople who I learned from: I began my journey in development with you. It was so much easier for me because I could afford to make choices which you could not. You still walked alongside me, with tremendous courage of conviction. You offered me a window into another reality, so generously, unthinkingly.

All the scholars whose work I built on: Over time, your names have grown familiar, and I have sometimes discovered a tick in the way you write and think. This has made you feel like old, dependable friends in this sometimes-solitary journey. I got so far, because I stood on your shoulders, because you tread before me.

Definitions[1]

- *Craft*: *Craft* is a broad, highly contested term, which is more easily described by what it is not, than by what it is. Craft is the antithesis to industrialization: before industrialization, everything was crafted. This book defines craft as a non-industrial production-to-consumption system that encompasses – but is not limited to – products (crafted objects), skills (craftsmanship), producers (craftsperson) (Risatti, 2007) and trades or occupations (crafts) (Ihatsu, 2002).
- *Design*: "Design is the act of deliberately moving from an existing situation to a preferred one by professional designers or others applying design knowingly or unknowingly" (Fuad-Luke, 2009, p. 5).
- *Developing Countries*: Countries in the bottom three quartiles of the Human Development Index – a composite index of three indices measuring countries' achievements in longevity, education and income – are termed as developing countries (Klugman, 2010).
- *Holistic Sustainability/Sustainability*: The systemic nature of sustainability begs that it be dealt with as a holistic construct, comprised of the sum of all of its conceptual sub-sets – including ecological sustainability, social sustainability, cultural sustainability and economic sustainability. While the adjective *holistic* is implicit in the construct of sustainability that underpins in this book, the chapters sometimes use the word *holistic* alongside *sustainability* for additional emphasis, as a pleonasm. This book defines (holistic) sustainability as "the possibility that humans and other life will flourish on the Earth forever" (Ehrenfeld, 2008, p. 49) through consciously maintaining the balance between different tenets – including ecological, social, cultural and economic ones.
- *Industrial design*: Industrial design is the professional service of creating "products, services and systems conceived with tools, organizations and logic introduced by industrialization" (International Council of Societies of Industrial Design, 2015).
- *Industrial materials*: Industrial materials include those commonly produced and processed with the tools and logic introduced by industrialization, for industrial production-to-consumption systems. These include mainstream versions of wood, metal, glass, textile, ceramic and plastic.

- *Industrial*: *Industrial* broadly means "of, relating to or resulting from industry" (Industrial, 2018). In this book, the term is defined as: of, relating to or resulting from industrialization.
- *Non-industrial materials*: Non-industrial materials include those materials produced and processed with the tools and logic introduced, pre-or post-industrialization, for non-industrial production-to-consumption systems. These include non-mainstream materials used for small production batches, including those used in craft production-to-consumption systems, such as natural fibers. This category may also include some exploratory sustainable materials which are not yet mainstreamed, such as recycled Tetra Pak board.
- *Production-to-consumption system*: A *production-to-consumption* system includes "the entire set of actors, materials and institutions involved in growing and harvesting a particular raw material, transforming the material into higher-value products, and marketing those products" (Belcher, 1998, p. 59). A production-to-consumption system includes three dimensions – the physical flow of materials, the set of players through whose hands the materials flow, and the labor and capital involved in these processes (Belcher, 1998).
- *Sustainability design*: Theories and practices for design that deliberately actualize the possibility that humans and other life will flourish on the Earth forever (Ehrenfeld, 2008, p. 49), by cultivating a balance between different the different tenets of sustainability – including ecological, economic, cultural and social conditions – are termed as design for sustainability or sustainability design.
- *Sustainable design*: "Theories and practices for design that cultivate ecological, economic, social and cultural conditions that will support human well-being indefinitely" (Thorpe, 2007, p. 13) are collectively called *sustainable design*.
- *Sustainable development*: The most widely accepted and used definition of *sustainable development* is, development that "meets the needs of the present generation without compromising the ability of future generations to meet their own needs" (Brundtland, 1987, p. 47).
- *Sustainable*: The term *sustainable* essentially means "that which can be maintained over time" (Heinberg, 2010, p. 25).
- *Unsustainability*: *Unsustainability* refers to the state or condition of being unsustainable (Wordnik.com, 2018). It is not the obverse of sustainability; the two are categorically different (Ehrenfeld, 2008, p. 54). Unsustainability is generally tangible and measurable, while sustainability is an aspirational, emergent property of a living system (Ehrenfeld, 2008).
- *Unsustainable*: *Unsustainable* is the antonym of sustainable, essentially meaning "not able to be maintained at the current rate or level" (Design, 2018).
- *Worldview*: A worldview is a fundamental set of "presuppositions (assumptions which may be true, partially true or entirely false) which we hold (consciously or sub-consciously, consistently or inconsistently) about the basic constitution of reality, and that provides the foundation on which we live and move, and have our being" (Sire, 1976, p. 19).

Note

1 Several of the main thematic areas of this book are comprised of abstract ideas, which have no commonly accepted definition. Therefore, in these cases, interpretations that best crystallized these concepts have been arrived at from literature to serve as reference points for this book. These key definitions are listed here and discussed further in the following chapters.

1 Introduction

The importance of renewable materials

The environmental damage caused by over-extraction of materials for human production-to-consumption systems has led to serious concerns about the Earth's carrying capacity, and highlighted the importance of renewable materials. Almost three-fourths (70%) of the materials we use post-industrialization – such as coal, natural gas and oil – come from the lithosphere (Thorpe, 2007). These materials take millions of years to form and are therefore considered *non-renewable*, as opposed to resources from the biosphere, which take a comparatively shorter time to regenerate, and are therefore *renewable* (Thorpe, 2007).

Bio-based materials are more energy-efficient than most commonly recycled materials because their production generally requires less energy (Van der Lugt, 2017). Most plastics, though recyclable, are not in fact recycled because recycled plastic is generally more expensive and of lower quality than virgin plastic (Van der Lugt, 2017). Metallic minerals, like aluminum and steel, can be recycled with minimal or no change in quality; however, there is simply not enough scrap metal to meet worldwide demand (Van der Lugt, 2017).

Therefore, an important rule of thumb in sustainability design is to use renewable input materials (Crul & Diehl, 2006) from the biosphere – such as wood, cotton, linen, hemp and bamboo.

The decline of traditional production-to-consumption systems for craft based on renewable materials

Renewable resources from the biosphere – such as grasses and other natural fibers, vegetables and fruits such as coconuts and squashes, and animal-based materials such as leather and sea shells (Risatti, 2007) – have traditionally been used as input materials for craft-based production-to-consumption systems around the world, due their easy availability in the natural environment. Craftspeople spanning several categories – including:

> the skilled master craftsman, the wage worker, the fully self-employed artisan, the village artisan producing wares for local use, the part-time artisan

whose craft activities supplement his meager earnings from the land, and the landless artisan – have historically been, and still are, employed in crafting these materials into products for the use of their own communities or for trade and export.

(Jaitley, 2001, p. 14)

Post-industrialization, craft-based production-to-consumption systems – and the craftspeople they encompass – are endangered with the influx of industrial products into their traditionally closed economies (Jaitley, 2001). This is a spin-off of the industrial and information revolutions, each of which has impacted access and reorganized economic activity (Humbert, 2007) across the world. The physical and virtual connectivity of the information revolution has exposed consumers in developing countries – including rural buyers – to globalized lifestyles, to which they now aspire. This preference for technology over tradition (Chaudhary, 2010), and for mass-produced substitutes over craft products, has disrupted traditional localized production-to-consumption systems, resulting in a loss of livelihoods for traditional producers in developing countries – thereby contributing to poverty and unemployment.

The unsustainability of livelihoods for craftspeople, given their lack of economic or productive skills, assets and options apart from craft, has forced many indigenous craftspeople to migrate to urban areas in search of wage labor (Reubens, 2010a; Society for Rural, Urban and Tribal Initiatives, 1995). This causes unsustainability at several levels. Several crafts have either vanished or are declining, and the pressure caused by mass-migration and unprecedented urbanization (Craft Revival Trust, 2006) makes it difficult to even imagine the possibility of sustainable development for all.

The opportunity and need for design vis-à-vis sustaining craft-based production-to-consumption systems

Globalization, the information revolution and unprecedented development – the same constituents which contributed to the unsustainability of craft-based livelihoods – offer a way forward for their sustainability. These same three phenomena have catalyzed a growing demand for sustainable products (Potts, van der Meer, & Daitchman, 2010), including products crafted by communities (Ihatsu, 2002). Sustainability-aligned markets are expanding faster than markets for conventional products, and are increasingly embracing initiatives that factor in a wider spectrum of sustainability criteria – including ecological, social and economic considerations (Potts et al., 2010; Sustainable Brands, 2017).

Despite being a good match, traditional craftspeople in the developing world are unable to access and navigate emerging markets for sustainable products, to which developed and organized regions have privileged access (Potts et al., 2010). The reason for this disconnect is that craftspeople are unfamiliar with new globalized markets where the producer and buyer are physically disconnected. These markets are in stark contrast to traditional craft production-to-consumption systems which hinge on the craftsperson-patron connection. The link between buyer and producer was severed during the process of industrialization, when industrial concepts such as standardization and economy of scale heralded the need to divide the integrated craft-based production-to-consumption process into specialized disciplines (Dormer, 1997) – including design, production and marketing – to increase the productivity of each process, in line with the new concept of division of labor (Cusumano, 1991).

In contemporary globalized value chains, craftspeople are able to function as producers, but there are several gaps which need to be filled with supplemental players in the value chain: actors (who directly produce, process, trade and own the products), supporters (who do not deal directly with the product, but whose services add value to the product) and influencers (who create and moderate the regulatory framework, policies, infrastructure, etc., at the local, national and international levels) (Roduner, 2007). Identifying and putting in place these value-chain actors, supporters and influencers can help bridge the gap between craftspeople and sustainability-aligned markets.

Designers, who have traditionally functioned as the bridge between production and marketing, are ideally positioned to bridge the gap between craftspeople and sustainability-aligned markets. Designers are equipped with the skills and tools to envisage distant scenarios and innovate accordingly, a skill most craft-producer communities lack. Designers are also able to internalize industrial concepts, such as batch production, productivity and quality checks, needed to maintain these markets. For these reasons and more, designers can be instrumental in enabling craftspeople to leverage sustainability-aligned markets, and thereby sustain their livelihoods.

Why existing design initiatives for renewable materials overlook the craft-livelihood connection

Emerging design initiatives and approaches already look at leveraging sustainability-aligned markets, including in the context of developing countries. Several of these initiatives have an ecological focus (Reubens, 2013b). They look at recontextualizing renewable materials – including those traditionally used in non-industrial craft production-to-consumption systems, such as cork and bamboo – using industrial techniques and technologies to create innovative products and systems for sustainability-aligned markets. While the resultant designs contribute to ecological sustainability, they miss out on the chance to address the outcomes of complex and interlinked social, cultural and economic unsustainabilities – such as poverty and unemployment – in the developing countries where these products are produced. Consequently, they bypass the need and opportunity for design to be a vehicle to address the social, cultural and economic dimensions of sustainability alongside its ecological aspect.

A case in point to illustrate this would be that of the International Network for Bamboo and Rattan (INBAR), an intergovernmental organization which aims to improve global bamboo production-to-consumption systems, through its programs on climate change, environmental sustainability, poverty alleviation, sustainable construction, trade and development. INBAR aims to generate equitable incomes from bamboo and rattan, by extending value chains and building stronger partnerships between consumer and producer countries through a cross section of approaches, including supporting – and broadening the application of – technological product innovation (INBAR, n.d.). Towards this end, in 2006, INBAR supported Pablo van der Lugt – a Ph.D. researcher from Delft University of Technology, the Netherlands – in studying why bamboo products only have a small market share in the EU, despite the potential of industrially processed bamboo as a fast-growing substitute for hardwood. The resulting report, titled, *Bamboo Product Commercialization in the West: A State-of-the-Art Analysis of Bottlenecks and Opportunities* (Van der Lugt & Otten, 2010) indicated that design intervention could aid in a greater acceptability of bamboo in the West. To facilitate this, van der Lugt organized a series of design workshops to encourage Dutch designers to work with bamboo, under the project *Dutch Design Meets Bamboo* (Van der Lugt, 2007), as part of his research work. The prototypes developed during the project received positive media attention as eco-friendly designer products, and some were successfully commercialized.

These design-led, industrially processed, engineered bamboo products demonstrated that through design, non-mainstream renewable materials could find commercial viability in sustainability-aligned markets. However, recent studies (Bailly, 2010; Williams, 2007) have questioned the ecological sustainability of these products, given their huge carbon footprint if they are transported from producers in developing countries to markets in developed countries. In addition to the energy spent in transportation, the energy used in producing engineered bamboo also increases its carbon footprint – in fact, even more so than transportation (Van der Lugt, 2017).

In addition to perhaps not being as ecologically sustainable as first imagined, industrially processed, engineered products also fail to leverage bamboo's potential to contribute to social and cultural sustainability by addressing issues of poverty and livelihoods (Lobovikov, Paudel, Piazza, Ren, & Wu, 2007). This is because these products do not translate into livelihoods for indigent bamboo producers in traditional MSMEs (micro, small and medium enterprises) in Asia, Africa and Latin America, where a substantial percentage of bamboo production takes place. These communities lack the financial capital to invest in the technology that these product lines require. Therefore, they go from being involved in, and therefore benefitting from, every node of non-industrial bamboo value chains to having limited involvement in industrial value chains – mostly in growing, managing, harvesting, transporting and processing bamboo at the most primary levels (Figure 1.1).

The scenario just discussed is not specific to bamboo. It is common to the value chains of several renewable materials – including cork, sea grass, rattan, hemp and jute – especially those which have traditionally been part of craft production-to-consumption systems. This sheds light on the fact that design efforts – even if aligned to sustainability markets and involving green materials – need to go beyond green design and commercial viability, if they are to impact all the

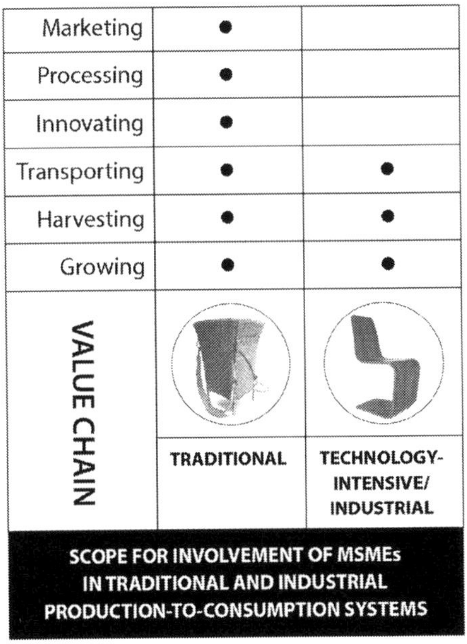

VALUE CHAIN	TRADITIONAL	TECHNOLOGY-INTENSIVE/INDUSTRIAL
Marketing	●	
Processing	●	
Innovating	●	
Transporting	●	●
Harvesting	●	●
Growing	●	●

SCOPE FOR INVOLVEMENT OF MSMEs IN TRADITIONAL AND INDUSTRIAL PRODUCTION-TO-CONSUMPTION SYSTEMS

Figure 1.1 Involvement of poor-producers in traditional and technology-intensive/industrial value chains

dimensions of sustainability in a balanced and holistic manner. To achieve this, there is a need to bridge the worlds of development and design, and to facilitate design which actively seeks to impact sustainability holistically in the context of developing world enterprises.

The need for sustainable alternatives to the traditional industrial design paradigm

Design for and in developing countries can be instrumental in realizing a holistically sustainable vision of development. Such development would rest on economic development, with a simultaneous increase in socially desirable phenomena (Lélé, 1991), and would also be mindful of ecological and cultural aspects. Design has already been able to align the renewable raw materials available in developing countries with sustainability markets – including, as discussed earlier, by using industrial processing to reconstitute these materials into new avatars. Though these new designs capitalize on sustainability markets, they do not leverage the huge workforce and cultural resources available in developing countries. Nor do they realize design's potential to orchestrate production-to-consumption systems which contribute to holistic sustainability, by simultaneously addressing social, cultural, economic and ecological dimensions, and their complex interlinkages.

In order to do this, design needs to facilitate production-to-consumption systems that are underpinned by technologies which have a high potential for employment, are not capital-intensive, and are highly adaptable to social and cultural environments (Jequier & Blanc, 1983). This, in turn, calls for design to challenge mainstream, technology-intensive industrial design approaches, which do not tackle the concept of sustainability in a holistic manner (Maxwell, Sheate, & van der Vorst, 2003). This is easier said than done, as the design-industrialization bond is deeply rooted; the discipline of design emerged as a result of the process of industrialization, and therefore inherently aligns to industrial logic and philosophy. This highlights the need for alternatives to mainstream design approaches which generate collective benefits to the ecology, society, economy (Maxwell et al., 2003) and culture in the context of developing countries.

This book focuses on this underexplored area and aims to improve sustainability design approaches, and thereby practice – especially in the domain of enterprises working with renewable materials in developing countries.

Sustainability is a new and emerging field, and offers no comprehensive answers yet. Therefore, we center on three main questions in this book:

1   To what extent does design address sustainability holistically – simultaneously considering all of its dimensions including social, economic, ecological and cultural dimensions – while working with non-industrial craft-based enterprises working with renewable materials in developing countries?
2   What could be a possible sustainability design approach that: a) is mindful of the pros and cons of the existing sustainability design approaches, and b) looks at addressing a holistic picture of sustainability – including its ecological, social, economic and cultural dimensions – in the context of non-industrial craft-based MSMEs working with renewable materials in developing countries?
3   What mechanisms would support and encourage the use and operationalization of a sustainability design approach that might be identified or developed in response to Question 2?

Our primary objective is to improve sustainability design practice so that it positively impacts sustainability in a holistic manner, especially in the case of craft-based enterprises in developing countries (Question 3). This question is underpinned by the existence of a sustainability design approach that better addresses sustainability holistically (Question2) and is mindful of existing scholarship and practice in this regard (Question 1).

The first step into our inquiry is to understand what *exists* – to what extent current design approaches to achieve sustainability address the topic holistically (Question 1). Chapter 2 focuses on exploring and crystallizing the concept of sustainability, based on which, chapter 3 explores current design approaches to actualize sustainability: *what exists* – including *why* and *how* it occurs.

2 Sustainability and development

2.1 How development shapes sustainability

Ironically, sustainability remains a fuzzy word with no single definition, despite the fact that achieving it has become non-negotiable, given the urgent crises our world is facing. These crises range from traditional development issues such as poverty, hunger, health and income security to new challenges such as climate change and globalization (Munasinghe, 2010). Having a clear understanding what sustainability is, and what shapes it, is imperative to investigate and address the causes of the acute and pressing manifestations of unsustainability that threaten human survival, and the survival of the systems that constitute our world. This chapter, therefore, focuses on sustainability, and aims to identify or put in place a definition for the term, to serve as a reference point for the discussions in this book.

The beginnings of production-to-consumption systems and unsustainability in the pre-industrial world

Concerns about sustaining our world are not a recent phenomenon; visionaries through the ages have deliberated on the impact of human activities on Earth's ecosystems (Pezzey & Toman, 2002). Scientists tell us that we are now in the Anthropocene – an epoch in which human activity shapes the planet's geological future, alongside natural occurrences such as ice ages and volcanic eruptions (Berkeley, 2011). The beginning of the Anthropocene, and unsustainability in general, is commonly traced back to the industrial revolution. The production-to-consumption systems which emerged during the industrial revolution facilitated unprecedented development and, thereby, tremendous ecological devastation, forcing public attention on the need to recognize and cultivate sustainability globally (Edwards, 2005). However, we argue that the industrial revolution was not an isolated event; the conditions for its full-blown take off (Rostow, 1960) were created over the course of human development and the production-to-consumption systems that underpinned this process.

Around 12,000 years ago, humans began transitioning from a forest-based subsistence to agriculture and animal rearing (Lloyd, 2008). The resultant food security led to the emergence of technologies and professions which were not based on producing food – such as craftspeople, who created things of daily use for settled tribes using natural materials (Lloyd, 2008; Overy, 2007). The trade of agricultural and non-agricultural surplus, in turn, led to the first pre-industrial production-to-consumption systems and value-chain actors: these included traders, account keepers and transporters (Lloyd, 2008; Overy, 2007). Over time, the production of surplus by pre-industrial societies financed both industrial development and the development of suitable trading and government institutions (Lloyd, 2008; Overy, 2007).

As civilizations flourished, global legacies of nature-worship (Lloyd, 2008; Overy, 2007) were remodeled. In South Asia, tribal nature worship crystallized into religions like Hinduism, Jainism and Buddhism (Lloyd, 2008; Overy, 2007). In other parts of Eurasia, religions like Judaism, Christianity and Islam (Lloyd, 2008) – coupled with the advent of Western scientific thought – shifted people's worldview from the pagan veneration of nature, to seeing nature as a hostile resource to be harnessed (Lloyd, 2008) under the shield of technology. These changes in worldview were actualized in the natural landscape. In 500 AD, more than 80% of the European landscape was forested, but by 1300 AD, less than 50% remained that way (Lloyd, 2008). Traders and raiders carried this new philosophy to distant communities, heralding the beginnings of globalization and a single worldview (Lloyd, 2008).

The growing needs of an escalating population in rapidly developing Europe demanded a maritime search for resource-rich colonies (Lloyd, 2008). The expansion of Europe caused large-scale global redistribution: flora and fauna moved across continents, there was mass human migration, mineral wealth was tapped and regional economic specialization and sea-transport facilitated trade realignment (Lloyd, 2008; Overy, 2007). Using the colonies as production bases for agricultural and non-agricultural export produce replaced their extant robust natural diversity (Lloyd, 2008; Overy, 2007) with a fragile monoculture. The influx of Europeans to the colonies as adventurers, entrepreneurs or refugees (Lloyd, 2008; Overy, 2007) saw several species of fauna – especially those which were hunted for their skin and fur – becoming endangered and, eventually, extinct. European incursions brought new diseases, violence and land appropriation, which caused several indigenous communities to become endangered and extinct as well (Lloyd, 2008; Overy, 2007).

Colonization and unsustainability

The growing dissent over the inequality between European colonizers and their colonies caused numerous uprisings, resulting in the independence of several colonies, including the United States. Simultaneously, the new notions of liberty, equality and individual rights reshuffled Europe's social and labor systems. The energy crisis – Britain had already moved from using wood to coal – and the simultaneous non-availability of slave labor because of Britain's slave-trading ban of 1807 (Lloyd, 2008; Overy, 2007) begged for an alternative, which took the form of the industrial revolution.

The demands of European industrialization created a renewed fervor to colonize, in order to gain control of land, labor, commodities and markets (Lloyd, 2008; Overy, 2007) around 1870. The economic gains of 19th-century Europe were made at the expense of the native populations of its colonies in Asia, Africa, Australia and America (Overy, 2007). By the time these colonies gained political independence, their land had been exhausted, their raw materials had been depleted and they were locked in rural and national debt due to trade agreements (Lloyd, 2008; Overy, 2007). The eventual emancipation of Asia and Africa, and the rise of Japan, saw the European Age give way to the age of global civilization in the early 1900s. Thousand-year-old pre-industrial agricultural systems were replaced by urban, industrialized and technocratic systems (Overy, 2007) during and post-colonization; this caused rapid increases in population and economic growth with a quality of life that did not match (Lloyd, 2008), laying the ground for the pressing unsustainability we face today.

The link between production-to-consumption systems, development and unsustainability

As previously discussed, the current state of unsustainability cannot be attributed to the industrial revolution, or to any other isolated phenomenon (Rostow, 1960). It is the cumulative result of the development process: development resulted in secure production-to-consumption systems, which resulted in population growth, which called for more resources, which in turn prompted more development (Nkechinyere, 2010). Thus, through the ages, development was both the cause and effect of incremental development, and simultaneous incremental unsustainability.

Each production-to-consumption system that emerged and evolved over the development process had significant direct and indirect impact on the world and its systems. The production input influenced raw material utilization and flows, i.e., ecological sustainability; the production process facilitated by technology affected the dynamics of labor and employment, i.e., social sustainability; and systems of exchange affected trade and development, i.e., economic sustainability. All of these were orchestrated by and orchestrated changing human worldviews (Ehrenfeld, 2008), thus affecting cultural sustainability. The tiniest change in each production-to-consumption system affected each of the world's complex, interlinked and dynamic systems in differing degrees – ranging from the profound to the insignificant. Sustainability – or the lack of thereof, i.e., unsustainability – is, therefore, the emergent property of the collective production-to-consumption systems that underpin development (Ehrenfeld, 2008).

Over the ages, the economic benefits of development have been optimized by globalization: production-to-consumption systems are now spread across nations, resulting in economies of scale and optimal outputs that are globally rationalized (Ehrenfeld, 2008). These economic benefits are not equitable within or across nations; invariably, the ratio is skewed in favor of the affluent (Munasinghe, 2010). Ecological costs are also inequitably distributed across and within nations:

developing countries not only host global production centers, but also bear their ecological costs – such as pollution and depletion of biodiversity and resources (Munasinghe, 2010). Unsurprisingly, the social costs caused by these relocated globalized production-to-consumption systems – including unemployment, inequity, breakdown of socio-economic community systems and income disparity (Stiglitz, 2002) – are also centered in developing countries. Globalization and media bombardment have caused developing countries to metamorphose too quickly for them to preserve and, sometimes, to even record their cultural capital, leading to cultural unsustainability.

Developed countries, which incurred similar costs during the industrial revolution, caution against the path of rapid industrialization – especially because the burgeoning populations and nascent levels of governance in the developing world will likely magnify the costs associated with the development process (Munasinghe, 2010). The developing countries' counter-argument is that the developed world has already used up a large part of Earth's ecological resources to fuel its own development and industrialization; the environmental policies these countries now lobby for would constrict potential economic growth for developing countries (Munasinghe, 2009).

The continued pursuit for development in both developed and developing worlds is unquestionable, despite their bargaining impasse. Equally obvious is that sustainability depends on this development not being based on the past paradigm whereby production-to-consumption systems existed at the cost of the ecology (The Economist, 2017), economies, societies and cultures. A possible way forward could be through development that is based on a holistic vision of sustainability: which is mindful of developed-country concerns such as resource depletion, unsustainable growth and pollution, alongside developing-country priorities such as poverty alleviation, equity and development (Munasinghe, 2010).

2.2   Sustainable development

Sustainability first began to crystallize as an ecological concept during the industrial revolution, following public dissent on the effect of unprecedented development on the environment (Hawken, Lovins, & Lovins, 1999). The links between ecological unsustainability and unprecedented industrialization-based economic growth became increasingly obvious amid growing awareness on sustainability all through the 1970s (Adams, 2006). The United Nations Conference on the Human Environment in 1972 – also known as the Stockholm Conference – was a turning point acknowledging the connection between the biosphere and human development, through the idea of *ecologically sustainable development* (Mann, 2011).

In 1983, the United Nations convened the World Commission on Environment and Development – also known as the Brundtland Commission – to address the "accelerating deterioration of the human environment and natural resources and the consequences of that deterioration for economic and social development" (Brundtland, 1987, p. 43). The Commission's 1987 report, *Our Common*

Future, presented the idea of *sustainable development* to the world as "development that meets the needs of the present without compromising the ability of future generations to meet their own needs" (Brundtland, 1987, p. 43). The report discussed how the world's economic systems could contribute to solving ecology-related issues, alongside development-related issues of equitable growth – including poverty and under-development – which had emerged in the 1960s (Munasinghe, 2010). This created a paradigm shift in understanding sustainability as a primarily ecological concept, as it married post-industrial ecological concerns with development – which has social and economic connotations (Barash & Webel, 2002).

The view that sustainable development needed to address social, ecological and economic aspects was revisited at the United Nations Earth Summit in 1992, against the backdrop of discussions on integrated economics and equity. The Rio Declaration asserted that the environment and social and economic development can no longer be viewed separately as isolated fields (United Nations Sustainable Development, 1992). The eight Millennium Development Goals (MDGs) outlined at the United Nations Millennium Summit in 2000 included poverty, education, gender, child mortality, maternal health, combating diseases, environmental sustainability and global partnerships for sustainable development. These reiterated the need for sustainable development to address diverse aspects, and were widely accepted by world leaders as indicators to measure progress. The MDGs were amongst the top priorities at the World Summit on Sustainable Development in Johannesburg in 2002, and resonated with the WEHAB thematic areas of water, energy, health, agriculture and biodiversity.

In 2012, the United Nations Conference on Sustainable Development – informally known as Rio+20 – proposed a set of Sustainable Development Goals (SDGs) in a document titled *Transforming our World: the 2030 Agenda for Sustainable Development* or, *Agenda 2030*, colloquially (United Nations, 2015). The SDGs took over from the MDGs (whose time period ended in 2015), and were mindful of and underlined the importance of precedents, including Agenda 21 and the Johannesburg Plan of Implementation. The SDGs are successors to development targets, which have – in response to persistent calls from diverse global forums and platforms – increasingly grown mindful of the need for development to address social, ecological and economic dimensions and their interlinkages in a balanced manner (Le Blanc, Liu, O'Connor,& Zubcevic, 2012). In contrast to the MDGs which seemed to have been underpinned by the notion that rich donors (the developed world) need to support the development trajectories of poor recipients (the developing world) to guard against unsustainability, the SDG's seem more universal: they put accountability on both factions by acknowledging that sustainability rests on the joint and holistic actions of both developed and developing countries (World Economic Forum, 2015).

Almost 200 world leaders adopted both the SDGs and Agenda 2030 at the UN Sustainable Development Summit in 2015. The international discourse on sustainability has grown steadily. The goals outlined towards achieving sustainable development have more than doubled (the eight MDGs gave way to

17 SDGs), and are being arrived at in a more inclusive way (the MDGs were developed by a group of UN experts, whereas the SDGs were arrived at through a highly inclusive process) (Kumar, Kumar,& Saxena, 2016). However, the goals decided upon have not been successfully attained so far, and the current set of goals – the SDGs – are heavily negotiated and non-binding (World Economic Forum, 2015). This is because there has been no collective political vision or will to take the leap towards the uncharted path to holistic sustainability; strategies and plans for sustainability have consistently prioritized the economic aspect. While most countries are on the same page in their pursuit of economic ascendancy, in general, the developed world prioritizes the ecological dimension, while the developing world prioritizes meeting basic needs through the social dimension (Figure 2.1). Global dialogue and action on sustainability has also reached an impasse because it is unclear who will bear the economic cost of achieving the SDGs, a figure pegged at approximately 4% of the world's gross domestic product (GDP) (Hickel, 2015): currently, the developed world pledges around 0.7% of GDP as aid, and only actually pays out one-third of that amount (The Economist, 2015). Meanwhile, the immediate crises – financial recession on one hand, and environmental catastrophe on the other (Narain, 2012) – need to be urgently addressed.

While *sustainable development* continues to be a powerful and, some argue, useful paradigm, it has been deeply criticized because its object is not *sustainability* per se, but rather, making *development* sustainable (Partridge, 2005). Unyoking the concepts of *sustainability* and *development* would allow the questioning of whether growth and *development* are central to the sustainability debate; it would also allow

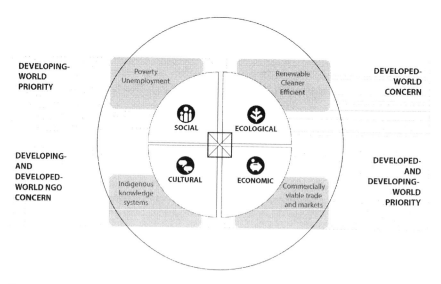

Figure 2.1 Developed- and developing-world sustainability priorities and concerns

Source: Reubens, 2016c

the exploration of currently marginalized critiques of pro-growth economics (such as *limits to growth* and *zero-growth* discourses) (McManus, 1996).

The calls that demand that we step back from the current anthropocentric paradigm (Sutton, 2004), which presupposes a certain type and scale of economic development (Jackson, 2009; Victor, 2008), are escalating. It is time for us to collectively revisit the larger non-negotiable outcome desired: sustainability (Latouche, 2010) – "the possibility that humans and other life will flourish on the Earth forever" (Ehrenfeld, 2008, p. 49).

2.3   The dimensions of sustainability

Sustainability is a multi-faceted concept with several dimensions (also known as domains, systems, areas, disciplines and pillars) (Mann, 2011). Early sustainability praxis focused on two dimensions – the ecology and the economy. This expanded to include the social dimension, identifying the three pillars of sustainable development – ecology, economy and society – which resonate with the Triple Bottom Line of sustainability reporting (people, planet and profit) (Elkington, 1998). Recent scholarship has sought to separate the cultural dimension from the social dimension, which traditionally subsumes it (Duxbury & Gillette, 2007), in order to present a clearer picture of sustainability. Each of the four identified dimensions of sustainability – ecological, economic, social and cultural – is discussed separately in the following sub-sections:

Ecological sustainability

Ecological sustainability focuses on maintaining the vitality and health of natural capital (Costanza, 2000), including the atmosphere, the hydrosphere, the lithosphere and the biosphere (Costanza, 1991). Everything we use comes from one of these spheres, and, when disposed of, returns to one of these spheres (Thorpe, 2007).

Ecological sustainability centers on managing human impact on the natural environment, and not on managing nature per se (Cuthill, 2010). The process of human urbanization and development is escalating damage and costs to nature, of which humans are a part, and without which humans cannot exist (Saunders, 1971; Sarkis & Zhu, 2017). We need to manage human impact on nature for our own survival – nature doesn't need people to survive; people need nature to survive (Conservation International, 2018).

In order to avoid catastrophic ecological-system collapse (Holling, 1986), we need to maintain safe thresholds and not exceed the carrying capacity of ecological systems (Ciriacy-Wantrup, 1952). This is complex, because the "ownership" of nature falls into the ambiguous space between public (collective) and private (individual). Up until the early 20th century, nature was an unregulated resource which was owned by "everybody" as part of the collective commons (Harding, 1968). In the last few decades, the collective responsibility to preserve biodiversity has been acknowledged (Oksannen, 2007)and actualized through agreements such as such as the Rio Convention for Biodiversity of 1992 – an international agreement that covers the conservation, sustainable use and equitable sharing of benefits arising from all ecosystems, species and genetic resources (United Nations, n.d.).

It is important to maintain all existing stocks of ecological biodiversity at a sustainable level, and not just those ecosystems which are of immediate direct use to human production-to-consumption systems. Natural systems are interlinked in a complex manner which we still do not understand clearly, and need continuity of ecological processes on micro- and macro-spatial scales in order to be resilient (Peterson, Allen, & Holling, 1998). Seemingly small changes in one system can have a magnified butterfly effect in another. A case in point is climate change, and the devastating natural disasters it causes – including floods, cyclones, hurricanes and wildfires. These events alter life as we know it, often with catastrophic spin-offs including loss of food security, shelter and lives. Preserving biodiversity offers a richer palette of resource-options to underpin regeneration in the face of such current and emerging challenges (Shiva, 2005) and thus, a better chance at sustainability. Maintaining biodiversity is also important because maintaining resilience – the ability to regain equilibrium after a disruptive shock (Pimm, 1984) – is more difficult for ecological systems than for anthropocentric systems, such as social and cultural systems (Munasinghe, 2010). This is because, unlike natural systems, human-centric systems are better able to plan their own adaptation (Munasinghe, 2010).

Economic sustainability

The underlying principle of economic sustainability is the maximization of income from a given capital – "a stock of instruments existing at an instant of time" (Fisher, 1906, p. 324) – while at least maintaining the capital which generated this income (Hicks, 1946). The concept of capital extends from economics to the several different types of capitals – including ecological, social and cultural – that economies require for their functioning (Hawken et al., 1999; Munasinghe, 2010).

The "spendable income" (Repetto, 1985) for an economy depends on the duration for which the capital is to be maintained and for whom – issues of intertemporal distribution and intergenerational equity (Anand & Sen, 2000; Arrow et al., 2004; Asheim, Buchholz,& Tungodden, 2001). There is a general agreement that it is incumbent upon current/existing generations to sustain society's broad stock of capital and productive capacity for future generations (Anand & Sen, 2000; Dworkin, 1981; Rawls, 1971; Sen, 1980). However, it is not clear how to value non-economic capital in monetary units, and, therefore unclear how much of which different types of non-monetary capital need to be sustained (Munasinghe, 2010). Dynamic efficiency – in other words, constant non-wastefulness – in production-to-consumption systems, therefore, becomes a pragmatic and proactive measure to remain on the path to economic sustainability (Stavins, Wagner, & Wagner, 2003).

While the concept of economic equity in the future is important, addressing economic equity in the present – intra-generational justice – is even more pressing. Currently, economic progress is judged by financial indications such as the per capita GDP, or the wealth that a community or nation accrues – neither of which reflects the inequity in wealth distribution. The equitable redistribution of a society's economic wealth – including through poverty alleviation measures, and related development areas of education, health and nutrition – is not important just from the perspective of deontological ethics. It also has economic consequences, as it raises the productivity of human capital, in turn potentially leading to higher present and future incomes and material prosperity (Anand & Sen, 2000).

Poverty alleviation helps to safeguard the productive capacity of the ecology, for the present and the future. In the struggle for day-to-day survival – and given their limited access to resources, property rights, finances and insurance – the economically backward are left with little option but to tap ecological resources, often illegally and in an unsustainable manner (Anand & Sen, 2000). Investing in human capital offers the possibility that the economically poor earn a living without needing to jeopardize ecological capital (Anand & Sen, 2000). This in turn impacts economic sustainability, because ecological capital is an important input to generate economic capital.

Social sustainability

Sustainability's social tenet has received less attention than its ecological and economic tenets (Koning, 2001; Cuthill, 2010; Colantonio, 2008). This is ironic because sustainability is essentially a social question (Partridge, 2005): it centers on how present societies choose to shape their actions so as to ensure the preconditions of future societies (Koning, 2001; Robinson, 2004).

Social sustainability rests on social capital; however, these two concepts are not synonymous: social capital focuses on processes, whereas social sustainability encompasses these processes, and also their outcomes. Social capital comprises two main components – the institutional (laws, norms or policies that govern behavior), and the organizational (the entities – individuals and institutions – that operate under the umbrella of the institutional framework) (Munasinghe, 2010). Social sustainability prevails when both, the institutional and the organizational components of social capital, support the possibility of equitable, diverse, interconnected and democratic communities (McKenzie, 2004) in both the present and the future.

Some of the key elements of social capital include trust, reciprocity and exchange between individuals, common rules, norms and mutually agreed upon sanctions which may be handed down within a society, and connectedness between networks or groups – including access to wider institutions (Carney, 1999). Social capital is augmented by use (Munasinghe, 2010; Putnam, 1995), unlike ecological and economic capitals, which are depleted by use.

High social capital can both positively and negatively impact social sustainability indicators (Koning, 2001). For example, high social capital could translate into a community working towards common social goals – such as reducing vulnerability or equity and poverty alleviation, thus increasing social cohesion. This would enable socio-economic systems to remain resilient in times of flux and transition, and bolster the coping mechanisms of disadvantaged factions of society (Munasinghe, 2010). This, in turn, would potentially minimize social unsustainability indicators – such as violence. On the other hand, high social capital could also translate into communities taking collective action which is unethical – including community-led riots, pogroms and ethnic cleansing. The accompanying violence and social distrust would be indicators of decreased social sustainability.

Vallance, Perkins, and Dixon (2011) outline *development* – a focus on meeting the basic needs of shelter and food – as a recurrent theme in social sustainability literature. *Development* is often pegged as *brown* or *developing world* agenda, and not relevant to the developed world, which already meets its basic needs, and therefore focuses on maintaining the levels at which its basic and higher-order needs are currently being met. For social sustainability to flourish, development needs to be address all present and future societies; it needs to meet basic human needs (Streeten, Burki, Haq, Hicks, & Stewart, 1981), and also go beyond this to afford human freedoms, such as social opportunities, political rights, economic facilities, guarantees of transparency and protective security (Sen, 1999), and facilitate human development, thereby expanding economic, social, cultural and political choices and leading to sustainability, productivity and empowerment (Haq, 1999).

Cultural sustainability

Cultural sustainability has traditionally been clubbed with social sustainability. However, since the 1990s, several international organizations (Committee on Culture of the world association of United Cities and Local Governments, 2015; European Commission, 2007; European Task Force on Culture and Development, 1997; United Nations Development Program, 2004) and scholars (Hawkes, 2001; Munasinghe, 2010) have argued that culture is a distinct dimension of sustainability. In 1995, UNESCO proposed culture as a key dimension of sustainability; and, in 2001, Jon Hawkes popularized it as the fourth pillar of sustainability. Culture has since been included as a key dimension of sustainability in several sustainability paradigms. These paradigms argue that a cultural shift in society's values and the way they are expressed is required to internalize the changes proposed by the new sustainability frameworks (Nurse, 2006) – and, thereby, to achieve sustainability (Hawkes,2001) – since culture affects all the dimensions of sustainability (Munasinghe, 1992).

While *culture* is a highly contested term (Hawkes, 2001), cultural anthropologists agree that two defining features of a culture are that it is learnt, and that it is shared by a certain community or group of people (Mead & Metraux, 1953). These groups are not only characterized by physical demarcations such as nations and geographies; they also exist at a micro-level within societies as smaller communities which share symbols, heroes, rituals and values (Hofstede, Hofstede, & Minkov, 2010).

Culture encompasses three aspects: a) values and aspirations or the worldview, b) the modes of developing and communicating the worldview, and c) the intangible and tangible manifestations of the worldview (Hawkes, 2001). Cultural capital includes tangible aspects such as artifacts and intangible aspects such as oral traditions and expressions, bioregional social practices and indigenous knowledge (Moreno, Santagata, & Tabassum, 2004).

Cultural sustainability hinges on the fine balance between preserving culture (United Nations Educational, Scientific and Cultural Organization, 2002) and allowing cultural metamorphosis (Hawkes, 2001). The amalgamation of indigenous cultures – which represent more than 90% of the total global diversity (Gray, 1991) – with state cultures is an inevitable corollary of globalization (Working Group on Culture of United Cities and Local Governments, 2006). While such an intermingling has both pros and cons (Gray, 1991), it is imperative that indigenous cultural capital, with its diversity of histories, geographies, actors and content, is safeguarded. This is just as important as preserving biodiversity (United Nations Educational, Scientific and Cultural Organization, 2002). Cultural sustainability is also underpinned by the ability to retain the cultural identity of a people, while simultaneously allowing change to occur in a manner which is mindful of their cultural values (Sustainable Development Research Institute, 1998). Therefore, inclusive and participatory governance in framing and assessing cultural policies is integral to cultural development (Committee on Culture of the World Association of United Cities and Local Governments, 2015) and sustainability.

2.4   Sustainability paradigms: integrating the compound picture of sustainability

The previous section discussed the dimensions of sustainability; here, we review paradigms that integrate these dimensions into a compound picture. This is important because holistic sustainability is much more than the sum of its parts (Munasinghe, 2010).

Several attempts have been made to elucidate, communicate, model and depict sustainability and sustainable development – including diagrammatically. These diagrams, like most diagrammatic representations and models, reveal the gaps of their sentential paradigms (Larkin & Simon, 1987). Most understandings of sustainability and their diagrammatic representations depict three dimensions of sustainability – ecological, social and economic. These diagrams locate sustainability or sustainable development at the center of, at the intersection of, or resting on, these dimensions (McKeown, 2002).

In 1987, the Brundtland Commission visualized sustainable development as resting on three pillars – social, environment and economy. The diagram (Figure 2.2) implies that each pillar is equally important and independent, and that together the three pillars support the roof – sustainable development (Mann,

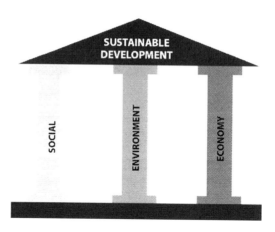

Figure 2.2 Brundtland's diagram for sustainable development (1987)

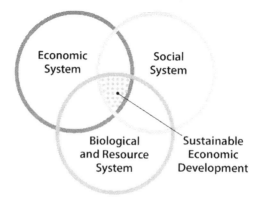

Figure 2.3 Barbier's sustainability Venn (1987)

2011). The idea of economic development, social development and environmental protection as independent and mutually reinforcing pillars was echoed in the Earth Summit in 2002, and the outcome document of the 2005 World Summit (Mann, 2011).

Several sustainability diagrams – including Barbier's sustainability Venn diagram (Figure 2.3) which is arguably one of the most recognizable sustainability diagrams – seem to imply that each dimension of sustainability is discrete and can be measured separately (Stanners et al., 2007). The sustainability Venn diagram depicts sustainable economic development at the intersection of the three dimensions of sustainability, thereby representing Brundtland's three separate pillars as interlinked, interrelated and inseparable (Mann, 2011).

Munasinghe's (1992) sustainable development triangle (Figure 2.4) connects the social, environmental and economic vertices with lines, emphasizing that the interaction between the three pillars is as important as the separate domains.

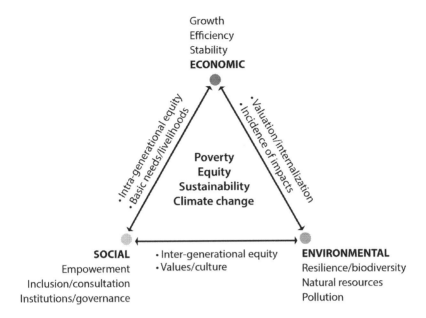

Figure 2.4 Munasinghe's sustainability triangle (1992)

Another issue with using the Venn diagram format to model sustainability is that the size of the circles seems to indicate the priority of the dimensions (Mann, 2011). Most sustainability Venn diagrams are comprised of equal circles, indicating that each of sustainability's dimensions is equally important. These represent *weak sustainability*, since they do not reflect the ecological constraints within which humans and other life forms, economies and social systems operate (Mann, 2011).

In contrast, *strong-sustainability* models – pioneered by Daly's (1996) bull's-eye diagram (Figure 2.5) – depict the overlapping circles of weak sustainability

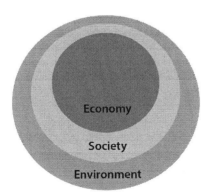

Figure 2.5 Daly's strong-sustainability bull's-eye diagram (1996)

models as concentric rings, in order to clarify the hierarchy of the dimensions and the dependency between them (Mann, 2011). The innermost ring, the economy, cannot exist without the exchange of goods and services between people in the middle ring – society. Society, in turn, cannot exist without the outermost ring – the environment – which is the source for the air, food and water required for existence, and fuel and raw material required for society's production-to-consumption systems.Figure 2.5 Daly's strong-sustainability bull's-eye diagram (1996)

Increasingly, sustainability models go beyond three dimensions. One such example is the Sustainability Integrated Guidelines for Management (Sigma) Project model (The Sigma Project, n.d.), which was launched in 1999 by the British Standards Institution, Forum for the Future and AccountAbility – a leading standards body, a leading charity and a think tank devoted to sustainability, and the international professional body for accountability, respectively – with the support of the UK Department of Trade and Industry. The Sigma Project model (Figure 2.6) replaces the three dimensions with five interlinked and overlapping *capitals* – social, human, man-made, financial and natural – from the

Figure 2.6 The Sigma Project's Five Capitals sustainability diagram (2003)

World Bank's *capital stock model*. This model resonates with the concept of strong sustainability, as it gives precedence to natural capital by circumscribing all the other capitals within it (Mann, 2011).

Culture has been factored in as a key dimension in several recent sustainability paradigms. Runnalls (2007) depicted the traditional three-circle Venn diagram circumscribed in the cultural dimension in her holistic systems approach to the four dimensions of community sustainability (Figure 2.7). While Runnalls's diagram seems to situate the pillars, the cultural dimension seems not to reach the sustainable core (Mann, 2011).

The Four Pillars model seems to call for more organic modeling, as it is difficult to depict more than three dimensions using Venn diagrams (Mann, 2011). A step in this direction is the Local Government Act 2002 of New Zealand, which depicts community sustainability as comprised of four interconnected dimensions (Figure 2.8) – cultural, environmental, economic and social – with overall well-being at the center (New Zealand Ministry for Culture and Heritage, 2006).

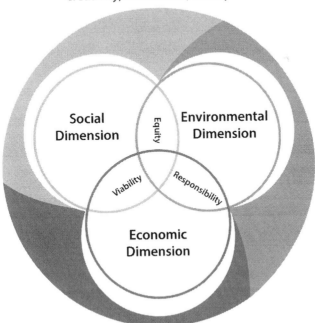

Figure 2.7 Runnalls's holistic systems approach to community sustainability (2007)

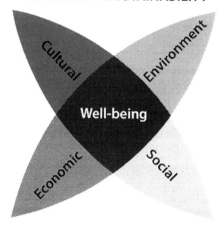

Figure 2.8 Four well-beings of community sustainability, according to the New Zealand Ministry for Culture and Heritage (2002)

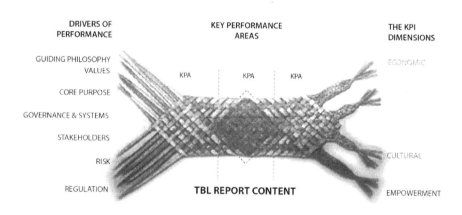

Figure 2.9 Landcare Research/Dunhan-Jones' braid (2010)

Another attempt to visualize sustainability is by New Zealand governmental research agency Landcare Research (Figure 2.9) and Dunham-Jones (2007), where sustainability is depicted as a braid. This representation shows interlinked social, environmental, cultural and economic dimensions which are stronger when interwoven together; when a single strand frays, it weakens the whole braid (Dunham-Jones, 2007).

2.5 Summary and conclusions

This chapter began by exploring when, why, how and where unsustainability began. The literature studied revealed that unsustainability did not originate at a particular time, and has no discrete cause or geography. It is an emergent process of the anthropocentric development process, underpinned by interconnected production-to-consumption systems. Development through the ages was both cause and effect of incremental development, and of simultaneous incremental unsustainability. The literature review also revealed that development and sustainability affect – and are affected by – multiple dimensions due to the interconnected, integrated systems of our world (Komiyama & Takeuchi, 2006; Shedroff, 2009; Thorpe, 2007). Some scholars explain the differences between growth and development rates of nations at a macro level on the basis of the economic dimension alone (Munasinghe, 1993). However, close examination reveals multiple causality and multiple dimensions at play. Economic behavior is the result of behavioral norms which stem from social conduct (Acemoglu, Simon,& James, 2001; Munasinghe, 2010; North, 1990) and which are orchestrated by a cultural orientation. This interconnectedness points to the fact that efforts to cultivate and maintain sustainable development must rest on a holistic concept of sustainability that is mindful of multiple dimensions.

The increasing human comprehension of sustainability's holistic nature is also evident in the sustainability diagrams we studied, which, over time, have expanded to include more dimensions. The evolution of these diagrams indicates that we are expanding our understanding of the dimensions of sustainability (Mann, 2011). Over time, the social (people), ecological (planet) and economic (profit) dimensions of sustainability have been supplemented by culture as a vital tenet (Duxbury & Gillette, 2007). In the future, more dimensions may be identified and dimensions that are currently under discussion – such as the political (O'Connor, 2007), temporal and/or ethical tenets – may be formally and commonly accepted. Important sub-dimensions may also be culled out from the identified umbrella dimensions, just as the cultural dimension was recently separately identified from the social dimension.

The prospect of expanding knowledge on sustainability juxtaposed with the fact that the sustainability crisis is real and urgent – and warrants immediate action – points to the importance of basing current sustainability efforts on a paradigm which reflects the current knowledge on sustainability, while being flexible enough to include and be enriched through future knowledge inputs. This flexibility is also relevant because a singular, absolute model defining the relationship, validity and priority of the tenets of sustainability cannot hold true for every situation, since the contexts of problems and their solutions are diverse (Komiyama & Takeuchi, 2006); trade-offs between the tenets are an unavoidable reality. Flexibility in structuring the scholarship and knowledge base of sustainability according to different situations may itself be a driving force for greater diversity; given that the homogenization of the models of sustainability and the approaches they offer will threaten the diversity of both Earth's regions and cultures, much as economic globalization does now (Komiyama & Takeuchi, 2006).

Therefore, in this book, we adopt a broad-based, inclusive and holistic definition of sustainability, underpinned by the Four Pillars model of sustainability, which is mindful of current knowledge and can contribute to further theory-building. Our scaffolding for our definition of holistic sustainability is the four pillar models, because its ecological, social, cultural and economic pillars encompass the broad themes contained in current and emerging discussions on holistic sustainability. The Four Pillars are also congruent with the set of 17 SDGs which outline the need for sustainable development to be holistic and balanced (Le Blanc et al., 2012).

Drawing on the literature review, in order to anchor our inquiry, this book defines *sustainability* as:

> A continual process of actualizing "the possibility that humans and other life will flourish on the Earth forever" (Ehrenfeld, 2008, p. 49) by maintaining the balance between different dimensions, including ecological, cultural, social and economic ones.

This definition will function as a reference point for holistic sustainability, which is an integral constituent of the questions this book centers on.

Using this definition of holistic sustainability as a reference point, the following chapter explores the extent to which designers address sustainability in a holistic manner.

3 Sustainability by design

3.1 Evolving design concerns: a mirror to dynamic social and historical processes

Papanek's (1971, p. 3) cult book, *Design for the Real World*, opens with the lines, "All men are designers. All that we do, almost all the time, is design, for design is basic to all human activity. The planning and patterning of any act towards a desired, foreseeable end constitutes the design process." However, since "everyone designs who devises a course of action aimed at changing existing situations, into preferred ones" (Herbert, 1969, p. 111), *design* is a highly contested (Julier, 2013), wide-ranging word that spans several disciplines and contexts (Fuad-Luke, 2009; Shedroff, 2009). Design has been classified in many ways, including by its several prefixes and suffixes (Fuad-Luke, 2009), and can refer to a process, the output of this process or also to an aesthetic or pattern (Walker, 1989).

Design is executed by trained, or *professional* designers, as well as by anonymous, or non-intentional, designers (Fuad-Luke, 2009). The prevalent mainstream design paradigm – which centers on the designer, design process and designed products (Walker, 1989), and the understanding that design is predominantly the domain of professional designers – emerged during the industrial revolution (Fuad-Luke, 2009; Walker, 1989). This emergence, and the shifts in design priorities that followed, cannot be examined in isolation; they need to be viewed as part of a larger dynamic social and historical process (Walker, 1989). Interestingly, both design and sustainability concerns – which have existed since time immemorial – crystallized during the industrial revolution.

The emergence of the design profession during industrialization

Before industrialization, products were parochially crafted in limited numbers (Walker, 1989). All the processes that were needed to envisage, make and sell a product were vested in a single craftsperson or guild of craftspeople. The industrial revolution divided integrated, artisan-based production-to-consumption systems into specialized disciplines (Dormer, 1997; Walker, 1989) – including design, production and marketing – in line with the concept of division of labor and the pursuit of increased productivity and efficiency (Cusumano, 1991) in

Europe and the United States (Walker, 1989). Industrial designers assumed the role of innovators, leaning on a logical design process to visualize big production batches for large, distant markets. Design began to be defined as "the art or action of conceiving of and producing a plan or drawing of something before it is made" (Design, 2018). It was only when designers were able to visualize the process – from concept generation to production – that *design* became exclusively coupled with *industry* (Greenhalgh, 1997a), and *industrial designer* was dissociated from *craftsperson* and *artist*. Consequently, "late-20thcentury Western culture saw the separation of 'design' from 'art' and 'craft,' and the separation in *having ideas* from *making objects*" (Peters, 1997, p. 18).

Social design concerns during and after industrialization

One of the first resistances to industrialization came in the form of the Arts and Crafts Movement. Proponents of the movement protested against the social, cultural and ecological evils – *unsustainabilities* – that industrialization heralded. They argued that craft revival would humanize society by restoring social equilibrium and the creative cultural ethos of the past. While the movement had little to boast of in terms of concrete achievement, it laid the foundation for future design ideologies that would reflect socialist concerns (Fuad-Luke, 2009). These concerns were evident in the pursuit of archetypical products that equalized their users, typical of Bauhaus design, and, later, in the rationalist, functionalist and modernist design that prevailed until World War II (Fuad-Luke, 2009). In a similar vein, communist ideals – including erasing all forms of social distinction – found expression through design, including by homogenizing fashion (Blaszczyk, 2011). It is interesting to note here that equalizing users is inherent in most pre-industrial craft, where archetypical products are produced in large numbers for communities.

Design and consumerism

The post-World War II generation, weary of one-size-fits-all design, demanded postmodern design pluralism (Fuad-Luke, 2009). With the war depleting manufacturing power in Europe, the United States became the hub of production. This saw the emergence of consumer-led design that celebrated the *American way* (Sheldon & Arens, 1932), which was based on high consumption and fueled by the constant exploitation of natural resources. Budding sustainability concerns were implicit in Sheldon and Arens' (1932) acknowledgement that, while the *American way* might be myopic and might need to draw on the more conservative European approach, "that time is not yet. . . . We still have tree-covered slopes to deforest and subterranean lakes of oil to tap with our gushers" (Sheldon & Arens, 1932, p. 15). Popular consumer-led design continued to hold its own in the West throughout the 1960s, alongside murmurs that design seemed more marketing-led than consumer-led (Whitely, 1993).

Design's social concerns take a backseat to ecological concerns in the 1970s

The global ecological and social concerns that had been brewing through the 1960s came to a head in the 1970s, and affected design as well. Papanek's (1971) book, *Design for the Real World*, urged designers to introspect deeply about how they could contribute meaningfully to global social and ecological issues. Papanek called on designers to be accountable to, and driven by, the world's ecological and social needs, rather than by the consumer-led economy. However, real-life ecological sustainability crises that were unfolding at the time seemed to drown out Papanek's call for social design, turning the spotlight almost exclusively onto ecological sustainability in the developed world. The West Asian oil price-rise crisis of 1973 forced design engineers in the global north to give serious thought to ecological issues such as energy efficiency; life-cycle thinking and life-cycle analysis emerged as a result (Fuad-Luke, 2009). While social concerns took a backseat to ecological concerns, they still popped up around the world through the mushrooming of alternative- and appropriate-technology practitioners, who proposed alternatives to capital-intensive industrial technology. The movement was popularized by Schumacher's (1973) book, *Small Is Beautiful: Economics as if People Mattered*, which had precedents in Gandhi's swadeshi ideology (Bakshi, 1987), which advocated domestic production-to-consumption systems.

Green design and Ecodesign in the 1980 and 1990s

Mounting global environmental awareness gave rise to the *green consumer* of the 1980s (Whitely, 1993); this was a driver for *green design*. John Elkington formulated *Ten Questions for the Green Designer*, for a 1986 UK Design Council booklet, inviting designers to reflect on life-cycle thinking and the green consumer (Chapman & Gant, 2007). Design for the Environment (DfE), or *Ecodesign*, subsumed green design in the 1990s. Ecodesign aimed to create a win-win situation by addressing both the ecology and the economy; it sought to minimize the negative ecological impacts of the product life cycle, while simultaneously offering financial benefits (Brezet & van Hemel, 1997). UNEP's manual on Ecodesign made the concept accessible to both for-profit and not-for-profit factions around the world, and galvanized the application of Ecodesign concepts.

The expanding scope of design post-2000

The scope of sustainability design grew rapidly post-2000. In the 1980s and 1990s, sustainability-aligned design approaches had centered on environmental stewardship and specifically on cleaning up unsustainability in the manufacturing process. Post-2000, this focus spread to transport, use and end-of-life issues – also looking at post-retail, and then the entire value chain: designers went beyond an environmental sustainability focus to engage with design for sustainability at a systemic and strategic level (Lønnea & Skjold, 2016).

Sustainability science has continually expanded to acknowledge and encompass escalating and pressing global issues – including climate change, violence, food security, social responsibility, inclusion and poverty. This has set the stage for alternative design praxis – including Design for Sustainability (D4S or DfS), slow design, social design, co-design, meta-design, design for the base of the pyramid (BoP), design activism, participatory innovation, jugaad and design participation. All of these alternatives look beyond ecological sustainability (Fuad-Luke, 2009) to address the different and often disparate aspects which come together to comprise a compound picture of sustainability.

3.2   Role and potential of designers to actualize sustainability

Design shapes production-to-consumption systems and, thereby, sustainability. Design decisions orchestrate production-to-consumption systems – including material production and processing, fabrication, distribution, use, repair and maintenance, and end-of-life handling (Lofthouse, 2017; Waage, 2005) – and thereby determine the flow of materials and human resources (White, Stewart, Howes, & Adams, 2008). These production-to-consumption systems, in part and in whole, and their collateral effects – including environmental, social (White et al., 2008) and cultural spin-offs – shape sustainability.

Innovation – "any novel product, service, or production process that departs significantly from prior product, service, or production process architectures" (McKinley, Latham, & Braun, 2014, p. 91) – is an inherent part of most design initiatives aiming to impact sustainability. However, despite the fact that innovation fundamentally calls for a departure from the status quo, most sustainability design initiatives stay close to traditional design's typical manufacture-use focus and design process. Most sustainability design happens in the domain of manufacture-use (Cuginotti, Miller,& van der Pluijm, 2008), and sustainability generally doesn't get addressed in the design process up until the operational product-design phase, which is traditionally design's stronghold. Addressing sustainability earlier in the design process, in the front-end stage – the phase when the design brief and initial concepts are formulated – can facilitate holistic and systemic sustainability design (Storacker, Wever, Dewulf, & Blankenburg, 2013). Several consequences of the product life cycle, which need to be *cleaned up*, could be eliminated or minimized by envisaging and addressing them earlier during front-end innovation (Dewulf, 2013) stage, which also offers the most opportunity for radical and out-of-the-box alternatives – such as replacing a product with a service.

Missing the opportunity to factor sustainability and innovation early on, not only in the domain of manufacture-use but in the entire production-to-consumption system, is also a missed opportunity for design to impact sustainability at a systems level (Dewulf, 2013) – whereby the properties of each individual system-component blurs and merges to form the whole system (Checkland, 1997; Jackson, 2003; Weinberg, 2001). Most sustainability design initiatives do not address system innovation, which Brezet (1997) identifies as the highest of the four incremental levels of innovation towards sustainability – product improvement, product redesign, function innovation and system innovation. The potential to achieve sustainability by using a traditional goal-based optimization approach seems bleak, as itis a system property and does not rest on individual components of the system: achieving it calls for a multi-scale, process-oriented and systemic approach (Ceschin & Gaziulusoy, 2016; Bagheri & Hjorth, 2007). One way to extend the scope of innovation from product to system could be by shifting the desired outcome of the design process from the product to be designed, to holistic and systemic sustainability (Cuginotti et al., 2008, Davis, Öncel, & Yang, 2010; Morelli, 2006). This shift – from designing products to designing the systems that underpin them – can potentially create the paradigm shift necessary to move beyond reducing unsustainability, towards proactively and strategically *designing* sustainability.

Getting inputs on sustainability challenges and opportunities from production-to-consumption system representatives, preferably in the front-end stage itself (White et al., 2008) could help designers understand the systems picture. While sustainability lies outside the expertise of traditional designers (White et al., 2008), they are ideally placed to facilitate such integrated and multidisciplinary front-end innovation teams. This is because designers' visionary, creative and analytical thinking (Jin, Crul, & Brezet, 2011) allows them to communicate with a cross section of stakeholders (Valencia, Mugge, Schoormans, & Schifferstein, 2015), and synthesize diverse and incomplete inputs and information, while maintaining a strategic overview of the process (Stappers, 2007).

Designers are future-oriented visualizers and problem solvers (Diehl & Christiaans, 2015). These attributes allow them to leverage challenges in dynamic and complex systems and scenarios – such as those at the intersection of sustainability and globalized production-to-consumption systems in flux – as opportunities for innovation. Unfolding scenarios lead to new socio-economic and cultural patterns, which translate into uncharted market potential – including for non-mainstream, niche products and systems with high social and cultural value (Morelli, 2006). The combination of generative and evaluative thinking (Stappers, 2007) allows designers to explore these evolving intersections of culture and market, because they can intuitively decipher the basis of emotions, values and meanings, and communicate abstract information (Maxwell et al., 2003).

This skill set – visionary, creative and analytical thinking (Jin et al., 2011), and the combination of generative and evaluative thinking (Stappers, 2007) – allows designers to go from designing sustainable products to designing sustainable behavior (Bhamra, Lilley, & Tang, 2008; Lockton, 2013; Wever, van Kuijk, & Boks, 2008). Designers are positioned to shape mainstream value systems (Wahl & Baxter, 2008) and design, because they have the skill set to understand people, and influence their values, attitudes and aspirations (Vezzoli & Manzini, 2008): they can design with the intention of influencing people to behave sustainably (Lockton, 2013). Bhamra et al. (2008) outline seven strategies of design for behavioral change: a) eco-information (encouraging consumers to make sustainable decisions by providing them with understandable sustainability information), b) eco-choice (enabling consumers to make sustainable decisions by providing them with sustainable options), c) eco-feedback (enabling consumers to make sustainable decisions by providing them with feedback on the sustainability of their choices), d) eco-spur (prompting sustainable behavior by rewarding it, and discouraging unsustainable behavior by punishing it), e) eco-steer (features embedded in the product design ensure that consumers make sustainable decisions), f) eco-technical intervention (design combined with advanced technology ensures that consumers adopt sustainable decisions), and g) clever design (the product is designed to automatically act in a sustainability-aligned manner, without raising user awareness or changing their behavior). Each of these strategies incrementally shifts control from the user to the designed product (Lockton, 2013).

Design shapes the world's production-to-consumption systems on which sustainability rests, and therefore, designers are key players in actualizing holistic sustainability. The potential and opportunity to design sustainability calls for designers to step out from their traditionally values-agnostic orientations (White et al., 2008) into the role of activists; it challenges designers to create counter-narratives (Fuad-Luke, 2009) to the mainstream design paradigm.

Designing holistic sustainability is more possible now than ever before, because design's expanding scope now positions designers to address larger issues – including sustainability. Valtonen (2005) describes the evolution of the designer's role in Finland over time. Initially likened to an artist, the designer became a core part of the industrial team – alongside the engineer and marketing experts – in the 1960s. In the 1970s, Finnish design became engrossed with user-centric issues, including ergonomics; in the 1980s, with design management; and in the 1990s, with brand-building and strategic design. In the new millennium, the focus of Finnish design is shifting towards creating a market edge in the rapidly globalizing world through new innovation. Valtonen's description of the Finnish design journey resonates with the expanding scope, role and power of designers around the world. Designers are increasingly positioned to move beyond design's traditional manufacture-use focus, to influencing and making strategic decisions which will determine production-to-consumption systems – and thereby sustainability – earlier in the innovation process (Lofthouse & Stevenson, 2013;British Design Council, 2004; Swedish Design Industry, 2004).

3.3 Drivers for sustainable design

We discussed the huge potential for design to impact sustainability in the previous section. Businesses are emerging as important stakeholders in actualizing sustainability design because the design function is housed within them (Ceschin & Gaziulusoy, 2016). The drivers for sustainable design can come from within the business (internal drivers) and also from outside the business (external drivers) (Dewulf, 2013). These drivers tend to move from external to internal over the company's sustainability journey. The initial push to embrace sustainability comes from two external drivers – regulatory frameworks and market demand – which we discuss below.

Formal and informal regulatory frameworks

One of the strongest external drivers for sustainable design and innovation is the growing importance of sustainability in the business landscape, and the consequent emergence of formal and informal regulatory frameworks (van Hemel & Cramer, 2002; Yoon & Tello, 2009;White et al., 2008;Williamson & Lynch-Wood, 2012). Businesses are being pressured to incorporate sustainability into their activities by different nodes of the value chain (PwC, n.d.; White et al., 2008). Policy and regulatory frameworks by governments – including those that demand compliance with labor and material standards – are increasing in both number and stringency (White et al., 2008; Howes et al., 2017). Failure to comply can mean the loss of future business, and even reversal of existing business by way of product recalls (PwC, n.d.; White et al., 2008).

Market demand and access

Demand (the carrot) is a seemingly stronger external driver than regulatory frameworks (the stick) (Mate, 2006; van Hemel & Cramer, 2002). Increasingly, urban consumers in both the developing and developed world – informed by product boycotts, media and NGO campaigns – are forming pressure groups which demand product transparency (Sarkar, 2013; Díaz-García, González-Moreno, & Sáez-Martínez, 2015; White et al., 2008). Driven by this, a plethora of companies are implementing green labeling, branding and marketing schemes. This pressures their competitors to follow suit in order to protect their market shares and also to tap into the widening sustainability-aligned consumer segments (Sarkar, 2013; White et al., 2008) such as the Lifestyles of Health and Sustainability (LOHAS) market sector demographic which is comprised of upscale and well-educated consumers interested in sustainable initiatives (Sarkar, 2013). Importers now demand integrated product audits (Social Compliance Initiative, 2015) which examine one or more factors, especially environmental factors (no lead paints, azo dye detection, etc.) towards citizen protection (low emission and low voltage). All of these compel businesses, and thereby design, to view sustainability not only as a market niche, but as a matter of market access (White et al., 2008), brand value and market credibility (Kumar & Christodoulopoulou, 2014).

3.4   Design approaches and assessment systems aimed at actualizing sustainability

In Section 3.3, we discussed how the changing business landscape has led to the emergence of drivers for sustainability design, and in Section 3.2, we saw how designers are ideally placed to leverage these opportunities. This section explores existing sustainability-aligned approaches and assessment systems, which can be scaffolding for designers' sustainability design practices. While we studied several approaches and assessment systems, we will limit our discussion to only those seminal approaches which position themselves as aiming to actualize sustainability design. This is because we argue that every design approach or assessment system can be more or less aligned to sustainability, based on how the design problem is framed and the designer's agency and propensity to practice sustainability design. Since classifying the suitability of existing design approaches and assessment systems for sustainability design use is beyond the scope of this book, we limited ourselves to only those with clearly stated sustainability-related intentions.

Sustainability approaches

1.   Natural capitalism

The Natural Capitalism Framework (Hawken et al., 1999) – also known as eco-efficiency (Schmidheiny, 1992) – centers on maximizing the productive value of natural capital. The framework argues that economies try to optimize the productivity of their scarcest resources in order to increase productivity and thereby profitability. During the industrial revolution, labor productivity was optimized as material resources were abundant. Post-industrialization, natural resources are growing scarcer, and they therefore need to be valued and optimized (Lovins, Lovins, & Hawken, 1999).

The framework advocates radical resource productivity (increasing the productivity of natural resources), ecological redesign (shifting to biologically inspired models), service and flow economies (shifting emphasis from products to services) and investing in natural capital (to build a strong resource base of finite natural resources) (Hawken et al., 1999). Natural capitalism seems intuitive, and while this makes it easy to understand, it offers no concrete methodology or tool to the designer. It has been criticized for not sufficiently addressing some aspects of production-to-consumption systems – such as waste (Shedroff, 2009). This approach centers on economic and ecological sustainability, and does not address the social and cultural aspects of sustainability.

Natural capitalism design example

Living Technologies cleans sewage water by running it through 'Living Machines', which are basically tanks containing water-purifying organisms, including bacteria and algae. The cost-efficient process doesn't produce toxicity and odor, and is located in a residential neighborhood.

(John Todd Ecological Design, 2018)

2.   Cradle-to-cradle

The Cradle-to-cradle Framework (Stahel, McDonough,& Braungart, 2002) – also known as C2C, or eco-effectiveness – focuses on closed-loop material flow of both technical and natural materials. C2C argues that there should be two material loop categories – products in the biosphere must be biodegradable, and materials in the technosphere should be continuously up-cycled (Stahel et al., 2002). Its key principles are materials health (safe materials that can be constantly recycled), materials reutilization (all materials must be constantly recycled), renewable energy (100% of energy used during product use and manufacture must be renewable), water stewardship (water must be managed to be clean) and social fairness (high labor standards) (Wever & Vogtländer, 2015).

C2C has been instrumental in motivating and inspiring businesses to pursue sustainability goals and radical innovation (Bakker, Wever, Teoh, & De Clerq, 2010). However, though it has helped open businesses up to the idea of sustainability, it has been critiqued for not being technically justified (Gauziulusoy, 2015). Critics of C2C argue that it does not adequately account for energy and resources used in converting waste into usable material streams. Neither does it consider the possibility that natural nutrients absorbed into ecosystems in the wrong quantities or locations (De Man & Brezet, 2016) can create an imbalance in bioregions and be hazardous for humans (Reijnders, 2008). A fundamental critique of C2C is that even if it were theoretically possible to create materials cycles with no waste, virgin materials would still need to be harvested to cater to growing populations and increasing development (Bjørn & Hauschild, 2013).

C2C has also been critiqued for being biased towards technical materials and technological solutions, as opposed to natural materials and traditional technologies (Shedroff, 2009), and advocating technical solutions, as opposed to exploring solutions centering on systemic socio-cultural possibilities (Amelung & Martens, 2008). Another critique is that C2C is too simplistic to be applied to complex products (such as consumer electronics): this seems corroborated by the fact that such examples are absent from the C2C roster (De Man & Brezet, 2016).

Designers need to have access to databases with material composition data in order to implement C2C. Currently, these databases do not exist or are not easily accessible, and first-hand information is difficult to come by as vendors today are spread over geographies (Bakker et al., 2010). The C2C framework offers detailed criteria and is accompanied by a tedious and stringent certification process (Shedroff, 2009); however, it calls for significant research and investments for new material-technologies.

C2C is ecologically focused, and does not address sustainability's cultural aspects at all. It touches upon some social aspects but neglects several key elements – including local production-to-consumption systems (Shedroff, 2009) and the possible hazards for humans through the release of excessive biological waste into the wrong ecosystem.

C2C design example

Climatex is upholstery which was designed by short listing 38 human and earth-friendly chemical formulations, from the many thousands used in textile production. This ensured the outflow of waste water from the mill was actually cleaner than the inflow, and that Climatex could decompose safely. The waste Climatex scraps were converted into felt, saving on disposal costs, and turning waste into another revenue stream. The felt is absorbed by local strawberry farmers as ground cover for their crops.

(Lumsden, 2014)

3.   *Biomimicry*

Biomimicry is an approach to innovation which seeks sustainable solutions to human problems by mimicking nature: the first level is mimicking forms; the second, mimicking processes; and the last, mimicking ecosystems (Benyus, 2002; The Biomimicry Institute, 2018). The approach advocates that designers use nature as model, measure and mentor (Benyus, 1997).

There are several tools and mechanisms available to integrate biomimicry into the design process. These include databases – the Chakrabarti system, the Biomicry Database and TRIZ, among others – which point designers in the direction of biomimicry information, inspiration and technical backstopping (Volstad, 2008). There are also tools to familiarize designers with biomimicry principles in designer-friendly formats: the Biomimicry Design Spiral, for example, presents biomimetic principles (principles arrived at by mimicking technical solutions from nature) in a format which is similar to the generic contemporary design process (Shedroff, 2009). Card decks have also been used as a tool to inform and inspire designers about biomimicry. Baumeister, Tocke, Dwyer, Ritter, and Benyus (2013) offer a handbook which covers several biomimicry methods and tools.

The assumption that biomimicry is sustainable just because it mimics nature has been critiqued. Shallow or reductive biomimicry (which involves mimicking natural forms) has been critiqued in particular, because it misses the potential for holistic design intervention, which deep biomimicry (which involves mimicking natural ecosystems) offers (Reap, Baumeister and Bras, 2005), especially when it is rooted in local systems (Ceschin & Gaziulusoy, 2016). Biomimicry falls short of addressing the social, economic (Shedroff, 2009), and cultural (Mathews, 2011) aspects of sustainability.

Biomimicry design example

The noise caused by the Shinkansen Bullet Train, which travels at 200 miles per hour, was so loud that it disturbed people living half a kilometer away. The noise was caused because every time the train emerged from a tunnel there were significant air pressure changes, producing loud thunder-like claps. Eiji Nakatsu, the chief engineer, identified the solution by looking for an exemplar in nature which travelled quickly and noiselessly between two mediums. The avid bird-watcher zeroed in on the kingfisher, which moved between water and air almost noiselessly. He modeled the front-end of the train on the bird's beak, resulting in a train that was quieter, and more aerodynamic, using 15% less electricity, even while going 10% faster.

(Biomimicry Institute, 2018)

4. *Ecodesign*

Ecodesign, or design for environment, is an approach which aims to reduce the environmental impact of products, systems and services throughout their life cycles from raw material extraction to end-of-life phase (Sherwin & Evans, 2000). The approach shifts towards more sustainable production and consumption by introducing ecological criteria alongside traditional product-design criteria – including functionality, ergonomics, aesthetics, profit and quality (van Hemel, 1998). It also does this by following the reduce-reuse-recycle waste hierarchy (Ceschin & Gaziulusoy, 2016).

Ecodesign is supported by different tools – including guidelines, checklists and handbooks, screening/management methodologies and tools – and linked life-cycle assessments and databases (Fraunhofer IZM, 2005; Vezzoli & Manzini, 2008). These tools help in quantifying environmental impacts, thereby enabling designers to make design decisions based on meaningful comparisons between products of the same category (Ceschin & Gaziulusoy, 2016). One of the earliest Ecodesign tools is the LiDs (Life cycle Design Strategy) wheel (Brezet & Van Hemel, 1997), also known as the EcoDesign Web (Bhamra & Lofthouse, 2003), D4S Strategy Wheel (Crul & Diehl, 2006), and the EcoDesign Strategy Wheel (Van Boeijen & Daalhuizen, 2014). This quick and dirty tool allows a comparison between two products in an easy, but sometimes subjective manner (Wever & Vogtländer, 2015).

Early Ecodesign addressed end-of-pipe issues, and over time progressed to looking at clean production, and then on to the entire life cycle (van Hemel, 1998). While later Ecodesign projects aimed to optimize the entire socio-economic system of the product, the approach's original economic and ecological focus (increasing prosperity while decreasing environmental costs) has prevailed as a priority (Diehl, 2010). This had led to the critique that Ecodesign lacks complexity (Gauziulusoy, 2015) and that its environmental and technical focus does not adequately address human factors (Bhamra, Lilley, & Tang, 2011). It disregards the social (Ceschin & Gaziulusoy, 2016) and cultural dimensions of sustainability, including those related to consumption (Ryan, 2003).

Ecodesign example

Yes Light is a 70 gm paper which is high on bulk, giving it the touch and feel of a 80gsm paper. Using this paper reduces 10% environmental load per sheet as compared to a regular 80gsm paper. This makes Yes Light an economical and eco-friendly substitute for office and home printing and general purposes.

(Yes Paper, n.d.)

5. *Design for Sustainability*

Design for Sustainability (D4S), or Sustainable Product Design, is an upgrade of Ecodesign: it goes beyond Ecodesign's environment and economic focus to integrate the social, ecological and economic pillars of sustainability (Crul & Diehl, 2006). It is one of the more inclusive sustainability design approaches for this reason, and also because it addresses sustainability assessment and business generation for emerging markets in the developing world. D4S fits well with small and medium enterprises in developing world because it aims to address the motivators for consumer choice – better quality and lower price – through sustainability strategies, including reuse, improved material sourcing and reduced energy (Clark, Kosoris, Hong, & Crul, 2009).

D4S outlines three levels of innovation for products and systems – incremental, radical and fundamental – and three sub-approaches to these – redesign, new product development and product-service system (Crul & Diehl, 2006). The D4S redesign approach comprises 10 steps with corresponding tools to facilitate these, including an impact-assessment matrix, D4S strategies and rules of thumb. The D4S approach also has a mechanism to compare the finished redesigned product with the original, so as to map the efficacy of the sustainable-design input (Crul & Diehl, 2006). In addition to supporting innovation and design, this approach offers tools to facilitate policy formulation and business creation (Castillo, Diehl,& Brezet, 2012), thereby looking at the envelope within design exists.

While D4S aims to address social sustainability, it retains the ecological and economic priority of its parent ideology – Ecodesign. It needs to address a larger spectrum of social issues, and include cultural issues in order to address sustainability holistically.

D4S design example

Moonlight is a chargeable, solar-powered lantern, designed as a sustainable substitute to potentially replace the kerosene lamps traditionally used in Cambodian households with no access to public electricity. The traditional kerosene lamps give a dim light, cannot be used on windy or rainy days, and are expensive to refuel. In contrast the MoonLight generates light equivalent to four kerosene lamps, and is a one-time investment as it is solar charged. It is easily portable, and can be hung from walls or ceilings or worn around the neck.

(Clark et al., 2009)

6. *Circular economy*

The circular economy is a concept that precedes the Brundtland commission's call for sustainable development (Wever & Vogtländer, 2015),and advocates that the mainstream industrial economy (with a linear make-use-waste production-to-consumption system) should be replaced by a circular economy with no waste. This is similar to C2C thinking; however, while C2C focuses on material flows, circular economy has a broader focus on the economy.

The current circular economy framework draws on principles from biomimicry, industrial ecology, cradle-to-cradle and blue economy (Ellen MacArthur

Foundation, 2013) towards creating an industrial economy which produces no waste or pollution, with separate biological and technical nutrient flows. The concept advocates looking at the systemic picture, rather than focusing on its separate components.

The methods to realize a circular economy include methods from the approaches on which it draws, and also from newer approaches such as ReSolve – regenerate, share, optimize, loop, virtualize and exchange (Zils, 2014). Newer strategies towards the circular economy also include creating longer-lasting products by reusing, repairing, refurbishing, remanufacturing, retrieval and recycling (Wever & Vogtländer, 2015).

The circular economy has been critiqued because its business-to-business focus generally results in techno-centric innovations in production systems (Wever et al., 2008): this limits design opportunity to engineering solutions, in line with Ecodesign. Expanding the scope of design within the circular economy framework would allow designers to also respond to socio-cultural and systems issues (Lofthouse & Prendeville, 2018). The circular economy retains the economic and ecological priorities of the approaches on which it draws. It fails to address cultural issues, and addresses social issues to a very limited degree (De Man & Brezet, 2016).

Circular economy design example

Pay-per-lux is an intelligent lighting system which Phillips developed collaboratively for and with architect Thomas Rau's lighting needs. Instead of designing a lighting device, they designed a lighting plan, which was mindful of available natural light, and charged Rau only for the amount of light consumed, and not for the fixtures. By selling the service rather than the product, Philips can better control the product's design, maintenance and recovery, and Rau only pays for the service he requires. This is a win-win not only for client and service-provider, but the energy-efficient design is also good for the environment.

(Ellen MacArthur Foundation, 2017)

7.   *Design for the base of the pyramid*

The base of the pyramid (BoP) consists of more than 4.5 billion economically challenged people (Prahalad & Hart, 2002). These people lack access to basic services (including health, education and shelter), and are characterized by social, cultural and political exclusion (Karnani, 2007). Design for BoP clients involves developing simple, functional and potentially open-source solutions, which can potentially transform their lives – including by enabling them to become self-reliant and empowered entrepreneurs (Smith, 2007).

There are two main approaches to design for the BoP: the first looks at the BoP as consumers (such that the focus is on developing and selling products/services to the BoP), and the second looks at the BoP as producers (such that the focus is on using the BoP as a labor input) (Rangan, Quelch, Herrero,& Barton, 2007). The concept alleviating poverty by targeting the BoP as consumers has been critiqued (Oosterlaken, 2008) because it can potentially exploit the BoP as low-cost labor who could, ironically, likely produce the products that are marketed to them. The second generation of BoP strategy, therefore, proposes to merge both first-generation BoP strategies: BoP as consumer and producer. This new strategy positions the BoP as a potential collaborator which can be empowered and involved in the innovation process, and the business resulting from it (Simanis & Hart, 2008). Several current BoP projects involve the client in the design process – including co-creation (Chakrabarti & Mason, 2014; Ben Letaifa & Reynoso, 2015) and participatory design. However, most of these strategies are still at a formative stage (Castillo et al., 2012).

   Several design manuals and tools support design for the BoP including the D4S (UNEP, 2006), the BoP Protocol (Simanis & Hart, 2008), and Human Centered Design Toolkit (IDEO, 2009). Gomez Castillo, Diehl, and Brezet (2012) have proposed a methodological framework to integrate these tools. Unlike most of the approaches reviewed in this chapter, which do not address sustainability's social dimension, the BoP framework focuses on socio-economic development, including by livelihood generation. However, because of its socio-economic focus, the BoP framework misses addressing ecological or cultural issues.

BoP design example

MittiCool is an Indian designed and produced clay refrigerator that is priced at around USD 40, making it affordable by the BoP. The fridge is tiny compared to its mainstream counterpart. At just 15x15x 12 inches, it can easily fit into BoP kitchens. The insides of the fridge remain around 8 degrees cooler than the outside temperature, keeping milk fresh for two days, and vegetables for four. MittiCool was developed by a traditional potter in India, who wanted to make a fridge that the poor could afford and use.

(Austa, 2015)

Sustainability assessment systems

8.   *Life-cycle Assessment*

The Life-cycle Assessment (LCA) assesses the environmental impact of the product over its life cycle, and is positioned to be a supporting tool to sustainability design approaches, especially those with an environmental focus. It examines the inputs (including the materials and energy consumed to make the product), and the resultant outputs (including the emissions and waste), throughout the product's life cycle – including during raw material extraction, processing, assembly, packaging, installation and use, upgrading and maintenance, and disposal and recycling.

   There are two ways of conducting LCAs. The classical (Wever &Vogtländer, 2015) and resource-intensive (White et al., 2008) process-based LCAs calculate the materials, energy and emission at each node of the production-to-consumption system or process (Shedroff, 2009). This makes it impossible to use unless the product exists, ruling out its use for the design-and-development stage (Shedroff, 2009).

The *fast-track* (Wever & Vogtländer, 2015) economic input-output LCA (EIO-LCA) model uses proxy data from reliable sources instead of measuring this first-hand: this makes it cost- and time-effective (White et al., 2008), but not necessarily as accurate as the process-based LCA model (Shedroff, 2009). The main steps of the EIO-LCA are a) establishing the scope and goal of the analysis, b)establishing the system, functional unit and system boundaries, c) quantification (of materials, energy, etc.), d) entering and calculating data, and e)interpreting data (Wever & Vogtländer, 2015).

LCA has been criticized as being opaque and not easily understood, and therefore not frequently used (Risz, Cammarata, Wellise,& Swibel, 2018). LCAs emerged in the 1960s, when environmental sustainability was emerging as a priority area (Guinée, 2016), and they retain their focus on ecological analysis (Shedroff, 2009). LCAs record only the direct ecological impact, and do not take into account the systems picture: there have therefore been calls for the deepening of the LCA framework in general (Guinée, 2016). LCAs fail to address social (Finkbeiner, Schau, Lehmann,& Traverso, 2010; Lehmann, Russi, Bala, Finkbeiner, & Fullana-i-Palmer, 2011), economic and cultural issues.

9.   Life-cycle Costing

Life-cycle Costing (LCC) computes the sum of the existing or potential costs which are directly related to a product over its life cycle. It is positioned to be used as an analysis and design decision-making tool, and is arguably most used in the construction sector.

Different variations of LCCs calculate different costs across different sectors. Conventional LCCs assess internal costs and benefits to the organization, while environmental LCCs additionally assess external costs and benefits which are anticipated to be privatized (Hunkeler, Lichtenvort,& Rebitzer, 2008). Societal LCCs (SLCCs) – which are still in their nascent stage – aim to assess private and external societal costs (United Nations Environmental Program, 2009), expressing social impacts in financial terms (Risz et al., 2018).

LCCs are usually carried out in four phases – a) defining the goal, scope and functional unit; b) calculating inventory costs; c) arriving at aggregate costs by cost categories; and d) interpretation of results. The definition of data availability and quality assessment, cost categories, and assurance are all challenges for the LCC approach (United Nations Environmental Program, 2009).

LCC focuses primarily on economic analysis; it does not address social (Lehmann et al., 2011; Finkbeiner et al., 2010), ecological or cultural issues. A variation of the traditional LCC is the upcoming Social Life-cycle Costing (SLCC), which focuses purely on social aspects: however, SLCCs are not as prevalent as LCCs (Risz et al., 2018).

10.   Social Life-cycle Assessment

Social Life-cycle Assessment (S-LCA) assesses the social and socio-economic aspects of products throughout their life cycles. S-LCA emerged from the growing critique that LCAs needed to include social aspects (Lehmann et al., 2011; Finkbeiner et al., 2010). The UNEP *Guidelines for Social Life Cycle Assessment of Products* (United Nations Environmental Program, 2009) summarize existing methodologies and approaches, and include methodological sheets (Finkbeiner et al., 2010). These documents outline socially relevant attributes to be assessed, the indicators for the analysis, and the recommendations for data assessment against five main categories of stakeholders – workers/employees, the local community, society (national and global), consumers and the value-chain actors (Life Cycle Initiative, n.d.). S-LCA needs to be integrated with mainstream LCA approaches, and cultural aspects need to be included towards addressing sustainability holistically (Finkbeiner et al., 2010).

11.   Life-cycle Sustainability Assessment

The concept of the Life-cycle Sustainability Assessment (LCSA) appeared in 2008 (Klöpffer, 2008) in response to the call for LCAs to broaden their ecological focus to include social and economic impacts, in line with the Triple Bottom Line model. Current LCSAs expand ecologically focused LCAs by combining them with S-LCAs and LCCs to look at broader impacts: LCSA = LCA + SLCA + LCC (Valdivia et al., 2013; Guinée, 2016). Guinée et al. (2011) have argued that LCSAs should also advocate broadening the level of analysis (from product-, sector- and economy-wide) and also go deeper into the systems picture and move beyond the technological focus to economic and behavioral linkages.

The LCSA is still in its nascent to middle stages, including its methodology, criteria and interpretation of results (Valdivia et al., 2013). One of the main challenges of the LCSA remains to develop practical and preferably quantitative indicators. There have been many indicators and methods proposed (Jørgensen, Le Bocq, Nazurkina, & Hauschild, 2008); however, there is still no single, agreed upon LCSA methodology yet (Clift, 2014). One of the reasons for this is because social indicators are not a natural fit with the LCA's ecologically focused structure (Clift, 2014). The lack of data and methods (specifically, SLCA indicators) remains one of the LCSAs strongest critiques (Guinée, 2016).

The LCSA seems like one of the most holistic assessment systems so far, as it goes beyond the ecological dimension to look also at the social and economic dimensions of the three-pillar model. It currently misses the cultural dimension of the Four Pillars model, but encouragingly, there have been calls for the LCSA to expand to include culture (Pizzirani, McLaren, & Seadon, 2014).

12.   Eco-costs/Value Ratio

The Eco-costs/Value Ratio (EVR) is an indicator which helps calculate both the environmental costs of a product or service and its value (Vogtländer, 2011).

When two products are compared through tools for ecological assessment, such as LCAs, it is assumed that the two products are identical in terms of market value. However, products with the same eco-cost may have different market values, and products which have the same market value may have differing eco-costs. EVR therefore evaluates both – the eco-cost and market value – in order to offer the best cost-benefit analysis. This enables the assessment of maximum value for the end user with the minimum environmental burden. Unlike the classical LCA, which can only be applied to a finished design, EVR can also be applied during the early stages of design to assess the feasibility of the proposed design using estimated data on costs and market value (Vogtländer, 2011). This possibility helps designers strike a balance between perceived product value and environmental costs. This results in strategic design which is mindful of the fact that green products and services need to offer good value to buyers in order to be viable in a free-market economy (Hendriks, Vogtländer,& Jansses, 2006). EVR focuses on both economic and ecological issues, but does not address social and cultural issues of sustainability.

Comparison of sustainability approaches and assessment systems vis-a-vis the dimensions they address

In Figure 3.1, we investigate the extent to which the approaches and assessment systems discussed above address sustainability holistically. The reference point for *holistic sustainability* was derived from the definition arrived at in the previous

Sr. No	Approach	Ecological Sustainability	Economic Sustainability	Social Sustainability	Cultural Sustainability
SUSTAINABILITY APPROACHES
1	Natural Capitalism	●	●		
2	Cradle-to-cradle	●	●		
3	Biomimicry	●			
4	Ecodesign	●	●		
5	Design for Sustainability	●	●	●	
6	Circular Economy	●	●		
7	Design for the base of the pyramid		●	●	
SUSTAINABILITY ASSESSMENTS
8	Life-cycle Assessment	●			
9	Life-cycle Costing	●			
10	Social Life-cycle Assessment			●	
11	Life-cycle Sustainability Assessment	●	●	●	
12	Eco-costs/ Value Ratio	●	●		

Figure 3.1 The extent to which sustainability-aligned approaches and assessment systems address sustainability holistically

Source: Reubens, 2016c

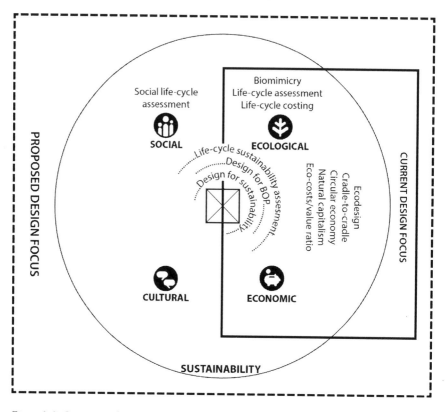

Figure 3.2 Current and proposed sustainability design focus vis-à-vis sustainability's tenets
Source: Reubens, 2016c

chapter: it indicated that, for sustainability to be holistic, it needs to address multiple dimensions including ecological, cultural, social and economic ones. The current and proposed design focus vis-à-vis sustainability's tenets are depicted in Figure 3.2.

3.5 The gap between sustainability theory and practice

The previous sections indicate that sustainability is growing in importance in the business landscape, that designers are ideally positioned to leverage the opportunities this presents, and that there are sustainability approaches and assessment systems available to underpin sustainability design practice. Despite all of these opportunities serendipitously lining up, the interest in sustainability and sustainable design (Lofthouse, 2006; Fuad-Luke, 2009) has not translated into frequent practice by designers in either developed (Aye, 2003; Kang, Kang, & Barnes, 2008; Kang & Guerin, 2009; Mate, 2006) or developing countries (Hankinson &

Breytenbach, 2012). While there is a paucity of literature on the percentage of design practitioners who use sustainable-design strategies and approaches (Bacon, 2011), the numerous studies which center on the barriers to sustainable design in themselves indicate that there is a deficit of sustainability design practice (Lofthouse, 2017). Some of the key barriers these studies reveal are as follow.

1. Lack of knowledge and information about sustainability

The lack of suitable and relevant information is one of the barriers to designers practicing sustainable design. Research with design students (Lofthouse, 2017) and design consultants (Stevenson, 2013) revealed that designers were not very confident using sustainability-related information because they did not clearly understand it. Designers need to understand the characteristics of sustainability and sustainable design in order to apply them (Kang & Guerin, 2009). Only when designers have sustainability knowledge and information, can they internalize their learnings as sustainable-design values, and then externalize these as sustainable design.

Sustainability knowledge impacts the likelihood of designers creating solutions that are mindful of formal and informal sustainability regulatory frameworks (Hankinson & Breytenbach, 2012). However, most designers do not learn about sustainability through their mainstream design education (Aye, 2003; Hankinson & Breytenbach, 2012), or later, through their professional practice or through professional peer-exchange platforms such as conferences (Lofthouse, 2017; Hankinson & Breytenbach, 2012). Consequently, they lack knowledge on sustainability – including on sustainable materials (Mate, 2006), their impact (Kang & Guerin, 2009) and sourcing (Hankinson & Breytenbach, 2012). Incidentally, designers who have a greater knowledge of eco-materials seem to use them more frequently (Mate, 2006).

Designers aiming to learn more about sustainability through literature are shortchanged, since most design literature cites *Ecodesign* as an umbrella term for sustainable design. Consequently, designers practicing sustainable design tend to focus on the ecological tenet and not on the holistic picture (Maxwell et al., 2003). In order to factor sustainability holistically into their designs, designers need to understand it as a systemic construct resting on interconnected tenets. Designers need to appreciate the links between the tenets and, better still, understand them (Shedroff, 2009).

2. Lack of overview on production-to-consumption systems and value chains

Designers, just like the other actors of industrial production-to-consumption systems, have lost sight of the systemic picture due to task specialization and division of labor. Because of this loss of overview, designers tend to address easily apparent and quantifiable challenges – such as ecological unsustainability – rather than exploring integrated issues, and aiming for holistically sustainable systems solutions (Maxwell et al., 2003). The difficulty in maintaining a holistic overview and assessing the reliability of product suppliers and manufacturers increases manifold with production-to-consumption systems now being spread across nations and geographies (Hankinson & Breytenbach, 2012). Most designers limit their design focus to the company they work with. They do not look at the company's forward and backward linkages (which comprise the entire production-to-consumption system) as a potential space for design intervention. This lack of holistic oversight becomes a barrier to holistically sustainable design. (Maxwell et al., 2003).

3. Failure to include sustainability at a strategic level in the overall approach

If the business does not incorporate sustainability at a strategic level, sustainability concerns do not generally trickle down to its key business systems – including design (Maxwell et al., 2003). Most companies resist sustainable design, and therefore designers working within their framework are not motivated to pursue it, either (Bacon, 2011). One reason for this is that the immediate and long-term benefits of sustainable design are not clear to companies (van Hemel & Cramer, 2002). Sustainable solutions sometimes cost more (Aye, 2003; Mate, 2006) and involve more time for sourcing and research (Aye, 2003; Bacon, 2011; Hankinson & Breytenbach, 2012; van Hemel & Cramer, 2002). Innovative solutions sometimes involve out-of-the-box thinking, including looking beyond designing a product to possibilities that do away with the product altogether – such as through a product-service combination (Maxwell et al., 2003) or by replacing the product with a service. The short- and long-term returns on such out-of-the-box thinking need to be clearly quantified in economic and non-economic terms for a company to take this route. Only then would sustainability be championed as a key part of an organization's strategic approach – even if it is perceived as requiring extra effort for benefits that may not be immediately clear (Hankinson & Breytenbach, 2012).

4. Failure to include sustainability criteria in the design brief

Factoring sustainability criteria early on in the design process, in the front-end stage itself (Dewulf, 2013), would minimize the need to *clean up* several consequences of the product life cycle later (White et al., 2008). However, sustainability is not frequently included in design briefs alongside traditional criteria such as market, customer, quality and production feasibility. One of the reasons for this is that sustainability is seen as an expensive add-on to the brief (Aye, 2003; Bacon, 2011; Mate, 2006), and often one that conflicts with the functional requirements of the product (Hankinson & Breytenbach, 2012; van Hemel & Cramer, 2002). Instead of being seen as a value proposition, sustainability is often seen as an additional project constraint – alongside deadlines, pricepoints, manufacturing and distribution channels, and legislation (Stevenson, Lilley, Lofthouse, & Cheyne, 2011).

There is no 'pull' to include sustainability in the design brief because most sustainability compliance is not yet mandatory (van Hemel & Cramer, 2002;Hankinson & Breytenbach, 2012). Designers cite client resistance (Aye, 2003), lack of client knowledge (Davis, 2001) and the perception that sustainable products are not yet needed by clients (van Hemel & Cramer, 2002) as reasons why sustainability is not included in the design brief. However, as discussed earlier in this section, it could be argued that designers do not push clients to include sustainability because they lack knowledge and information on sustainability themselves (Lofthouse, 2017), and cannot therefore make a strong and clear case for its inclusion.

5. Lack of a collaborative design process

Sustainable innovation calls for design to go beyond its typical manufacture-use focus (Dewulf, 2013); it calls for the integration of sustainability concerns and opportunities from across the value chain and the production-to-consumption system, into the innovation process (White et al., 2008). Each design, and the way it impacts sustainability, is not shaped by the designer alone. It is the result of inputs from all of the different functional units within the organization, and also the different occupational groups and stakeholders across the supply chain (White et al., 2008). Therefore, inputs from these stakeholders – including actors and groups who may not traditionally be part of the innovation team – need to be included during the sustainable-innovation phase (White et al., 2008).

Designers naturally assume the role of deciding when and how to factor in diverse viewpoints (White et al., 2008) from multidisciplinary collaborators during the sustainable-innovation process. However, each of these collaborators comes with the baggage of their specialization, viewpoint, and jargon, which makescommunication challenging (Maxwell et al., 2003). This is further compounded by the fact that sustainability lies outside the traditional domain of design, and so designers are not traditionally trained to coordinate the sustainable-innovation process (Maxwell et al., 2003). The lack of support from in-house experts (Aye, 2003) with regards to practically incorporating industry requirements vis-à-vis sustainability, is an additional barrier to the collaborative sustainable-design process.

6. Lack of tools

Designers cited that they do not practice sustainable design because they lack the appropriate tools to do so (Aye, 2003). Research indicates that the several Ecodesign tools availableare not widely used (Lofthouse, 2004; Perez, 2016; Stevenson, 2013). Lofthouse (2006) argues that this is because they are misaligned with design requirements. While these tools provide insights on the process and outcomes of designing sustainably (White et al., 2008), and also outline issues related to sustainable design, designers are not clear on how to use them (Lofthouse, 2006). Designers want tools that have accurate and accessible information

(Aye, 2003; Davis, 2001; Hes, 2005) packaged together in a manner which makes referring to them not tedious (Lofthouse, 2006).

Designers also cited the difficulty in measuring sustainability a barrier (Bacon, 2011). They added that clients unwilling to invest in the additional cost sustainable design entails could be convinced if its long-term economic savings could be quantified (Hankinson & Breytenbach, 2012). Tools to quantify sustainable-design achievements and communicate them through different mechanisms, such as ratings, could help legitimize sustainability efforts as credentials (Hankinson & Breytenbach, 2012).

Most of the available sustainable-design tools focus on cleaning up the life cycle and do not support the front-end innovation process (Walker, 1998) – which holds the greatest design opportunity for innovation which will impact sustainability.

7. Failure to keep the design team in the loop during product actualization

Designers do not perceive including or achieving sustainability as their responsibility (van Hemel & Cramer, 2002). It would appear that designers should be responsible for sustainability, given that the innovation process is vested with them. However, the final design is actually not designed just by the designer: it is the result of several iterations by different functional groups – including design, production, marketing and merchandizing (White et al., 2008). Each of these functional groups receives iteration by the previous group working on the product, which they work on and then pass to the next group in the pipeline. Most of these functional groups work in isolation and so do not understand why the groups before and after them in the design pipeline made changes to an iteration (White et al., 2008). So, even if a functional group – including design – tries to factor in sustainability, another functional group may not be mindful of this, and might make changes that reverse or lessen these considerations while working on their iteration (White et al., 2008). In the end, none of the functional groups takes ownership or accountability for the final design outcome, because none of them was involved with design decisions before or after they created their iteration.

Unless designers are kept in the loop from the front-end stage, right up to final product actualization, they cannot maintain their vantage view of the process (White et al., 2008), and therefore will not take responsibility for the outcome.

3.6   Summary and conclusion

This chapter explored our first question: to what extent do designers address sustainability holistically? In order to situate the subject, we mapped evolving design concerns against unfolding world phenomena, and discovered that design concerns through the ages have mirrored and responded to unfolding human processes and concerns – such as current sustainability concerns. The growing importance of these concerns has, in turn, changed the business landscape, giving rise to sustainability design drivers including market demand, and regulatory and non-regulatory frameworks. Designers are ideally placed to actualize the opportunities offered by these drivers due to their inherent skill-sets, and the expanding scope, role and power of the design professional the world over.

We studied and analyzed existing sustainability approaches and assessment methods which seemed best positioned to underpin designers' sustainability design practices, and explored how holistically they approached sustainability. We arrived at the reference point for this in the previous chapter, which indicated that, in order to address sustainability holistically, multiple dimensions – including the ecological, cultural, social and economic tenets – should be considered. Our analysis revealed that, while all of the approaches and assessment systems prioritized the economic and ecological aspects of sustainability – with the exception of BoP and SLCS, which prioritized the social dimension – none of them looked at sustainability in a holistic manner. However, the fact that the newer and hybridized frameworks and assessment systems – including DfS, LCSA and EVR – increasingly recognize and attempt to go beyond ecological and economic aspects to address multiple dimensions confirms the need and gap for a holistic sustainability approach and assessment system. The evolution of the original LCA – among the few inter-subjective ISO certified tools – to the SLCA which looks at social issues, and then on to the LCSA, which attempts to address ecological, social and economic dimensions together, also points to this gap and need.

All of the approaches and assessment systems we studied were created in the developed world, and this could account for their eco-centricity. The developed world is characterized by sufficient income and social security, and enormous consumption: this could explain the focus on reduction of eco-impacts as opposed to basic needs. The exception to this was the BoP approach, which, though created in the developed world, prioritized the developing world's low-resource setting; it gave precedence to the social aspect – and little attention to the ecological aspect. There is a growing discourse on the cultural dimension in the developing world, against the backdrop of concerns about cultural appropriation and the endangerment of cultural industries due to globalization, and calls for indigenous representation in decision-making. All of these seem to indicate that while a holistic approach to sustainability should address all the dimensions of sustainability, an innate bias towards situational priorities might be inevitable and even practical – in line with the "think globally, act locally" logic.

Our findings revealed that the interest in sustainability and sustainable design has not translated into frequent practice by designers in either developed or developing countries. In order to gain a deeper insight into the reasons behind this, we studied existing scholarship on the barriers to sustainability design. The findings were thematically grouped into seven distinct meta-barriers to sustainability-design practice, discussed in Section 3.5.

These can again be grouped into two categories (Figure 3.3) – barriers which are linked to the organization, and barriers which are fundamental to the design process. The grouping revealed that designers need support from the businesses

No.	Barrier	Organization Linked	Design Process Linked
1	Lack of knowledge about sustainability		●
2	Lack of holistic overview on production-to-consumption system and value chains	●	●
3	Failure to include sustainability at a strategic level in the overall approach	●	●
4	Failure to include sustainability in the design brief	●	●
5	Lack of a collaborative design process	●	●
6	Lack of tools		●
7	Failure to keep design team in the loop during product actualization	●	●

Figure 3.3 Grouping the seven barriers to sustainable design into organization-linked gaps and design-process-linked gaps

Source: Reubens, 2016c

within whose frameworks they work, in order be able to address almost all of the barriers. The only exceptions to this was Barrier 1 (lack of knowledge about sustainability), and Barrier 6 (lack of tools), which arise due to knowledge and mechanism gaps in the design process itself.

Overall, this chapter indicates that, while sustainability is growing in importance in the business landscape, and while designers are ideally positioned to leverage the opportunities this presents, the existing sustainability approaches and assessment systems available to designers do not address sustainability holistically. Unsurprisingly, designers in both developed and developing countries do not frequently practice sustainable design. Further action on improving sustainability design approaches could draw on the meta-barriers identified in this chapter, especially those intrinsic to the design process – namely, lack of knowledge about sustainability, and lack of tools.

4 To craft, by design, for sustainability

4.1 The broad phases of craft in the developing countries

In the previous chapters, we looked at sustainability and design for sustainability. This chapter looks at craft in the developing world. This is the final piece of the puzzle that we need to examine in order to answer our first question: to what extent do designers address sustainability holistically while working with non-industrial, renewable materials and craft-based MSMEs in developing countries?

Craft, like *design* and *sustainability*, is a highly contested, broad term, which evades a single, commonly accepted definition (Kouhia, 2012). Several themes – including 'products', 'handmade', 'minimal use of machinery' and 'hand-tools', 'substantial skill and expertise', 'element of tradition' and 'livelihood' (Liebl & Roy, 2000) – recur in literature that centers on craft. While each of these elements embodies *craft* singly and jointly, there is no consensus on these themes, nor on their hierarchy in relation to *craft*. In order to anchor this book, we define *craft* as a non-industrial production-to-consumption system that encompasses products (crafted objects), skills (craftsmanship), producers (craftspeople) (Risatti, 2007) and trades or occupations (craft) (Ihatsu, 2002). In order to understand how craft evolved in the developing world, we trace its journey from pre-industrial times to the present.

Pre-industrial craft: flourishing

Craft was the common mode of manufacture in the pre-industrial world. Before industrialization, everything around the world was parochially (Hill, 1997) handcrafted by craftspeople using simple tools and minimal machinery. The direct linkage between craftspeople and buyers, and the scale of production, made it possible for craftspeople to internalize and perform multiple roles in the value chain, including innovation, production, marketing and entrepreneurship (Vencatachellum, 2006). Craft production-to-consumption systems ranged from the *traditional* or *vernacular* – the collective cultural and utilitarian expressions of a rural community (Greenhalgh, 1997a) – to the *fine* and *decorative* art commissioned by wealthy patrons including churches, temples (Heslop, 1997), political rulers such as royalty and courtiers, and wealthy men such as the leaders of guilds (Jaitley, 2001) and merchants. Most pre-industrial rural craft catered to local markets within the city walls. In most instances, production surplus was only exported to distant markets on secondary priority (Diez, 2013). However, history also contains several examples of flourishing craft industries – including India's textiles and China's porcelains – which centered on non-local markets. In these scenarios, craftspeople were federated through different mechanisms – including as members of artisans guilds (Khan, n.d.) or through village-wise product specializations (Fanchette & Stedman, 2010) – in order to optimize production and trade.

Post-industrial craft: decline

Industrial production-to-consumption systems displaced craft value chains in both Europe and its colonies. However, whereas in Europe this displacement brought increased employment, economic wealth and development, in the colonies, it brought poverty and a decline of their flourishing craft-based economies (Rother-mund, 1992). Thriving craft-based export industries – such as India's handloom sector – were systematically sabotaged by colonial policies designed to reduce exports, while simultaneously leveraging the colonies as lucrative markets, which could absorb industrialized imports (Khan, n.d.). While this led to the decline of craft-based export industries, rural craft in the developing world survived because the lack of infrastructure and accessibility did not allow industrialization to pene-trate into the villages (Rothermund, 1992). Only in the late19th century – when the developing countries embarked on their own development trajectories – did industrial products percolate down to their rural areas.

Some developing countries, such as Vietnam, replaced traditional systems of craft production and organization (such as guilds, and individual and family pro-duction units) with cooperatives in order to try to accelerate their industrial potential (Fanchette & Stedman, 2010). This led to a decline of robust craft industries because coopretivism destroyed the link between craftsperson and buyer: post-cooperativism, craftspeople could only connect with their buyers through the craft-cooperative, making the government the mandatory intermedi-ary for all production and distribution transactions (Fanchette & Stedman, 2010). Craft in developing countries survived cooperativism and the growing trickle of industrial products by lowering product costs (Jaitley, 2005) – including by using imported low-cost industrial raw materials, tapping into a cheaper exploitable workforce comprising women and children (Afacan, n.d.), and deskilling – thereby becoming an industry for the poor run by the poor (Roy, 1999).

Post-information revolution craft: need and potential for revitalization

The final blow to craft in developing countries was dealt by the information revolution, which facilitated the penetration of low-cost, high-volume industri-alized goods into previously inaccessible markets and, more importantly, into the psyche of consumers. A substantial market segment for craft – including rural buyers – now have access to globalized media, and demand industrialized technology over tradition (Chaudhary, 2010). Over the last few decades, craftspeople in developing countries have found themselves disconnected from their buyers: they are unable to cater to distant markets and, therefore, have no takers for their products (Jaitley, 2001). Several crafts have vanished or are declining (Jaitley, 2001), and the available low-cost craft comes with hidden costs – including environmental degradation, unsafe and unhealthy working conditions, and unfair wages (Chotiratanapinun, 2013).

Figure 4.1 depicts our findings on existing market equations for both design- and craft-led production-to-consumption systems. The column on the left describes the pre-industrial craft production-to-consumption system, where craftspeople processed renewable materials using craft techniques for traditional markets. The column on the right describes how, post-industrialization, designers took over the bastion of innovation: they designed products produced from industrial materials, meant to be produced using industrial means of production, for mainstream markets. Until the information revolution, the left column was still prevalent in rural pockets where industrialization could not penetrate due to a lack of development. However, post-information revolution, industrial products have penetrated traditional markets, thereby significantly reducing the share of craft in traditional rural markets.

Parallel to this, the past 15 years have seen a surge of interest in craft (Ferris, 2009) from the developed world, and also from urban areas in the developing world. Consumers in these segments have higher incomes, which allow them to look beyond meeting basic needs to purchasing differentiated hand-crafted products with an ethnic identity (United Nations Development Organization, 2002).

Both of these scenarios – the decline of traditional rural craft markets and the growth of urban markets – indicate the need and potential to reposition the place, purpose and relevance of craft in post-industrial societies (Ferris, 2009). Recent academic discourse – including through academic platforms such as the Making Futures Conferences (Plymouth College of Art, n.d.), the *Craft+Design Enquiry*

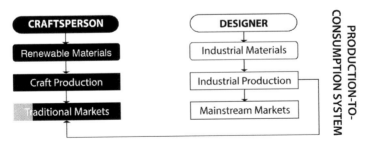

Figure 4.1 Production-to-consumption systems pre- and post-industrialization, and post-information revolution

Source: Reubens, 2016c

journal (Craft+Design Enquiry, n.d.), and the *Craft Research* journal (Intellect, n.d.) – touch upon the need to reposition craft more closely with contemporary economic, social, cultural and ecological scenarios, including sustainability concerns.

4.2   The analogous agendas of craft, sustainable development and sustainability

We discussed in the previous section the unsustainability of traditional craft production-to-consumption systems in the developing world, and the simultaneous demand for recontextualized craft production-to-consumption systems globally. These parallel phenomena encompass the agendas and opportunities for both sustainability and sustainable development because of the issues inherently linked to them – including social and environmental degradation, inclusive development, gender issues, globalization, localized livelihoods, urbanization and distress migration (Chatterjee, 2014). The UN's recent development agenda echoes the need to address these issues in its call for sustainable development with inclusive economic growth, decent employment, social justice and protection, and environmental stewardship, towards addressing global challenges with local solutions (Moon, 2014). Craft has the potential to be the vehicle to achieve all of these, holistically (Chatterjee, 2014), and thus impact all four tenets of sustainability. The opportunities for synergy between craft in developing countries and the four tenets of sustainability are examined in the following sub-sections.

Ecological sustainability vis-à-vis craft

Ecological sustainability rests on sustaining environmental or natural capital (Harte, 1995). Since traditional craft generally works within a localized production-to-consumption system, it has a strong sense of stewardship towards local natural capital. Traditional craft production-to-consumption systems have evolved over centuries, with due consideration to the strengths and vulnerabilities (Gaur & Gaur, 2004) of their respective bioregions. Craftspeople, therefore, value and are mindful about preserving natural resources within their bioregions, which they recognize, value and use for medicine, food and craft (Salmon, 2000), and as a basis for innovation (Chatterjee, 2014).

Traditional communities often have systems of custodianship and stewardship of the natural environment embedded in their religious, social and cultural practices and worldviews: they hold kin-centric and animistic worldviews, whereby man and nature are an interrelated part of an extended ecological family (Salmon, 2000). In some traditional cultures, a ritual bond is created between humans and nature through totems and taboos. Totemic animals and/or plants are assigned to specific social groups which revere and protect those species and some animal/plant species are off-limits for human consumption through taboos (Dovie, Witkowski, & Shackleton, 2008; Gaur & Gaur, 2004). Another mechanism to safeguard ecological resources is ancestral sanction, whereby each generation is entrusted with handing over a specific ecological resource to the next. An example of this is Japan's sacred groves which are linked to Shinto shrines and are still conserved today because they are deeply embedded in Japanese culture.

Traditional craftspeople are mindful of common-property natural resources – such as forests and rivers – to which they have historically had free access, because they depend on these for the sustenance of their craft. Since the ethos of resource conservation and optimization are deeply entrenched in the worldviews and practices of traditional craftspeople, they generally harvest only what they require; ensuring the sustainability of the community's common stock of natural capital, and their craft and livelihoods as well. The practice of *molong*, prevalent among Malaysia's Penan tribe, is an example of community-specific mechanisms to ensure sustenance of the ecological resource base. *Molong* means never take more than is necessary (Lloyd, 2008). When the Penans harvest a tree, they mark it with a *molong* cut, so that other harvesters are aware that it has already been tapped and needs time to regenerate.

Craftspeople, like most poor communities, create and suffer from ecological degradation (Anand & Sen, 2000). They are deeply affected by ecological degradation caused by non-local agents, and the consequent scarcity of natural resources – including flora, fauna, water and earth, which are input materials in their craft (Chatterjee, 2014). The community is therefore a check and balance for unsustainable production-to-consumption systems. Craft production systems which may be ecologically sustainable when catering to local demand may become ecologically unsustainable with an increase in the scale of production. For example, when village dyers upscale their activities to cater to a market beyond their traditional local demand, they may release increased effluents into local water bodies beyond the carrying capacity of the local ecosystem, and this will cause unsustainabillity, such as causing fish to die. In most of these instances, since the community is directly impacted by the unsustainable production – in this case, the polluted water and the dead fish – and since the producer is also part of the same ecosystem, there is a strong inbuilt check and balance and monitoring mechanism. Globalized production-to-consumption systems lack such a feedback loop, making it difficult to monitor and regulate systemic instances of unsustainability, including resource depletion or degradation (Thorpe, 2007).

Social sustainability vis-à-vis craft

Traditional socio-economic systems of exchange and subsistence linked craftspeople to the wider community, such that their productivity was not directed purely towards economic gain, but also addressed maintaining community life as a whole (Society for Rural, Urban, and Tribal Initiatives, 1995). Since these systems of social obligation were not based purely on monitory transactions, they afforded craftspeople security in times of scarcity (Society for Rural, Urban, and Tribal Initiatives, 1995), in line with the concept of social security.

The loss of livelihoods and the consequent breakdown of socio-economic systems have negatively affected the social sustainability indicators of traditional craft producers, including their health, education, safety and human rights. Given their dwindling market and landlessness (Reubens, 2010a), craftspeople are forced to distress migrate to cities and take on any work they can. Once in the cities, they join the ranks of the urban poor, and the livelihoods they are forced into – as unskilled laborers and, in some extreme cases, sexworkers (Kodapully, n.d.b). This indicates a deep social unsustainability and inequity. Sustainining and reviving craft production-to-consumption systems would promote sustained, inclusive and sustainable economic growth, full and productive employment and decent work for all – essentially, the Eighth UN Sustainable Development Goal (United Nations, n.d.). This, in turn, would allow these communities to actualize the remaining UN goals, including those focusing on the social mandates of health, education, food security, inclusiveness and shelter.

Craft capital is a resource that marginalized communities – such as ethnic minorities – can leverage towards economic and, thereby, social benefit (United Nations Development Organization, 2002). If this is done through a community-based organization, it could potentially strengthen the community's cohesiveness, which further empowers its members to negotiate issues of social inclusion (United Nations Development Organization, 2002).

Addressing the female workforce – often invisible in craft production – is a means to address the issues of gender equality and women's empowerment (Chatterjee, 2014). Despite being exploited, women continue to work in craft production, because it offers them flexibility of work location and timing. Reorganizing women craftspeople to enable them to get more equitable returns on work – such as through fair trade self-help groups – would recognize their economic contributions, unlike traditional gender-wise task division (Veillard, 2014). This, in turn, would empower women at different levels (Guadalupe, 2012), impacting practical needs (including well-being, income and ownership of assets) and also their strategic needs (including better access to the means of production and benefits) alongside their ability to renegotiate power relationships (Moser, 1989).

Economic sustainability vis-à-vis craft

Craft-based enterprises employ a large part of the workforce in developing countries (Hallberg, 1999), and are a significant source of livelihood, second only to agriculture (Chatterjee, 2014). Their sheer numbers establish craft's relevance to economic development. Craft-based enterprises are intrinsically labor-intensive (Hallberg, 1999): they are integral to developing countries' socio-economic fabric because of the employment they generate. Revitalizing craft-based enterprises translates into livelihoods, higher standards of living and social stability for craftspeople, and also overall socio-economic sustainability for the country through the development of value-added sectors and domestic markets (United Nations Development Organization, 2002). Craft enterprises contribute to a more equitable distribution of income, given that most of their owners and workers fall in the lower half of the income-distribution spectrum (Hallberg, 1999).

Most craft practice in developing countries is comprised of micro and small enterprises (MSMEs). Literature indicates that SMEs are more efficient than both larger and smaller firms: they are small enough to be flexible, and therefore respond to dynamic demands (Hallberg, 1999), while simultaneously being big enough to maintain quality (Snodgrass & Biggs, 1996). An economy which includes a substantial number of SMEs – including craft-based MSMEs – therefore allows for more economic resilience and flexibility, growth potential and employment opportunities (United Nations Industrial Development Organization, 2013). This positions craft-based MSMEs to be a potential asset to the emerging private sector in developing countries (Hallberg, 1999). It also positions them to become vehicles for holistically sustainable and inclusive expansion of production capacity, and value addition through development (Yong, 2013).

Craft-based production-to-consumption systems are traditionally localized. This dovetails with the concepts of community-based economics and regional trade, which are perhaps the truest models of localized economic security. Essentially, this means a community is largely self-reliant in terms of producing what it needs to survive. Economic sustainability and growth become endogenous when most of the economic and human resources are local (Moreno, Santagata, & Tabassum, 2005), and the entire production-to-consumption system is locally anchored, as well.

Cultural sustainability vis-à-vis craft

Craft consists of a body of cultural capital which is passed down from generation to generation (Ihatsu, 2002). The transmission mechanisms of craft – including the oral traditions and expressions, social practices and indigenous knowledge – translate into intangible cultural heritage (Moreno et al., 2005) and capital. Figure 4.2 outlines the cultural capital repositoried in indigenous knowledge, which can be leveraged for the creative industries through product differentiation, resulting in knowledge-based products and services with cultural relevance (United Nations Development Organization, 2002).

The craft sector is among the nine economic sectors which the government of the United Kingdom categorizes as creative industries (Department for Culture, Media &Sport, 2016). United Nations Educational, Scientific and Cultural Organization (UNESCO) recognizes the craft sector as an industry within the core cultural domain, and also therefore, as a creative industry (UNDP & UNESCO, 2013). UNESCO (2005) argues that craft's cultural capital, including craftspeople, is an enduring resource of the developing world. United Nations Industrial Development Organization (2002) views the same creative resource as an asset to development because it underpins differentiated employment and income. Aligning

Sr. No.	Type of Indigenous Knowledge	Examples
1	Information	Trees and plants that grow well together, indicator plants, flora-fauna and seasonal patterns
2	Practices and technologies	Seed treatment and storage, medicines, nature-based processing technologies, craft-technologies
3	Beliefs	Stewardship of natural resources and resource allocation, and sharing vested in belief systems
4	Tools	Tools and implements including utilitarian craft products for agriculture and subsistence
5	Materials	Bioregional input materials for construction and craft
6	Experimentation	Trial and error towards improved knowledge of bioregional resources
7	Biological resources	Indigenous flora and fauna
8	Human resources	Socio-economic systems of labor, exchange and specialization
9	Education and knowledge-transfer mechanisms	Oral traditions, apprenticeship
10	Communication	Folk media, rituals

Figure 4.2 Types of indigenous knowledge
Source: Reubens, 2016c, adapted from Rao (2006)

the craft sector with the creative economy can therefore be a means for inclusive development.

Thailand is an example of a country whose craft sector has successfully aligned with the creative economy. Thailand's "One Tambon, One Product" (OTOP) initiative was set up to deal with the rural economic crisis and the replacement of Thai craft exports with lower-cost substitutes from other countries. The OTOP initiative therefore adds value through indigenous knowledge and "Thai-ness": this differentiation is further reinforced through branding and marketing strategies (Chotiratanapinun, 2013).

Countries and communities that support and promote craft-based industries inherently create a cultural shift towards sustainability – something that is increasingly being recognized as a key driver for future development, given non-negotiable issues including resource constraints (United Nations Industrial Development Organization, 2013). This is because indigenous belief systems held by traditional craft communities – such as the Indian concept of *vasudhai-vakutumbakam*, i.e., the Earth family (Shiva, 2005) – resonate with the sustainability ethos.

4.3   Need and potential for craft to take the innovation-led, value-added manufacturing route, aligned to sustainability markets

We argue that one potential direction for craft is the innovation-led, value-added manufacturing route, aligned to sustainability markets. We discuss our three main reasons for this in the following sub-sections.

Emerging sustainability-aligned markets

Craft is poised to address new markets that are aligned to sustainability because many overarching concepts of sustainability – such as environmental responsibility, social justice, cultural diversity and economic inclusion (Borges, 2013) – underpin craft practice (Rees, 1997). These sustainability-aligned markets are expanding faster than markets for conventional products. Increasingly, these markets are looking beyond ecological considerations to include a wider spectrum of sustainability criteria (Potts et al., 2010). Interestingly, mainstream markets also display a huge trend towards mass-produced designer goods which embody handmade qualities – such as uniqueness (Na, 2011), imperfections, authenticity, familiarity and nostalgia – generally associated with craft (Greenlees, 2013).

The information revolution's knowledge class

The information revolution replaces capital and labor – the key factors of production of the industrial revolution – with knowledge and information (Humbert, 2007). The information revolution paradigm links the economy with knowledge and culture. It acknowledges the potential of knowledge, creativity and access to information to be engines of economic growth and development in a rapidly globalizing world (United Nations Conference on Trade and Development, 2008).

Craft is positioned to capitalize on the growing importance of knowledge and information, and growing *knowledge class* (Humbert, 2007) of the information revolution. This is because craft is underpinned by tacit indigenous knowledge systems (discussed in Section 4.1). These systems can be the basis for innovative value-added products crafted by communities (Ihatsu, 2002) which target the promising sustainability markets (Craft Revival Trust, 2006) discussed previously. Capitalizing on craft's tacit knowledge would enable craftspeople to dovetail with the growing *knowledge class* (Humbert, 2007) of the information revolution. If craft's indigenous knowledge is not recognized or leveraged, the perilous situation of craftspeople will grow even more untenable, because of their lack of formal education and formalized knowledge (Bhaduri, 2016).

The production-to-consumption systems of products that are underpinned by craft's tacit knowledge can potentially contribute to sustainable development and community development, by the repositioning of craft as a repository of knowledge, techniques and philosophy (Akubue, 2000). This is also in line with the concept of *creative industries*, which can potentially create wealth and generate income by leveraging cultural capital towards knowledge-based goods and services (United Nations Educational, Scientific, and Cultural Organization, 2005).

The potential to bypass the unsustainability of the mainstream development paradigm

Leveraging craft's tacit knowledge capital towards value-added manufacturing can help developing countries to bypass the unsustainability of the traditional industrialization paradigm. In the generic industrialization paradigm, when countries embark on their development trajectories, they first focus on utilizing their resources through manufacturing, then on making this manufacturing more efficient through capital-intensive technology, and – finally – on going beyond process innovation to product innovation (United Nations Industrial Development Organization, 2013). During the product innovation stage, the focus is on creating differentiation to set the product apart from competitors in the market. This is done by improving quality, and through innovations in products and services – including in upcoming areas such as green technology and sustainability, which are increasingly becoming important drivers for structural change in development (United Nations Industrial Development Organization, 2013).

Generally, when the technology focus of the second phase and innovation focus of the third phase align, manufacturing becomes innovative and value-added – while simultaneously remaining efficient – by maintaining reduced labor and increased capital (United Nations Industrial Development Organization, 2013). Both reduced labor and increased capital are not desirable outcomes or underpinnings for a developing world context which is characterized by unemployment and poverty. An out-of-the-box possibility for developing countries would therefore be to bypass the second phase altogether, and instead try to align the labor-intensive first phase with innovation-centric last phase. This would help developing countries to industrialize in a manner that addresses challenges of poverty and unemployment (United Nations Economic and Social Council Economic Commission for Africa, 2013). Craft is ideally positioned to actualize this possibility of innovation-led, value-added manufacturing, with large-scale employment opportunities, because it is intrinsically knowledge-based, labor-intensive and manufacturing-related. Moreover, it inherently aligns with sustainability; a strong prospect for differentiation in the third phase.

The possibility of innovation-led, value-added manufacturing is not only a potentiality, but also a need for craft. During the initial phases of a country's development, there is a rise in employment in the informal sector (United Nations Industrial Development Organization, 2013) – including in craft MSMEs. This rise in informal-sector manufacturing leads to economic development, and the resulting prosperity raises both the standard of living and labor costs (United Nations Economic and Social Council Economic Commission for Africa, 2013). At this juncture, only enterprises which have something to offer beyond low labour costs flourish – the enterprises with staying power would be those with differentiation including that based on high-skill labor, value addition and innovation (United Nations Economic and Social Council Economic Commission for Africa, 2013). Therefore, if craft enterprises are to survive in the long run in an industrializing world, they need to look at differentiated value-added products. These products would also help them stand their ground against the globalized high-quality, low-cost imports (United Nations Economic and Social Council Economic Commission for Africa, 2013) that are flooding their traditionally closed economies. As discussed earlier (Section 4.1), the inability to compete with globalized substitutes is one of the important reasons why craft has languished in developing countries (Borges, 2013) – despite encompassing local, national and international production-to-consumption systems, and spanning the spectrum from utilitarian to luxury goods (Jaitley, 2001).

4.4 Role of design in actualizing craft's potential to be a vehicle for sustainable development

The information revolution creates both a push and a pull for craft to leverage emerging sustainability-aligned market opportunities. However, as discussed in earlier chapters, craftspeople are unable to access these lucrative markets for sustainable products (Potts et al., 2010). We argue this is because of an information gap.

> While the "know-how" (how to make things – knowledge and skills) exists abundantly in the crafts sector, there is a severe shortfall in the "know-what" (what to make – strategies and designs) that curtails the ability of crafts communities to survive intense competition or, better still, develop value-added solutions in a complex economic and social matrix in which they exist.
>
> (Panchal & Ranjan, 1993, p. 14)

A synergistic collaboration between craft and design that centers on innovation, responding to contemporary needs and sustainability issues seems to offer a way forward (Figure 4.3) (Greenlees, 2013).

Figure 4.3 Craft-design collaboration to target sustainability markets
Source: Reubens, 2016c

Master's students at Centre for Environmental Planning and Technology (CEPT) University in Ahmedabad, India categorized the span of craft-design collaboration into seven distinct paradigms, based on the ideology that underpinned them (Agarwal et al., 2018). These are as below:

1   **CONSERVATION:** In this paradigm, the focus is on restoring and/or preserving and/or recreating authentic and traditional craft practice as it was historically practiced. Recreating traditional lime and plaster architecture authentically, for the extension of a heritage lime-plaster building, is an example in this direction.

     Keywords: restoration, preservation, heritage

2   **DIGITAL CRAFT:** This paradigm encompasses craft-design produced by the inputs of both the maker and digitalization. In some cases, the actual making could be completely digitalized, such as in 3-D printing, but the *mark of the maker* would be evident in the creation and actualization of the design. The distinguishing feature of this paradigm is that the process is haptic and that the final output cannot be arrived at without either the maker or digitalization. Digitally produced wallpaper, created by digitally repeating the image of a motif that was originally created by hand block-print, is an example in this direction.

     Keywords: haptic, humanizing technology, digitally-crafted

3   **GLOCAL:** In this paradigm, a contemporary version of traditional craft is arrived at through a global design sensibility. The result is a craft-design with a sense of placelessness, while simultaneously still retaining a strong sense of handcraftedness. Using a traditional seat weaving technique and material (such as wicker) on a structure made from a non-traditional material/form (such as plastic instead of the traditional wood), or both, is an example in this direction.

     Keywords: contemporary-handmade, contemporizing tradition, placeless craft

4   **OPULENCE:** In this paradigm, contemporary wealthy patrons commission craft in line with the traditional model of craft patronage. The final output is expensive because of the material or process, or both, and portrays great wealth and luxuriousness which in turn becomes a status-symbol for the patron. Highly embellished couture garments which use intricate traditional embroidery are an example in this direction.

     Keywords: status symbol, luxury, intricacy, better-than-machines

5   **IMAGERY:** In this paradigm, the feeling of craft is evoked through a 2-D representation of the authentic craft. This could, for example, be a poster of a gilded wall paneling which is used as a backdrop for an exhibition of gilded objects; here, the visual depicts what the craft encompasses without the craft actually being used in the production of the poster.

     Keywords: thematic, visual, inauthentic

6   **SUSTAINABLE DEVELOPMENT**: In this paradigm, the focus is on the creation of livelihoods for craftspeople through their crafts, towards their socio-economic upliftment. The numerous interventions by development agencies in the developing world where designers create designs to be produced by communities and sold in urban markets are examples in this direction.

Keywords: livelihoods, communities, development

7   **SUSTAINABLE FUTURING**: This paradigm centers on deconstructing traditional craft into different elements. One or more of these elements are then used as building blocks towards creating a new craft-design aligned towards sustainability. Often, the craft is used in such a deconstructed format without its cultural connotations towards a contemporary output, which aims to impact the future of the systems of our world, rather than only the themes of livelihood and development. The use of hand-crafted bamboo strips to create paneling for an airport, not because bamboo is part of craft traditions but because it is relevant to the sustainability crisis, is an example in this direction.

Keywords: sustainable craft materials, future crafts, DIY

Of the seven listed paradigms, sustainable development is arguably the most ubiquitous format for craft-design collaboration: here craft-design collaborations are initiated by international development agencies, NGOs and governments, who interface with community-based organizations (Rhodes, 2011). These interactions are intended to widen the reach of products crafted by communities (Borges, 2013), and to also serve as a vehicle to achieve sustainability agendas – particularly the social-development themes of economic empowerment, poverty alleviation and livelihood generation. The common modus operandi for most craft-design interactions is through *design intervention*, in which craft communities feature as a skilled – and often low-cost – workforce, which produces designs developed by a professionally trained designer (Borges, 2013; Frater, 2009; Kodapully, n.d.a). The resulting products are positioned as being inspired by local culture. The aim of several of these projects is to link languishing traditional crafts to wealthier markets in the West, through design assistance (Murray, 2010). The ubiquity of this model is evidenced in the several transnational examples of designers leveraging developing-country craft, to create products with a *Western* aesthetic (Chotiratanapinun, 2013). These products are projected as bridging the global north/south by combining *northern* design expertise with *southern* craft traditions (Murray, 2010).

Several projects that follow the model previously described have indeed widened the reach of community-crafted products, and may be construed to be fair – if all the concerned parties are clear on the nature of the transaction and agreeable to the terms of payment (Borges, 2013). However, these projects have not been so successful in addressing the theme of social development: they cannot actually be deemed social design projects, because they lack an equal exchange, continuity and respect for the local culture (Borges, 2013). Several craft-design projects, which are positioned as *aid to artisans*, in reality facilitate dependency relationships, rather than contributing to their eradication (Bonsiepe, 2011; De Waal, 2002; Lyon, 2006; Scrase, 2003). One of the reasons for this is that the design paradigm – due to its deep connection with industrialization – overlooks craft, and thereby craftspeople, craft culture and indigenous knowledge systems (Kodapully, n.d.a). Even though the ultimate beneficiary of several of these projects is meant to be the craftsperson and not the private sector (Murray, 2010), the limitation of perception and perspective affects designers' ability to facilitate livelihood solutions for craftspeople (Kodapully, n.d.b).

The insufficient internalization of the systemic craft scenario – including technique and context – can also lead designers to inadvertently intensify the problem of craftspeoples' livelihoods. Borges (2013) narrates an example of such a situation in Paraguay, where potters were provided with loans to purchase kilns that were intended to improve the quality of their pottery. The new ovens changed the firing process, and thus the color of the final product – something the designers had not anticipated. The eventual designs in the new color were not well received by markets, leaving craftspeople with no new income from the product line, while simultaneously struggling to pay off the loans.

Sometimes, the unintended adverse effects of design interventions run deeper than a missed market opportunity; they extend to the erosion of the communities' cultural capital and well-being. Design interventions which fail to capitalize on the indigenous knowledge contained in craft do not actualize their potential to align with sustainability markets. Worse, such approaches may dilute and diffuse the communities' cultural capital – thereby jeopardizing the very resource that can provide the basis and direction for differentiation, which can help these craft products find their place in a globalized world (Frater, 2009).

Our review of craft-design interactions in the developing world revealed several examples of top-down designer-led approaches, which failed to contribute to social sustainability or impact the socio-economic status of craft communities (Frater, 2009). Some of these interactions were criticized for their negative impact – eroding the cultural capital of communities (Frater, 2009). The ecological dimension has not been addressed in any of the interactions.

While literature contains several examples of top-down designer-led approaches which fail to contribute to the sustainability of craft communities in terms of their income or social status (Frater, 2009), it also contains some heartening examples that showcase the benefits of collaboration in craft-design interactions. Rhodes' (2011) research describes how Western makers worked in collaboration with craft communities in Africa, translating craft capital into activities that generated eco-income. Murray (2010) describes Martina Dempf's co-creation of grass-based jewelry with Rwandan women. Following the project, both Dempf and the women created their own version of the designs, reflecting equity in ownership, opportunity and creativity. Marchand (2011) – over the course of his research with Yemeni minaret builders – developed an approach to leverage social knowledge towards social innovation solutions, which are facilitated – but not dictated – by designers and development institutions.

Benchmarks of craft-design synergies include the Italian model, whereby sophisticated design and fine craftsmanship have been used synchronously as a mode of economic and cultural development (Secondo, 2002). In a similar vein, several countries – including Japan, Taiwan, South Korea, Switzerland, Germany, Italy and Scandinavia in general – attribute their success in design and manufacturing to their craft legacy (Chatterjee, 2014).

Also encouraging is the emerging action research and scholarship which looks at positioning craft as a methodological framework (Ferris, 2009), through which to impact and leverage social, economic, cultural and economic sustainability (Borges, 2013). This could provide the basis for an alternative craft-design paradigm, the main challenge of which would be the same as that facing social innovation and design projects – namely, avoiding the highly criticized path of imposing top-down solutions on local communities, by engaging the community in the innovation process; and recognizing the community's values, priorities and character (Greenlees, 2013).

4.5   Summary and conclusion

Craft has a huge potential to contribute to sustainable development in developing countries. It is labor intensive and comprises a substantial part of the economic fabric of developing countries. It also has the potential to dovetail with the information revolution's knowledge and creative economy to access new and lucrative sustainability-aligned markets. For these reasons, it provides developing countries with the opportunity to side-step the generic development paradigm, provided it can dovetail with the innovation-led, value-added, manufacturing-oriented paradigm.

Design can have an important role in actualizing craft's potential to align with the creative economy through craft-design collaborations. However, our review of craft-design interactions in the developing world revealed that most of these were top-down and designer-led, and did not address sustainability holistically. Several of these interactions had failed to contribute to social sustainability or significantly raise the socio-economic status of craft communities (Frater, 2009), and some of these had been criticized for eroding the cultural capital of communities (Frater, 2009). The ecological dimension has not been addressed in any of the interactions.

These findings, along with the findings from the previous chapter on sustainability design approaches, and assessment systems and practice, indicate the answer to our first question: design does not currently address sustainability holistically in the case of non-industrial craft-based MSMEs in developing countries working with renewable materials. Existing sustainability design praxis in general focuses on ecological and economic dimensions, though this focus seems to be expanding slowly but surely. In the case of craft-based MSMEs, the design focus and impact seem to be primarily in the economic dimension. Although social and cultural priorities are cited, the extent to which they have been achieved, and the means of achieving them are questionable. The existing design praxis we studied did not contain examples whereby design, craft and sustainability have been successfully harnessed together for holistic sustainability.

Emerging scholarship and discourse is beginning to recognize design's potential and intention to position craft as a methodological framework (Ferris, 2009), through which to impact and leverage social, economic, cultural and economic sustainability (Borges, 2013). However, this potential is yet to be realized – and the proposed means to realize this are few and far between. Currently, craftspeople are very vulnerable in craft-design exchange. Craftspeople are dependent on external middlemen for a range of functions – including accessing market information, design and technology inputs, finance and distribution. Whether these functions exploit or support craftspeople depends on their capacity to negotiate (Borges, 2013). This is why it is essential to articulate, and recognize the skill and knowledge that both, craftsperson and designer bring to craft-design collaborations. Designers bring information about modern markets, thus helping craftspeople cope with the process and consequences of industrialization (Craft Revival Trust, 2006). Craftspeople bring indigenous knowledge, which is a route to accessing the systems of integrated and holistic sustainability that underpins craft. In contrast to industrial design, which is driven by industry (Rees, 1997), craft is driven by the integration of tacit knowledge, innovation, skill, bioregional knowledge (Ihatsu, 2002) and traditional practices – which are all links into a single system determined by the interconnectedness between people, land, materials and energy (Ihatsu, 2002; Lea, 1984; Naylor, 1980).

The premise that craft capital can potentially be leveraged towards tapping sustainability markets and thus influencing sustainable development, and the wisdom of craft-design collaborations as a way to actualize this potential, seems well-founded. However, the paucity of models which have realized this potential points to the urgent need for mechanisms which can actualize craft's potential for value-added manufacturing, within the context of sustainability and sustainable development (Greenlees, 2013).

Simultaneously, there is also a need for tools to help validate existing and future craft-design paradigms (Murray, 2010). Both of these needs resonate with our second question: what can be a possible sustainability design approach that would: a) be mindful of the pros and cons of pre-existing sustainability design approaches, and b) address a holistic picture of sustainability – including its ecological, social, economic and cultural dimensions – in the context of non-industrial craft-based MSMEs working with renewable materials in developing countries?

We will attempt to answer this question in the following chapters by iteratively developing such tools. These tools will be developed based on the findings of the literature we reviewed, and conclusions drawn thereon.

5   The Rhizome Framework

5.1   Understanding the Rhizome Framework

The previous chapters offered an overview on, and insights into, the production-to-consumption systems of non-industrial craft-based MSMEs working with renewable materials in developing countries. The overview revealed a systemic problem: several traditional craft production-to-consumption systems in developing countries are being jeopardized due to shrinking markets, and the subsequent loss of livelihoods for craftspeople. This is forcing craftspeople to migrate to urban areas in search of employment, causing tremendous socio-economic unsustainability. Since craftspeople can generally only find employment as de-skilled labor, their craft languishes due to lack of practice. This leads to an erosion of the very cultural capital which can constitute the basis of a differentiated market for them. The urgent need, therefore, is to connect craftspeople to viable new markets, thus enabling them to continue to earn a sustainable livelihood through their craft. The resulting craft practice and income security would have positive spin-offs on the social, economic, cultural and ecological dimensions of the currently unsustainable scenario.

As the previous chapter discussed, designers can help craftspeople connect to viable new markets by supporting the value-chain nodes of design, production and marketing of the generic craft production-to-consumption system. We could not identify any framework or methodology in place in to navigate this terrain and the possibilities we argue it encompasses. We therefore developed a framework – which we call the Rhizome Framework – which outlines potential directions for craft-design collaboration aimed at connecting traditional craftspeople in the developing world to viable markets.

The framework is underpinned by a systemic perspective, and therefore offers more than one potential direction for viable craft evolution. We argue that a model which pinpoints a single direction for craft re-contextualization and evolution would not be justified because of the diversity of elements that make up the craft sector in the developing world – including crafts, craftspeople, skill set and bioregion. No single direction for traditional craft evolution can do justice to the opportunities which the complex natures of craft and sustainability hold. Therefore, we offer the Rhizome Framework (Figure 5.1) towards a model which will

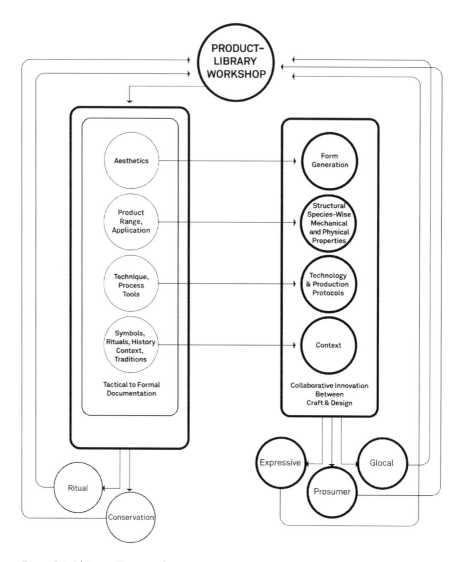

Figure 5.1 Rhizome Framework
Source: Reubens, 2010a

conserve cultural capital, in addition to offering different directions for craft evolution. We have designed and intend the framework to be flexible, so that it can be adapted to different contexts, while remaining strongly rooted in sustainability and the interconnections between its tenets. The intention is to avoid creating cookie-cutter solutions which do not work effectively because they do not take into account the nuances of different contexts: we advocate promoting the diversity of design solutions based on different contexts.

The Rhizome Framework is named after bamboo's complex, underground rhizome system. Each rhizome is an underground stem, which either sends up a shoot or sends down a root, and networks itself to other rhizomes to form a stable mesh that prevents soil erosion. The botanical rhizome system is a metaphor for our Rhizome Framework: we intend it to function like a rhizome system in the sense that it will connect both craftspeople and designers, and form a stable mesh that prevents erosion of sustainability.

Philosophically, we drew on Deleuze and Guattari's (1987) use of the rhizome to symbolize theory and research that allows for multiple, non-hierarchical entry and exit points in data representation and interpretation. The principles of a rhizome outlined by Deleuze and Guattari (1987), and which the Rhizome Framework aspires to cultivate, follow:

- *1 and 2*: Principles of connection and heterogeneity – "any point of a rhizome can be connected to anything other, and must be" (Deleuze & Guattari, 1987, p. 7).
- 3: Principle of multiplicity – "it is only when the multiple is effectively treated as a substantive, 'multiplicity,' that it ceases to have any relation to the One as subject or object, natural or spiritual reality, image and world" (Deleuze & Guattari, 1987, p. 8).
- 4: Principle of asignifying rupture – "a rhizome may be broken, shattered at a given spot, but it will start up again on one of its old lines, or on new lines" (Deleuze & Guattari, 1987, p. 10).
- 5 *and* 6: Principles of cartography anddecalcomania – "a rhizome is not amenable to any structural or generative model" (Deleuze & Guattari, 1987, p. 12); it is a map, and not a tracing.

The Rhizome Framework draws on these principles and therefore looks at three distinct directions, which are independently and interdependently sustainable, and prevent the erosion of social, economic, ecological and cultural capital.

The generic process of designing artifacts, and the deconstruction of the constituents that make up this process, was the scaffolding for the Rhizome Framework. This included the key elements of design – including function, aesthetics, material and production possibilities and socio-cultural concerns – which are part of foundational industrial design education (Nugraha, 2010). In similar vein, Papanek's (1995) model of a *six-sided function matrix* of a designed object identifies method, use, consequence, aesthetics, association and need as the six interlinked aspects of a designed object.

How the Rhizome Framework works

The first step in the framework is to create a physical library of products – a product-library. This product-library will function as a cultural repository of the aesthetics, products, techniques and contexts of the craft practice. The cultural repository serves two purposes: a) it formalizes and records indigenous knowledge as cultural capital; and b) it creates a repository of cultural capital that can serve as an input for innovation, including innovation in a collaborative craft-design framework. We suggest this physical library is created through a product-library workshop (described in detail in Section 5.2) where the complete range of craft products of a community, is recreated by craftspeople at a common location, using their own tools, in actual scale (Reubens, 2005). This process is documented by resource people – including designers and community mobilizers.

We recommend that designers and craftspeople collaboratively analyze the cultural repository created by the product library and identify and isolate distinct cultural markers from it (Hickey, 1997). These markers can then be factored into the collaborative innovation process as building blocks for design inputs. The aesthetics derived from the cultural repository provide reference points for form generation; the product range and applications provide insights into the species-wise structural, mechanical and physical properties of renewable materials; the traditional techniques, processes and tools are important inputs to build on innovate technologies and viable production protocols; and the symbols, rituals, history, context and traditions offer a context and rich material culture.

Some of the products in the library would fall under the *ritual*: they would continue to be used in traditional rites and ceremonies and contribute to the vitality (Hawkes, 2001) of the community's cultural capital. We argue that this set of products should continue to be authentically crafted only for and by the community as far as possible, because these products are reference points to substantiate the cultural identity of the craft community and its material culture. For this reason, we recommend exercising restraint and sensitivity when drawing on this set for design and development. We argue that this set should be treated as cultural heritage, and therefore, be key to conservation efforts by and for the community, including through community museums, as artifacts of anthropological, ethnographical and cultural relevance.

The Rhizome Framework proposes three potential directions for craft evolution (discussed in detail in Section 5.3), namely *expressive, prosumer* and *glocal*. These directions target potential markets for the outputs of craft-design collaboration which are likely to be both sustainable and viable.

5.2   Product-library workshop: a methodological tool

As discussed earlier, the Rhizome Framework proposes the creation of a cultural repository of craft tradition and practice through the product-library workshop – a methodological tool that we first developed and used in 2002. The workshop is based on a *making-for-documenting* process, as opposed to the typical *observing-and-documenting* process. The basic methodology involves the craftspeople assembling at a common location, and crafting a complete range of actual-scale traditional products (including obsolete and in-use products) using their own tools. The exercise is designed to put in place baselines for the existing product range, technique and skill level of the craft community against which future interventions can be benchmarked. Information along the entire value chain, including on material harvesting, material usage patterns, process and technique, tools and product range, and their applications and cultural practices, is collected through interactions with the assembled craftspeople. Since there are several craftspeople, this information can be validated on the spot through focus-group discussions. Designers, community mobilizers and other resource persons meticulously document this exercise. Designers record information on aesthetics, product range, application, techniques, processes, tools, history, tradition and symbolic, ritualistic and utilitarian contexts through pictures, videos and notes. Community mobilizers facilitate individual and focus-group discussions, which are documented through notes and photographs.

The output of the workshop is a set of actual-scale products that serve as a *library* of products for further reference. The entire physical product-library and the process of crafting its contents are documented in electronic format, through photographs and video, and archived for easy circulation and access. The resulting documentation functions as a baseline indicator, and also as a cultural repository. This is a resource from which both craftspeople and designers can isolate indigenous cultural markers on which to base further innovation. The workshop, and the physical products that result from it, provide an opportunity for documenters to see and record, and also to observe and analyze at a later date.

The product-library workshop gives a focused and holistic insight into craft, especially when compared to traditional methods of craft documentation which rely on field visits. While in-situ visits to craft communities give an honest account of the craft practice, they do not always reveal the exhaustive repertoire of product range or techniques; there are always waning products and techniques which – though not being produced by the current generation of craftspeople – are not yet extinct and can be reproduced on demand. Products which are used and produced seasonally are also not reflected, unless the field visits are regular and over all the seasons. The product-library workshop circumvents these failings, and, when supported by field visits, provides a holistic and realistic picture of the craft range that exists and is being practiced.

5.3   Directions of innovation

The Rhizome Framework proposes three potential directions for craft evolution: *expressive, prosumer* and *glocal*. These three directions are in line with the three elements which Greenhalgh (1997b) argues comprise the ideological and intellectual underpinning of craft constituency: decorative art, the vernacular and the politics of work. The Rhizome Framework identifies opportunities for the craftsperson to be an artist (*expressive*), and/or a vernacular producer and the marketing link of an interdependent sustainable community (*prosumer*), and/or a producer and perhaps an entreprenuer (Greenhalgh, 1997b) rooted in producing sustainable (*glocal*) products. The directions also align with the three reasons Greenhalgh (1997b) gives for promoting handicrafts in opposition to machine based production: the economic, psychological and aesthetic (Greenhalgh, 1997b). The economic, because technology destroys labor opportunities (*prosumer*), the psychological, whereby society loses its creativity to think because of mechanization (*expressive*), and the aesthetic, whereby human expression is better than machine-made standardization (*glocal*).

Expressive

The *expressive* direction proposes that the cultural repository created through the product-library workshop forms the basis for product lines which align craft with art – which are deeply rooted in maintaining cultural capital. This direction has several conceptual precedents, including haute couture, and the studio crafts, both of which aim to realign craft with art. The philosophy of Judy Frater, who conceived and founded the first design school for traditional artisans of craft and textiles in India – the Kala RakshaVidhyalaya – is inspiring: the idea of exquisite craftsperson-led innovation mirrors the idea of the artist-maker. Frater argues that "the top-down solution to design innovation may dilute or diffuse the essence and strength of traditions; the unique quality which can enable artisans to survive in an increasing commoditized world" (Frater, 2009, p. 44). These limited edition and exclusive artifacts will create an aspirational market for the craft, which will trickle down and add value to crafted products aligned to art and design. In this way, the relation between art and craft can begin to be viewed not as problematic but as productive (Adamson, Cooke, & Harrod, 2008).

Prosumer

Futurologist Alvin Toffler (1980) coined the term *prosumer* in his book *The Third Wave*, wherein he envisions the need for mass production of highly customized products. This is ideologically in line with the traditional craft process, whereby craftspeople custom-crafted pieces based on close interactions with their consumers. The principle also extends to professions like architecture, where the consumer interacts closely with the innovator/maker.

Another parallel is in the idea of *meta data*, whereby designers provide *seeds* or aesthetic *codes* which users then use as a basis for their own creations, e.g., self-building housing, based on a general framework from an architect (Thorpe, 2010). The *prosumer* direction proposes that cultural markers – drawn from the cultural repository created through the product-library workshop – form the point of departure for product lines that are based "on self-sufficiency through production networks" (Bersalona, 2002). The aim is to create products that craftspeople can craft for themselves and other rural communities in the region – the idea being a self-provisioning rather than a commodities approach (Thorpe, 2010).

In *Wikinomics: How Mass Collaboration Changes Everything*, Tapscott and Williams (2006) devised the term *prosumption* to refer to the creation of products and services by the same people who will ultimately use them. Given that many corporations are viewing rural markets as important production and market bases (Humbert, 2007; Prahalad, 2004); the framework aims to allow the rural *prosumer* greater independence from the mainstream economy. Movements such as cooperative self-help that sprang up during great economic crises, and the more recent voluntary self-sufficient communities, are all precedents for this direction. In similar vein, M.P. Ranjan's (2009) *Katlamara Chalo* initiative aimed to design products which bamboo craftspeople could produce using limited resources and which were relevant in local markets.

Glocal

Several not-for-profit organizations – such as Aid to Artisans in the United States, and Dastkar in India – engage designers to develop new product lines inspired by the craft of specific artisan groups; the craft groups then produce these designed products. The aim is that, "through innovation, craft can rise above subsistence into a satisfying and profitable business" (Hnatow, 2009, p. 5). This approach is ubiquitous to design intervention in developing countries, where craft is struggling to make the transition from "viable economic activity" to "ideological cultural property" (Adamson et al., 2008, p. 6), and where craftspeople need to be linked to lucrative markets. An example in this genre includes Patty Johnson's North-South Project (Johnson, n.d.), whereby products are produced by African craftspeople in a manner that is mindful of the sustainability of the region's community and economy.

The *glocal* direction proposes that the cultural markers drawn from the cultural repository form the basis for product lines that target sustainability-aligned markets. This direction targets both domestic and foreign urban markets, where there is a demand for sustainable products. It builds on the fact that while there are several designed economically viable, eco-friendly products – e.g., bamboo board – these do not capitalize on the social and cultural potential of materials for sustainability. Products targeting urban markets, and produced by marginalized (socio-economic) craftspeople (cultural), do this effectively. *Glocal* has its precedents in the numerous occasions when designers have drawn inspiration from the craft process and tradition (Dormer, 1997) to develop avant-garde consumer products.

5.4   Areas that would benefit from design-craft interaction

Art, craft and design are part of a spectrum (Rees, 1997). Though they are conceptually divided, their boundaries are porous, such as in the case of haute couture, whereby a limited edition, statement (art) designer bag (design) may be produced by traditional leather craftspeople (craft) with extreme attention to detail, then finished in Europe, in line with the strong artisan-influenced culture of high-quality personal accessories (Dormer, 1997). Therefore, we have sought to move beyond the debate on the relevance, justification and suitability of design intervention in traditional craft practice – a debate which is fraught with incongruent arguments and opinions (Craft Revival Trust, 2006). Instead, we focus on the comparative advantages that both designers and craftspeople bring to the innovation process. Some of the areas which would gain from a meaningful interaction between designers and craftspeople, and which are factored into the Rhizome Framework, are discussed in the following sub-sections.

Market access

Most traditional craftspeople are unable to perceive and cater to markets outside their villages because they are accustomed to traditional markets which function at an inter-village level, where there is a direct link between producers and buyers (Panchal & Ranjan, 1993; Vencatachellum, 2006). As discussed in Chapter 4, while the *know-how* (knowledge and skills) exists abundantly in the crafts sector, there is a severe shortfall in the *know-what* (strategies and designs) that curtails the ability of craft communities to survive intense competition or, better still, develop value-added solutions in the complex economic and social matrix in which they exist (Panchal & Ranjan, 1993). Designers hold the potential to elucidate modern markets for the craftspeople through collaborative innovation, and thus enable them to cope with the process and consequences of industrialization (Craft Revival Trust, 2006).

Equitable access to gains from production

It is important for traditional craft producers to reorganize themselves if they are to be able to access a portion of the economic profits of the information revolution. "The actual issue is how we want the production gains of the information revolution to be distributed, how we want the coming world to be" (Humbert, 2007, p. 17).

Technology causes radical changes in the social, economic, ecological and cultural worlds and to sustainability in general. The Rhizome Framework therefore deliberately focuses on craft technologies, in order to secure craftspeople a higher place in the value chain. This will bring greater equitability into who controls the means of production, who labors and who profits. The Rhizome Framework advocates being *low-tech* as opposed to *technology-intensive* or following the *technology-push* ideology, in order to allow the crafts practiced by thousands of craftspeople to evolve organically (Dormer, 1997) towards a sustainable end. It places squarely on the designer the onus to reference the triad of traditional material, technique and context (Metcalf, 1997), and to design the crafted contemporary artifact in collaboration with craftspeople.

Recording and protecting cultural capital

The Rhizome Framework creates a cultural repository through the product-library workshop and the craft documentation linked to it. This cultural repository records and preserves indigenous knowledge and practices which is key to concretizing the cultural capital of traditional communities as intellectual property rights, and putting in place geographical indicators to protect craft capital (Craft Revival Trust, 2006). The process of creating a cultural repository enables the formalized archiving of tacit knowledge, which is traditionally transmitted orally (Craft Revival Trust, 2006), or through the apprenticeship mode, in the craft tradition. This formalization is important, because the breakdown of generational craft practice calls for complementing and supplementing traditional transmission mechanisms of craft knowledge. If this is not done, the knowledge-transfer link between generations can be broken and indigenous knowledge can be lost permanently.

Indigenous knowledge-based craft-design collaboration for sustainability

The collaboration between designer and craftsperson maximizes the skill and knowledge that each brings to the innovation process. The craftsperson brings indigenous knowledge and practices that have been validated over time as being more sustainable than not. As discussed earlier, many of the concepts of sustainability underpin craft practice (Rees, 1997), e.g., the use of local materials, or expertise and production in a single material which allows for ease in sourcing, production and repair, and also in eventual disassembly and recycling. The designer brings value with his access to information and technology on current issues, including sustainability. Both inputs are complementary and supplementary. The Rhizome Framework advocates adopting principles of social sustainability such as fair wages, fair trade and banning child labor, etc., in each of the directions offered. Incidentally, these principles are inherent in the indigenous craft process; child labor and labor unions both surfaced during the process of industrialization. The framework aims to bring in sustainability by addressing the politics of labor – i.e., to address unemployment, exploitation of labor, the environment, and globalization.

5.5   Summary and conclusions

This chapter presented the Rhizome Framework, a construct which proposes three potentially viable directions for the evolution of tradition craft – the *expressive*, *prosumer* and *glocal* – through craft-design collaboration. Such meaningful collaboration would empower craftspeople to access viable markets, access equitable gains from production, record and protect their cultural capital, and leverage indigenous knowledge in craft-design collaborations. The need and basis for the development of the Rhizome Framework is discussed in this chapter: it centers on linking craftspeople to viable markets so they can have sustained livelihoods, which in turn will positively impact sustainability in a holistic manner.

Craft is a vital force in communicating and validating the culture and tradition of craftspeople. Simultaneously, craft's huge commercial potential can be leveraged to help contribute to large-scale employment of craftspeople who do not have much capital but are rich in indigenous knowledge and have a strong skill and resource base (Ranjan, 1995). Therefore, the Rhizome Framework aims to deconstruct indigenous knowledge so that it can be used as a design input during innovation. The framework functions as part of a holistic system, whereby natural-resource management, community mobilization and organization, market analysis, design and development, skill training, capacity building, production streamlining and institution building are part of a comprehensive strategy.

The following chapter offers a methodology we developed to actualize the Rhizome Framework. This approach to design is named after the Rhizome Framework, which it aims to make actionable – it is called the Rhizome Approach.

6 The Rhizome Approach

6.1 The Rhizome Approach: towards meaningful craft-design collaborations for sustainability

The previous chapter offered a construct called the Rhizome Framework, which proposes three potential directions for the evolution of traditional craft. Each of these directions is actualized by craft-design collaboration aiming to create products which align with viable markets. The livelihood arising from the production of these products would positively impact the sustainability of the craft and the craftspeople, and also holistic sustainability in general.

The described scenario is underpinned by two premises: a) that design can be a sustainability enabler, and b) holistic sustainability can result from collaborative innovation between designer and craftsperson.

We discovered that the enormous potential of the first premise – design as a sustainability enabler – remains untapped. We discussed this in detail in Section 3.2, where our study of literature revealed that the interest in sustainability and sustainable design (Fuad-Luke, 2009) has not translated into frequent practice by designers in developed (Aye, 2003; Kang et al., 2008; Kang & Guerin, 2009; Mate, 2006), or in developing countries (Hankinson & Breytenbach, 2012). Our study of literature threw up seven reasons for this (Section 3.5): a) lack of knowledge about sustainability, b) lack of holistic overview of production-to-consumption systems and value chains, c) failure to include sustainability at a strategic level in the overall approach, d) failure to include sustainability criteria in the design brief, e) lack of a collaborative design process, f) lack of tools, and g) Failure to keep design teams in the loop during the product actualization process.

The second premise – holistic sustainability through craft-design collaboration – also remains unrealized. Currently, most designers working towards sustainability with "craft" materials – such as bamboo, cork and sea grass – tend to focus only on the material's ecological and economic potential. While the resulting designs are eco-friendly (ecologically sustainable) and marketable (economically sustainable), they do not capitalize on the potential of these materials to contribute to social and cultural sustainability. This is a pity, because these materials are well-placed to impact holistic sustainability and inclusive development. This is because they are traditionally part of production-to-consumption systems which involve a large number of indigent producers – including marginalized groups such as women, craftspeople and ethnic minorities. We argue that design-craft collaboration can be the vehicle for innovation which can go beyond impacting the ecological and economic tenets, to addressing all the dimensions of sustainability holistically. This, in turn, would open up the possibility of side-stepping the various unsustainabilities of the mainstream industrial paradigm, especially with regards to MSMEs in developing countries.

Craft offers a valuable input into sustainable design, and also counter-balances the mainstream industrial design ethos (Tonkinwise, 2015). In contrast to industrial design – which is driven by industry, craft is driven by the integration of tacit knowledge, innovation, skill, bioregional knowledge (Ihatsu, 2002) and traditional practices. All of these link into a single system determined by the interconnectedness between people, land, materials and energy (Ihatsu, 2002). If design manages to tap into craft's slowness, richness (Tonkinwise, 2015) and indigenous knowledge systems, it can also leverage the systems of social, ecological, cultural and economic sustainability that underpin them. Collaborating with craftspeople offers designers the opportunity to orchestrate and be part of value chains that are localized, systemic and relatively transparent – where stakeholders have greater accountability, both to each other and to the outcome of the production-to-consumption system in general.

Collaborative innovation also offers the potential of going beyond designing products to designing the production-to-consumption systems that underpin them. Through interaction with their craft collaborators, designers are exposed to the specific problems and opportunities in developing-country scenarios – including the need and potential for systems which are non-industrial, labor-intensive, localized and community-centric.

While the idea of collaborative innovation is not new, we did not find a particular methodology to support it. We therefore created the Rhizome Approach towards a methodology to support collaborative innovation and to actualize the Rhizome Framework. This methodology is mindful of the barriers to sustainable innovation we identified. We offer it towards a methodology to equip mainstream designers to design to impact sustainability holistically – especially in the context of design for and in developing countries, with renewable materials, and with craft production-to-consumption systems. The Rhizome Approach advocates the re-emergence of systems thinking in the design process towards understanding and being mindful of the entire system that sustainability rests on. It is a flexible methodology to ensure that is adaptable to different scenarios, rather than becoming a cookie-cutter template. The Rhizome Approach – like the Rhizome Framework – is named after bamboo's complex underground rhizome system, and has its philosophical underpinnings in work of Deleuze and Guattari (1987). A detailed discussion on this is offered vis-à-vis the Rhizome Framework (Section 5.1); this also holds for the Rhizome Approach.

6.2   The Rhizome Approach

Figure 6.1 offers an overview of the Rhizome Approach, including the barriers which informed its seven steps, the steps, their aims and the envisaged method for operationalizing the steps.

Step	Barrier	Aim	Method
1	Lack of knowledge about sustainability	Inform designers about sustainability, and the connections between its tenets	Provision of background reading material covering the connections between sustainability, design, material and the production-to-consumption system
2	Lack of a holistic overview of the production-to-consumption system	Sensitize designers to the systemic production-to-consumption system	Exposure visits to stakeholders of the different nodes of the value chain and production-to-consumption system
3	Failure to include sustainability at a strategic level in the overall approach	Factor sustainability into the strategic blueprint of the enterprise	Introducing a blueprint, towards which all the participants of the collaborative design process will work together collectively
4	Failure to include sustainability criteria in the design brief	Articulate sustainability criteria in the design brief so that it can be factored into the front-end design phase	Clear brief supplemented by the Sustainability Checklist to clarify desired design and its impact on each tenet of sustainability
5	Lack of a collaborative design process	Provide inputs from different stakeholders towards a collaborative design process	Constant linkage and interaction with stakeholders of the production-to-consumption system during the design process
6	Lack of tools to measure holistic sustainability against indicators	Increase designers' accountability to factor sustainability into their designs and provide a tool to measure the sustainability achieved	Evaluation of the design against the Sustainability Checklist by the designer and two external evaluators
7	Failure to keep the design team in the loop during product actualization	Keep designers in the loop until final product actualization, thereby retaining their responsibility for the product's sustainability	Involving the design team in all iterations of the design, up to final product actualization

Figure 6.1 Overview of the Rhizome Approach
Source: Reubens, 2016c

The seven steps of the Rhizome Approach are elaborated upon in the following sub-sections. The barriers on which these steps are based are discussed in detail in Section 3.5:

Step 1: providing knowledge and information on sustainability

Designers cited the lack of knowledge and information on sustainability as a barrier to their practicing sustainable design. Designers need to understand the specific characteristics of sustainability and sustainable design, in order to apply these (Kang & Guerin, 2009). Most designers do not learn about sustainability through their mainstream design education (Aye, 2003; Hankinson & Breytenbach, 2012), through their professional practice or through professional peer-exchange platforms such as conferences (Lofthouse, 2017; Hankinson & Breytenbach, 2012).

The first step of the Rhizome Approach, therefore, advocates bridging the theoretical knowledge gap on sustainability, by providing designers with information through focused presentations and reading material.

Step 2: enabling a holistic overview on production-to-consumption systems and value chains

Designers tend to focus on the business, but not on its forward and backward linkages (Maxwell et al., 2003). Looking at the entire picture – and thereby being able to assess the reliability of suppliers and vendors – is becoming increasingly challenging and important, given that production-to-consumption systems are now spread across nations (Hankinson & Breytenbach, 2012). Designers tend to focus on addressing easily visible problems – such as ecological unsustainability – rather than exploring integrated, invisible issues and reaching holistically sustainable systems solutions (Maxwell et al., 2003).

Step 2 therefore advocates supplementing the didactic learning from Step 1 with hands-on exposure to the entire production-to-consumption system. The aim is to facilitate experiential learning – including by first-hand visits to the different nodes of the value chain – in order to understand how the independent actors of the production-to-consumption system collectively impact sustainability. Realistically, this understanding will probably not translate into designer's influencing the behavior of each actor in the production-to-consumption system. However, understanding the collective motivations and compulsions of the actors that comprise the system can be the basis for the design of an optimal solution that weighs and prioritizes the trade-offs between the individual motivations and compulsions of each actor.

Step 3: including sustainability at a strategic level

A business would need to include sustainability at a strategic level for its key systems – including design – to internalize sustainability concerns (Maxwell et al., 2003). Sustainability often seems to involve extra effort (Hankinson & Breytenbach, 2012) and cost more (Aye, 2003; Mate, 2006). In addition, sustainable solutions require more time (Bacon, 2011; Hankinson & Breytenbach, 2012) for sourcing (Aye, 2003) and research (Hankinson & Breytenbach, 2012). In order for sustainability to be factored into innovation and design – especially because it calls for extra effort with no clear immediate benefits (Hankinson &Breytenbach, 2012) – it needs to be championed as a key part of an organization's strategic approach.

Step 3 therefore focuses on introducing sustainability into an organization's strategic blueprint, towards which all the participants of the collaborative design process will work together collectively.

Step 4: including sustainability criteria in the design brief

Sustainability is often not included in the design brief because it is seen as an expensive (Aye, 2003; Mate, 2006; Bacon, 2011) add-on to the design brief that conflicts with the functional requirements of the product (Hankinson & Breytenbach, 2012; Van Hemel & Cramer, 2002). Including sustainability in the design brief – right in the front-end stage (Dewulf, 2013) – would minimize the need to clean up several consequences of the product life cycle (White et al., 2008). Step 4 therefore advocates including sustainability in the design brief and clearly outlining the criteria desired in the design, and their impact on the four tenets of sustainability. We created a tool to do this, called the Sustainability Checklist (Figure 6.2).

The starting point for the checklist was the seven meta rules of thumb with 105 detailed rules developed in the *Design for Sustainability (D4S) Manual* (Crul & Diehl, 2006). The precedents for the rules of thumb in the *D4S Manual* were Module B ("Optimization of the End-of-life System") and Module G ("The Environmental Problem") of the Dutch *PROMISE Manual for Ecodesign* (Brezet, Horst, & Riele, 1994), the *Life-Cycle Design Guidance Manual* (Keolian & Menerey, 1993), the Office of Technology Assessment's *Green Products by Design* (United States Congress, 1992), the German standards VDI 2243 guidelines and compatibility tables for recycling (VDI 1993)and the GEP *Design for Recycling* guide (Industry Council for Electronic Equipment Recycling, 1993). The Sustainability Checklist was developed by creating a list by grouping and short listing the rules of thumb from the D4S Manual (Crul & Diehl, 2006). We supplemented this list with inputs from the ILO's international declaration on fundamental principles and rights at work and its follow-up (ILO 1998) and conventions and recommendations (ILO 2016) (Figure 6.3). The final list was mapped against a generic production-to-consumption system, and the Four Pillars of sustainability and craft.

The Sustainability Checklist illustrates a generic product's production-to-consumption system and the sustainable-design parameters relevant at each stage. This offers the designer an insight into the interlinkages between the tenets of sustainability and production-to-consumption. The tenets of sustainability strongly influenced by each parameter are indicated, along with the potential of craft practice to address and be fortified by these parameters. By understanding

	Production-to-consumption Chain	Sustainable Design Parameter	Ecological tenet	Economic tenet	Social tenet	Cultural tenet	Craft process
1	Material selection considerations	Cleaner	●				●
2		Renewable	●				●
3		Low energy consumption	●	●			●
4		Biodegradable	●				●
5		Recyclable	●				●
6		Recycled	●				●
7		Supplied by poor/ marginalized/ local producers	●	●	●		●
8		Fairly traded	●		●		●
9		Sustainably harvested and managed	●		●		●
10		Minimum treatment for processing	●	●			●
11		Background of local/ indigenous production systems			●	●	●
12	Production considerations	Minimum material	●	●			●
13		Less harmful/ sustainable combination materials	●		●		●
14		Indigenous treatments and processes	●		●	●	●
15		Less emissions	●		●		●
16		Minimum production steps	●	●			●
17		Renewable energy used	●				

Figure 6.2 Sustainability Checklist

Source: Reubens, 2016c adapted from Crul & Diehl, 2006 + ILO directives

#	Category	Description					
18		Less waste generated/ waste reused	•	•		•	•
19		Material reduction through efficiency	•	•			•
20		Healthy and safe working environment			•	•	•
21		Fair wages and benefits to producer			•	•	•
22		Non-discriminatory			•	•	•
23		Employment to marginalized producers			•	•	•
24		Capacity-building of producers		•	•	•	•
25		Producers involved in decision-making			•	•	•
26		No child and/ or forced labor			•	•	•
27		Respect for human rights of producers			•	•	•
28		Indigenous representation in decision-making affecting indigenous resources			•	•	•
29	Distribution considerations	Minimum weight	•	•			
30		Reduction in distribution volume/weight	•	•			•
31		Minimum packaging	•	•		•	•

Figure 6.2 (Continued)

32		Clean/cleaner packaging	•			•	•
33		Reusable packaging	•			•	•
34		Recyclable packaging	•				•
35		Packaging made from reused/ recyclable material	•			•	
36		Energy efficient transport for distribution	•				•
37		Localized production and distribution systems to reduce physical production to delivery gap	•	•	•	•	•
38	Consumer use considerations	Low energy consumption during usage	•			•	•
39		Clean energy consumption during usage	•			•	•
40		Reduction of disposable auxiliary materials through permanent product feature	•				•
41		Efficient use of consumables during usage	•				•
42		Use of clean consumables during usage	•				•
43		Safe for users' health	•		•		•

Figure 6.2 (Continued)

44		Customizable		•		•	•
45		User-friendly		•	•	•	•
46		Affordable			•		•
47		Easy to maintain and repair	•			•	•
48		Easily upgradeable	•			•	•
49		Classic design	•			•	•
50		Promote a strong user – product relationship			•	•	•
51		Locally repairable and maintainable	•		•		•
52	End-of-life handling considerations	Classic design and robust quality, enabling product to be passed down and reused	•		•	•	•
53		Designed for disassembly	•				
54		Mono-material	•		•	•	•
55		Recyclable	•				
56		Toxic harmful materials easily isolatable for separate disposal	•		•		
57		End-of-life handling facilitates employment for local communities through recycling			•		•

Figure 6.2 (Continued)

Production-to-Consumption System	Sustainability Checklist	D4S Rules of Thumb	ILO Conventions and Articles
Material considerations	Renewable	Use renewable materials	–
	Minimally treated	Avoid additional surface treatment	–
		Do not use paint if possible	–
		Use efficient painting techniques	–
	Recyclable	Use recyclable materials	–
	Recycled	Use recycled materials	–
	Local materials	Use local materials	–
	Fair trade	Use fair trade materials	–
		Use certified materials	–
		Use materials with social benefits	–
		No toxic materials or additives	–
		Avoid materials from intensive agriculture	–
		Avoid energy-intensive materials	–

Figure 6.3 First version of the Sustainability Checklist developed with inputs from D4S and ILO
Source: Reubens, 2016c

Production considerations	Minimum material			
	Minimum production steps	Reduce number of production steps	–	
	Renewable energy	Use renewable energy sources	–	
		Save energy for production	–	
		Avoid toxic substances	–	
	Less emissions	Use low-emission techniques	–	
		Use water treatment systems	–	
		Recycle production residues	–	
	Less waste generated	Reduce production waste	–	
	Waste reused	Reuse production waste	–	
		Reduce number of rejects	–	
	Indigenous treatments and processes	Use natural treatment	–	
		Preserve local culture	–	
	Indigenous representation in decision-making		•	Indigenous and tribal peoples have the right to "decide their own priorities for the process of development as it affects their lives, beliefs, institutions and spiritual well-being and the lands they occupy or otherwise use, and to exercise control over their economic, social and cultural development." (Convention 169: Article 7)

Figure 6.3 (Continued)

Healthy and safe work environment	Safe and clean working place	• Employers need to ensure that the machinery, processes, and any substances used at the workplace are "reasonably safe and without risk to health"; • Employers should also provide employees with protective clothing and equipment, emergency measures including first-aid, and training in health and safety norms; • Employees need to cooperate with their employers in maintaining a safe and healthy workplace; employers cannot force employees to work in an unsafe environment. (Convention 155: Article 16–19)
Fair wages and benefits to producers		• Both social factors (needs of workers and their families, cost of living/inflation, social security benefits) and economic factors (job creation, productivity, competitiveness) should be considered while setting the minimum wage. (Convention 131: Article 3) • Wages must be paid regularly, in full, and only in legal tender. (Convention 95) • Workers are obliged to perform only up to 56 hours per week; • Employers need to prominently display the start and end times for the workday or shift; • Overtime pay should not be less than 125% of the regular rate. (Convention 1: Articles 4–9) • Such compensation should be in addition to the remuneration paid for the same work performed during the daytime. Workers who have to perform work on weekly rest days or public holidays must be compensated for these days additional to the normal wage rates, for working on these days. (Convention 1: Article 8) • On completing a year of service, every worker should get paid leave of three working weeks each year. (Convention 132: Article 3)

Figure 6.3 (Continued)

	• At least 14 weeks of paid maternity leave. (Convention 183) • Workers should receive a sickness benefit, of 45% of the normal wage rate. (Convention 102)
No child labor	• Any work which is likely to jeopardize children's health, safety or morals should not be done by anyone under the age of 18; or 16 under strict conditions. • Minimum age for basic work should not be lower than the "the age for finishing compulsory schooling," or 15 years, whichever is higher. • However, developing countries may initially set the lower minimum age of 14 years (12 years in case of light work). (Convention 138)
No forced labor	• States must suppress use of forced labor: as a means of political coercion; for purposes of economic development; as a means of all types of discrimination; or as a punishment for participation in strike. (Convention 105: Article 1)
Capacity building of producers	—
No discrimination	• Employers may not discriminate – exclude or show bias against – employees or potential employees on the grounds of: race, color, sex, religion, political opinion, national extraction or social origin, age, HIV/AIDS status, disability, family/marital status (family responsibilities), trade union membership and related activities in terms of employment and remuneration. (Conventions 87, 98, 100, 156, 158, 159, 162 and 183) • No discrimination against indigenous workers. (Convention 169: Article 20)

Figure 6.3 (Continued)

Distribution considerations		Strive for gender equality	Occupational sex segregation is a form of discrimination. (Convention 111)
Distribution considerations	Respect for human rights	Contract local workers	–
		Create social opportunities	–
	Minimum distribution volume	Reduce transport/storage volume	–
		Make design foldable or stackable	–
		Design knock down products	–
	Minimum distribution weight	Reduce weight	–
		Aim for rigidity by construction	–
	Energy-efficient transport	Use energy efficient and clean transport	–
	Localized production-to-consumption system	Contract local distributors	–
	Minimum packaging	Reduce amount of packaging	–
	Reusable packaging	Use reusable packaging	–

Figure 6.3 (Continued)

	Recyclable packaging	Give packaging an extra function	–
	Packaging made from reused/recycled material	Use low impact materials	–
		Use standardized bulk packaging	–
Consumer-use considerations	Low/clean energy-consumption during usage	Use clean energy source	–
		Reduce energy consumption	–
	Reduced and clean consumables during use	Reduce or recycle consumables	–
		Reduce water consumption	–
	Safe for users health	Ensure safe usage	–
		Avoid harmful substances	–
	Customizable	Use modular design structure	–
	User friendly		–
	Affordable		–
	Easily upgradeable	Design for upgradeability	–
	Classic design	Strive for classic design	–

Figure 6.3 (Continued)

Promote a strong–user product relationship	Provide instructions to avoid misuse	–
	Give usage a social value	–
	Strengthen product – user relationship	–
Locally repairable and maintainable	Increase reliability and durability	–
	Make maintenance and repair easy	–
	Limit maintenance and repair	–
	Use local maintenance and repair systems	–
End-of-life handling considerations	Mono-material	Reduce material complexity	–
		Make it safe for composting	–
		Avoid downcycling of materials	–
	Designed for disassembly	Design for dismantling	–
		Design for reuse	–
		Avoid extra elements such as stickers	–

Figure 6.3 (Continued)

		Use universal fasteners	–
		Minimize the use of fasteners	–
End-of-life disassembly facilitates employment for local communities		Use existing take-back and recycling systems	–
		Develop new take-back and recycling systems	–
		Avoid incineration	–

Figure 6.3 (Continued)

the systemic perspective through the deconstructed parameters, the collaborative craft-design object can be strategized to be culturally, ecologically, socially, economically or holistically sustainable.

The checklist makes the innovator aware of the potential and desired criteria that can make a product more holistically sustainable at a product-development stage.

Step 5: collaborative design process

The final design is not shaped only by the designer; the inputs of each of the different occupational groups and stakeholders across the supply chain shape the final design, and thereby sustainability (White et al., 2008). Designers need to collaborate with these groups and stakeholders in order to factor in sustainability concerns and opportunities from across the production-to-consumption system (White et al., 2008) and be able to go beyond design's typical manufacture-use focus (Dewulf, 2013).

Step 5 therefore advocates creating platforms that allow for collaborative decision-making by encouraging and actively facilitating a constant linkage and interaction between designers and actors, facilitators and enablers of the production-to-consumption system – including those who are not traditionally recognized as part of the innovation team.

Step 6: providing tools for sustainability design

Despite the plethora of sustainability tools available, designers cited the lack of appropriate tools was still cited as a barrier to sustainable design (Aye, 2003). This suggests that the existing tools are misaligned with designers' requirements (Lofthouse, 2006) – tools with accurate and accessible information (Aye, 2003; Davis, 2001; Hes, 2005) packaged together in an easy-to-refer-to manner (Lofthouse, 2006).

Designers also cited the need for tools which could help them to measure, quantify and communicate sustainable-design achievements. Such tools – including ratings – would help legitimize sustainability efforts as credentials (Hankinson & Breytenbach, 2012), and help them convince their clients to invest in sustainability as a quantifiable value proposition.

Step 6 of the Rhizome Approach addresses these issues through the same Sustainability checklist introduced in Step 4. Step 6 involves a 360-degree evaluation of the finished product against the checklist, by three evaluators. These could include producers, other designers, industry experts and other evaluators relevant to the process. Each evaluator can rank the product 1 = low, 2 = medium, and 3 = high. The final "grading" for the product would be the triangulated mean of the three grades.

Having three sets of evaluations would reduce the discrepancy between the scorings through investigator triangulation (Denzin, 1978). The final score gives designers the opportunity to reconsider aspects of their design, and develop a more sustainable iteration if needed. The grading can be represented visually in several

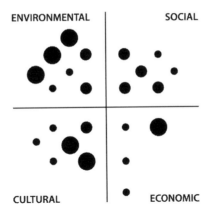

ENVIRONMENTAL | SOCIAL

CULTURAL | ECONOMIC

Figure 6.4 Sustainability landscape, to represent results of assessment against the Sustainability Checklist

Source: Reubens, 2016c

ways. For example, one solution would be representing the grading through color. For example, a red dot can represent a low grading, a yellow dot can represent a medium grading, and green dot can represent a high grading. This grading can be reflected on a *sustainability landscape* which can consist of a matrix depicting the identified four tenets of sustainability. Or the same information can be conveyed through different sizes of dots, where the smaller the dot, the lesser the sustainability (Figure 6.4). For example, low energy-consumption affects both ecological and economic tenets, so there will be one dot each in each of these *regions*. The final sustainability quotient can be reflected as a little *map* (Figure 6.4) which will allow consumers to see at a glance what tenets of sustainability the product addresses the most and those tenets which are neglected.

The quantitative output of the checklist can be used to showcase the sustainability achieved, including through a branding and labeling initiative. Chapter 7 offers a case when the checklist was used as a tool to assess sustainability.

Step 7: keeping the design team in the loop until final product actualization

As we discussed earlier, the final design is the result of several iterations by different functional groups – including design, production, marketing and merchandizing (White et al., 2008). In the end, none of the functional groups – including design – takes ownership or accountability for the final design outcome, because they were not involved with design decisions before and after their iteration. If designers are to be held accountable for factoring sustainability into the product, they need to remain involved and invested in the entire innovation process and have ownership of it.

Step 7 therefore advocates keeping designers in the loop from the front-end stage to right up to final product actualization so they can maintain an overview of the process (White et al., 2008), and ownership of the design outcome.

6.3   Summary and conclusions

This chapter presented a methodology, called the Rhizome Approach, which was developed towards equipping designers to leverage craft production-to-consumption systems in developing countries for holistic sustainability design. Most sustainability design centers on the ecological tenet; the Rhizome Approach proposes a methodology which centers on and facilitates a holistic focus on all the four tenets of sustainability. The approach advocates the re-emergence of systems thinking in the design process towards sustainability design, through collaborative innovation.

The seven steps of the Rhizome Approach correlate with the seven broad thematic barriers to sustainability identified in the literature review: a) lack of knowledge about sustainability, b) lack of holistic overview of production-to-consumption systems and value chains, c) failure to include sustainability at a strategic level in the overall approach, d) failure to include sustainability criteria in the design brief, e) absence of a collaborative design process, f) lack of tools, and g) failure to keep design teams in the loop during the product actualization process.

The efficacy and relevance of the Rhizome Approach, step-wise and as a whole, was validated through a questionnaire that was e-mailed to 15 designers located around the world. Their feedback, especially vis-à-vis alternatives to each step of the approach, is discussed in Chapter 8.

The Sustainability Checklist was further refined through a second phase of iterations. This phase was mindful of the fact that design's influence on sustainability is limited without support from the outside envelope, comprising the company, the market and the policy. This aspect is discussed further in Chapter 9, which centers on our third question – possible mechanisms to support the operationalization of our sustainability design approach.

The following chapter discusses how the Rhizome Approach was demonstrated and tested in India through a craft-design collaboration workshop in India.

7 The bamboo space-making craft workshop

7.1 Trialing the Rhizome Framework and Approach

The two previous chapters offered a construct called the Rhizome Framework, and a methodology to actualize it called the Rhizome Approach, respectively. The Rhizome Framework proposes that traditional craft evolve along three potentially viable directions through craft-design collaboration. We did not find a methodology to support such collaborative innovation, especially one at the intersection of craft, design and sustainability. Therefore, we developed the Rhizome Approach towards a methodology to support collaborative innovation and to actualize the Rhizome Framework. The Rhizome Framework is therefore the proposed end, and the Rhizome Approach is the proposed means to this end.

We conducted a space-making craft workshop in India to trial the Rhizome Framework and Approach. The workshop centered on craft-design collaboration between Indian designers and the Kotwalia, a traditional Indian bamboo-working tribe (Figure 7.1). The number of Kotwalia who continue to craft agrarian bamboo products is dwindling, because the demand for their baskets has all but vanished due of the influx of industrially produced substitutes. In addition, the forests to which the Kotwalia traditionally had free access for their raw material are now the property of the state, and off limits for them. The Kotwalia currently have almost no access to raw material, almost no market – and therefore, almost no income. This income loss forces them to migrate seasonally in search of wages, because they do not have any economic or productive skills other than bamboo working, or land to farm. Like members of several other traditional craft communities, the Kotwalia urgently require focused strategy development to allow them to access viable new markets. The income security will then help them address their own forms of unsustainability – social, economic, cultural and ecological.

We conducted the Space-making Craft Workshop from January 20 to February 2, 2011, at the Design Innovation and Craft Resource Centre (DICRC), at CEPT (Centre for Environmental Planning and Technology) University, Ahmedabad. The overall workshop structure was based on a technical-training format, involving didactic learning, supervised hands-on training and unsupervised experience-building (Baille & Ravich, 1993). The underlying effort was to provide a

Figure 7.1 The Kotwalia area traditional Indian bamboo-working community

learning experience with relevance, reflexivity and continuity (Strand, 2011). An important consideration of both the Rhizome Approach and the workshop design was to take the designers through three independent, but closely interconnected, modes of thinking: a) connective or systems thinking, b) critical thinking or the ability to critique existing and established mental models, and c) personal thinking, or self-awareness.

The didactic-learning module was designed to be brief and relevant, and to establish core concepts. Field visits confronted the participants with the trade-offs and disparity between the different elements that shape sustainability, and the need for design to respond to this complex and holistic picture. This was intended to create experiential learning, and also to instill reflexivity and objectivity. The collaborative design process that followed built on the learning so far, and was largely unsupervised. While there were inputs from different factions, including facilitators, the effort was to rely on personal thinking.

Participants and facilitators

The workshop included an equal number of designers and craftspeople as participants, in line with the emphasis on craft-design collaboration towards sustainability design, which is central to both the Rhizome Framework and Rhizome Approach. The 24 design participants included design students from the Faculty of Design, CEPT University, Ahmedabad, and the Indian Institute of Craft and Design (IICD), Jaipur, in addition to professional designers and civil engineers. The 24 craft participants were Kotwalia bamboo-working trainees from Waghai town, who were linked to two social sector organizations, namely, the Tapini Bamboo Development Centre (TBDC) and the Eklavya Foundation.

The facilitators included assistant professors from CEPT University and IICD, a resource person from the Eklavya Foundation, mastercraftspeople/production heads from the TBDC and us, representing both Delft University and our sustainability design firm Rhizome.

Structure of workshop

The day-by-day outline of the workshop is presented in Figure 7.2.

Day	Activity
1	• Presentation and discussion on linkages between sustainability, bamboo and design • Introduction to the Rhizome Framework • Exploring the product range of the Kotwalia community, created through the product-library workshop (see Section 5.2)
2 3	• Field visits for exposure to stakeholders in the bamboo production-to-consumption chain, including Kotwalia craft enterprises and the forest department
4	• Icebreaking exercises • Forming three groups as per the Rhizome Framework—*expressive, glocal* and *prosumer* • Design brief and introduction to the Sustainability Checklist • Sub group-wise brainstorming session for the entire design team and the entire craft team to come up with potential applications and design directions in line with their respective subgroup. The groups presented their findings to the remaining groups, and also to varied stakeholders following the discussion on Day 3
5	• Concept development by designer–craftsperson teams
6–12	• Design and prototyping
13	• Evaluation against the Sustainability Checklist
14	• Exhibition in Ahmedabad

Figure 7.2 Day-by-day outline of workshop

Overview

An overview of the workshop vis-à-vis the Rhizome Approach is presented in Figure 7.3.

Each of these seven steps is discussed in detail in the following seven sections. The first part of each section discusses the workshop design; the next part, how the design was actualized during the workshop; and the last part, the relevant findings from the questionnaires administered on the efficacy of the step.

Step	Barrier	Aim	Method	Workshop-specific mechanisms
1	Lack of knowledge about sustainability	Inform designers about sustainability, and the connections between its tenets	Didactic knowledge through knowledge kit to provide information and knowledge on the core concepts on sustainability	• Knowledge kit containing pre-workshop reading material • PowerPoint presentations by institutional representatives • Our presentation on the holistic picture of sustainability

2	Lack of a holistic overview of the production-to-consumption system	Sensitize designers to the systemic production-to-consumption system	Experiential learning through exposure visits to different nodes of the production-to-consumption system	• Exposure visits to:
				  ○ Handicraft-scale MSMEs
				  ○ Design-led MSME enterprise
				  ○ Industrial-scale enterprise
				  ○ Bamboo resource-growing area

3	Failure to include sustainability at a strategic level in the overall approach	Factor sustainability into the strategic blueprint	Classroom sessions and experiential learning to internalize sustainability and introduce it into the strategic blueprint	• Sharing and explaining Rhizome Framework as a common goal
				 • Concept mapping exercises on
				  ○ Is craft relevant?
				  ○ What is the impact on each direction of the Rhizome Framework on the tenets of sustainability?
				  ○ What are the product possibilities of each direction of the Rhizome Framework?

Figure 7.3 Overview of bamboo space-making workshop vis-à-vis the Rhizome Approach

4	Failure to include sustainability criteria in the design brief	Articulate sustainability criteria in the design brief	Clear brief supplemented by the Sustainability Checklist to clarify desired design decisions and their impact on each tenet of sustainability	• Clear brief to design a commercially-viable bamboo product, using local production capacities, that leverages indigenous knowledge systems • Clear outline of which direction of the Rhizome Framework on which the design would center • Explanation of the Sustainability Checklist and provision of a copy to each innovation team

5	Lack of a collaborative design process	Provide inputs from different stakeholders towards a collaborative design process	Constant linkage and interaction with stakeholders of the production-to-consumption system to facilitate collaborative design	• Icebreaking, team-building and energizing exercises
				  o Animal-sounds exercise
				  o Three-secrets exercise
				  o Hand-drawing exercise
				• Constant feedback from experts and stakeholders
				  o Eleven talks from different resource experts
				  o Constant feedback from facilitators in their area of expertise

6	Lack of tools to measure holistic sustainability against indicators	Increase designers' accountability to factor sustainability into their designs and provide a tool to measure the sustainability achieved	Evaluation of the design against the Sustainability Checklist by three evaluators	• Self-evaluation by designers using the Sustainability Checklist • Cross-validation of evaluation by one community expert and one design expert
7	Failure to keep the design team in the loop during product actualization	Keep designers in the loop until final product actualization	Involving design team in all iterations of the design, up to final product actualization	• Involvement of designers in all changes required for product actualization until final prototype is resolved

Figure 7.3 (Continued)

7.2   Step 1: inform designers about sustainability, and the connections between its tenets

Step 1 of the Rhizome Approach advocates bridging the information and knowledge gap on sustainability. This is actualized by orienting the participants on core sustainability concepts, including the connections between sustainability, design, material and technology, and production-to-consumption systems.

Step 1 workshop design

During the workshop, the designers had inputs in sustainability through a combination of didactic and experiential learning. Multiple learning methods were employed to cover different core concepts – including craft, sustainability and sustainability design – which their mainstream design education may not have covered in depth. In order to better structure this chapter, the experiential-learning component of the workshop is elaborated upon in Step 2 (Section 7.3); this section covers the didactic-learning phase.

Didactic learning sets the tone for, and begins the learning process by delivering factual information succinctly (Domask, 2007). It ensures that seminal and core concepts are covered, thus providing a foundation for the participants' overall learning and internalization of it. The didactic-learning phase of the workshop included digital presentations followed by discussions. This was supplemented by a knowledge kit comprised of focused reading material (Baille & Ravich, 1993).

Step 1 workshop actualization

Sustainability is a vast and complex domain. It is therefore very important that designers access sustainability information that is relevant and applicable to design practice (Strand, 2011). This would optimize time and avoid information overload: as discussed earlier, designers do not want tedious or lengthy information which is difficult to absorb. Therefore, information closely related to the overall domain of the workshop's design project was selected.

Reading material

Before the workshop, the designers were provided with a knowledge kit, which they could use for reference and study. This kit comprised the following reading material:

- INBAR Technical Paper 60, titled *Bamboo in Sustainable Contemporary Design* (Reubens, 2010b), which discusses the linkages between bamboo, sustainability and design.
- Article from the *Journal of Craft Research* titled "Bamboo Canopy: Creating New Reference Points for the Craft of the Kotwalia Community in India

Through Sustainability" (Reubens, 2010a), which discusses the Rhizome Framework against the background of the Kotwalia community.
- Diagnostic study report for development of the bamboo craft cluster in Tapi district under the participatory cluster development program of NABARD (National Bank for Agriculture and Rural Development) (Reubens, 2010c), which discusses the bamboo production-to-consumption system, especially vis-à-vis the Kotwalia community.

Digital presentations

The didactic-learning phase included the following digital presentations followed by interactive discussions:

- Orientation sessions by the institutions involved – DICRC, IICD, the Eklavya Foundation, TBDC, Rhizome and Delft University of Technology. These presentations brought out the synergies between the mandates of the institutions, and the different institutional perspectives on sustainability.
- We gave a presentation on the concept of sustainability, discussing how it is an evolving and holistic concept.

Apart from the presentations listed above, different expert resource persons linked to the areas of craft, design, bamboo and sustainability gave presentations every morning through the course of the workshop. While these also comprise the didactic-learning module, for reasons of structuring this chapter, they are discussed in Section 7.6.

Step 1 workshop findings

Digital presentations

Most of the participants found the presentations, *Sustainability and the Rhizome Approach*, and *Introduction to DICRC and Space-Making Crafts*, to be the most useful in Step 1 (Figure 7.4).

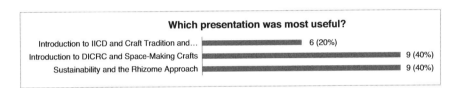

Which presentation was most useful?

Introduction to IICD and Craft Tradition and...   6 (20%)
Introduction to DICRC and Space-Making Crafts   9 (40%)
Sustainability and the Rhizome Approach   9 (40%)

Figure 7.4 Findings from 24 respondents on the most useful presentation

7.3 Step 2: sensitize designers to the systemic production-to-consumption system

Step 2 of the Rhizome Approach advocates sensitizing designers to the systemic production-to-consumption system, including through exposure visits to different nodes of the value chain and stakeholders of the production-to-consumption chain.

Step 2 workshop design

The exposure visits were an important part of the experiential-learning component of the workshop design, which included both major categories of experiential learning – field-based and classroom-based (Schwartz, n.d.). This section dwells on field-based learning, which is the oldest and most established form of experiential learning. The classroom-based experiential-learning modules are discussed in the following sections.

The field-based experiential-learning module built upon the didactic-learning inputs of Step 1, whereby the participants were introduced to seminal concepts around sustainability. The exposure visits were intended to expose participants to real-world issues, which they could connect back to the theoretical inputs of Step 1. The exposure visits would offer participants the opportunity to groundtruth for themselves the inputs on sustainability-related issues, actors and dynamics, to which they were exposed through the didactic learning of Step 1 (Alvarez & Rogers, 2006).

The exposure visits aimed to give the participants a real-world experience of cause and effect. Exposure visits would help the participants to connect the theory and dynamics to which they were exposed in Step 1, to the local impacts on people located thousands of miles away from the decision-makers (Domask, 2007),which they experienced in Step 2. This was intended to enable designers to internalize how relatively invisible design decisions could have deep, and sometimes unintended, impacts on different groups.

The exposure visits to the different nodes of the production-to-consumption system were intended to provide the participants with the opportunity to see the systemic picture (De Déa Roglio & Light, 2009), and to understand how each production-to-consumption system was a small sub-set within it. The participants needed to identify and internalize the interlinkages between dynamic systems, and develop a genuine concern for sustainable development, in order to be able to engage with the world as a systemic construct (De Déa Roglio & Light, 2009). Also important was that they develop the ability to identify the interconnections between different elements that constitute a problem context, and understand how these impact different spheres – including society, culture, economy and ecology (De Déa Roglio & Light, 2009). This, in turn, would help them to go beyond a myopic, short-term and business-centric perspective (Atwater, Kannan, & Stephens, 2008; Ghoshal, 2005; Strand, 2011) – and beyond design's typical manufacture-use focus.

Step 2 workshop actualization

The field-based experiential-learning module involved an intensive exposure visit to Waghai, a town located an overnight journey away from the city of Ahmedabad. The participants and facilitators stayed at a government ecotourism facility, which was the base for capsule exposure visits. Participants visited and had discussions with the different actors, enablers and supporters of the nodes of the production-to-consumption system. There was peer-to-peer learning through the designers' sharingexperiences through informal and formal discussions among themselves. The entire process resulted in the designers becoming aware that sustainability could potentially be realized through paradigm shifts in the production-to-consumption chain – including changes in the production volume, focus on livelihood opportunities, preservation of the social and cultural nucleus, and the use of materials (Walker, 1998).

The capsule exposure visits were as under:

- *Kotwalia village (Handicraft-scale MSMEs)*: The participants were divided into three groups, each of which visited a different Kotwalia village. The groups observed and documented the day-to-day life of Kotwalia families in order to internalize a handicraft-scale bamboo production-to-consumption system. Each group was accompanied by a facilitator and an interpreter, to enable the participants to interview and converse with the families. Several of the participants tried their hand at bamboo working.
- *TBDC-Eklavya-Rhizome production unit (Design-led MSME-scale enterprise)*: All of the participants visited the production unit of the TBDC-Eklavya-Rhizome consortium, where bamboo products are handcrafted for contemporary markets. The participants had a chance to see the impact of training and use of power tools and design on the productivity and product range of the same Kotwalia community in an MSME-scale production-to-consumption system. The participants interviewed and had discussions with the unit's resource people – including the producers, production managers and community mobilizers.
- *Vanil Udhyog (Industrial scale)*: All of the participants visited Vanil Udhyog, an integrated wood-working unit established by the government. The unit has state-of-the-art equipment – including conventional and solar-seasoning plants, and a saw-mill and finishing departments. The participants observed how more than 100 tribal workers worked under the supervision of qualified engineers to manufacture ISO-compliant products in an industrial-scale production-to-consumption system.
- *Waghai Botanical Garden (Resource-growing area)*: The participants saw different bamboo species of different ages at the Waghai Botanical Garden and biodiversity conservation center. This gave them the opportunity to understand the morphology of bamboo discussed during the presentation in Step 1. We gave a short talk, which provided inputs on field-identification of bamboo species, and the bamboo plant's morphological characteristics.

Step 2 workshop findings

A questionnaire was administered to the participants to check their learning on the Kotwalia bamboo production-to-consumption system. The aim of this was to ascertain the efficacy of the design and actualization of Step 2.

Level of learning on raw material source

A majority of the participants could correctly answer that the forest is the primary source of bamboo for the Kotwalia community. The remaining wrongly cited subsidiary sources as the primary source (Figure 7.5).

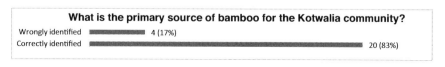

What is the primary source of bamboo for the Kotwalia community?

Wrongly identified   4 (17%)
Correctly identified   20 (83%)

Figure 7.5 Findings from 24 respondents on primary source of bamboo for the Kotwalia community

Level of learning on raw material transportation

None of the participants could correctly assess all three ways in which the Kotwalia community transports bamboo – themselves, through private transporters and through the government. While a majority of participants correctly assessed the one major way that the Kotwalia community transports bamboo – themselves – only a few could identify two ways of transportation; and some wrongly answered that members of the Kotwalia community do not transport bamboo themselves (Figure 7.6).

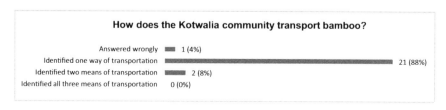

How does the Kotwalia community transport bamboo?

Answered wrongly   1 (4%)
Identified one way of transportation   21 (88%)
Identified two means of transportation   2 (8%)
Identified all three means of transportation   0 (0%)

Figure 7.6 Findings from 24 respondents on raw material transportation of the Kotwalia community

Level of learning on design and innovation

More than four-fifths of participants correctly assessed that open-source craft tradition and inputs from traditional users/patrons are the primary source of design and innovation for products produced by the Kotwalia community. Of these, over half answered open-source/traditional craft tradition, and the rest answered traditional patrons (Figure 7.7).

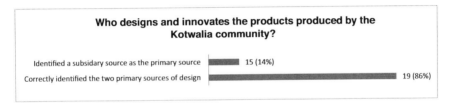

Figure 7.7 Findings from 24 respondents on design and innovation of products crafted by the Kotwalia community

Level of learning on processors

More than half of the participants correctly answered that all three constituents of a Kotwalia family – men, women and children – are involved in bamboo craft. The rest cited only men, or men and women, as being involved (Figure 7.8).

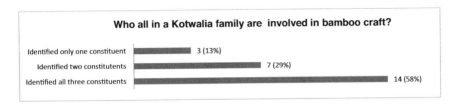

Figure 7.8 Findings from 24 respondents on involvement of family in processing

Level of learning on treatments

A little more than half of the participants could correctly identify the two traditional methods of bamboo treatment – smoking and water soaking; the rest could identify only one of the two methods, and one wrongly identified painting as a traditional method of bamboo treatment (Figure 7.9).

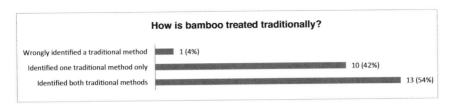

Figure 7.9 Findings from 24 respondents on traditional treatment methods of bamboo

Level of learning on type of bamboo used

A little over two-thirds of the participants could correctly answer that the craftspeople use green bamboo for traditional products (Figure 7.10).

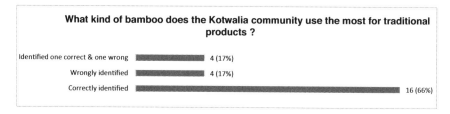

Figure 7.10 Findings from 24 respondents on type of bamboo used for traditional products

Level of learning on transfer of craft knowledge

The Kotwalia learn craft both intergenerationally and through training. Almost three-fourths of the participants could correctly identify only one way by which the Kotwalia learn craft (Figure 7.11).

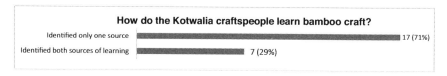

Figure 7.11 Findings from 24 respondents on transfer of craft knowledge

Level of learning on status of craft practice

A whopping three-fourths of the participants could correctly answer that the number of Kotwalia traditionally crafting bamboo had reduced compared to in the past; the remaining gave the wrong answer. Of the two respondents who didn't go to the field visit, one could not answer at all, which points to the importance of experiential learning (Figure 7.12).

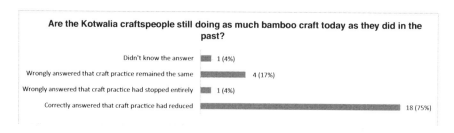

Figure 7.12 Findings from 24 respondents on the status of craft practice

Level of learning on marketing

Only a few of the participants could correctly identify all four ways in which the Kotwalia sold their products – within the village, at nearby villages, at towns and at tourist places. The remaining could identify between one to three ways of how the Kotwalia sold their products. The one respondent who didn't join the field visit didn't know the answer at all, again pointing to the importance of the exposure visits (Figure 7.13).

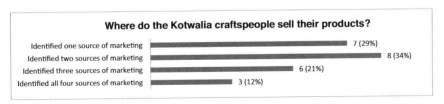

Figure 7.13 Findings from 24 respondents on the marketing of traditional products

The overall analysis of the findings, depicted in Figure 7.14 seems to indicate that the participants were able to grasp the design perspective the best, perhaps as they were from a design background. The most wrong answers were related to the resource, probably because the participants did not see resource harvesting or transportation first hand (Figure 7.14).

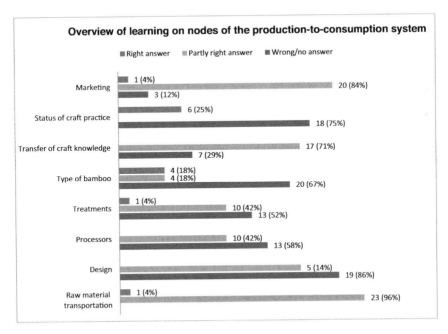

Figure 7.14 Overview of learning on different nodes of the production-to-consumption system; the 24 participants are assessed separately for each item

Overall participant experience

Two of the participants did not go on the field exposure visit. Both of these participants could not answer several questions on the craft production-to-consumption system, despite having access to the knowledge kit in Step 1, which contained all of this information. All of the participants who visited the Kotwalia community answered that they were better able to understand the production-to-consumption value chain more clearly and thoroughly after the visit. This indicates the efficacy of exposure visits in understanding production-to-consumption systems.

All of the participants answered that they thought that there are differences between industrial and non-industrial, or craft, set-ups in terms of production, design requirements and potential, and that the exposure visit had helped them understand the difference.

7.4   Step 3: factor sustainability into the strategic blueprint

Step 3 of the Rhizome Approach advocates factoring sustainability into the strategic blueprint, towards which all of the actors of the collaborative design process will work collectively.

Step 3 workshop design

Step 3 centers on sharing the Rhizome Framework with the participants, followed by classroom exercises to help the participants to internalize the holistic sustainability ethos that underpins it. These exercises also ask the participants to apply and reflect upon the learning from their primary experiences in Step 2 – the field and exposure visits.

Classroom exercises, where learning from primary experiences is applied, work at three levels: first, they prevent participants from forgetting the learning from primary experiences; second, the need to reflect upon and apply the learning from the primary experiences bolsters the primary experiences and learning from them; and third, the very act of reflection generates secondary experiences (Wurdinger, 2005). The exercises used in the workshop were shortlisted and/or designed based on a study of existing adult classroom-based experimental learning modules, mechanisms and strategies – including games, role-play, simulations, case studies, presentations and group work (Schwartz, n.d.). The underlying aim of these exercises was to pose problems whose resolution would require participants to think and to do, thereby facilitating reflection, internalization and retention of the consequent learning – as opposed to requiring participants to remember information by rote (Wurdinger, 2005). The exercises are aimed at facilitating critical thinking – the ability to become aware and question tacit mental models which guide decision-making at an individual and/or group level (De Déa Roglio & Light, 2009).

The exercises were designed keeping in mind Moon's (2004) methods, including:

- *Concept maps*: These reveal the participants' perception; sharing the maps allows for exchange between participants' perceptions.
- *Asking participants to explain and apply*: This leads participants to deeper critical thinking and reflection.
- *Questioning*: Posing open and leading questions, especially when set as problems, encourages critical thinking and reflection.

Step 3 workshop actualization

On our return to Ahmedabad, we had a PPT presentation of the Rhizome Framework for both design and craft participants. This was followed by an interactive discussion, after which the craft and design participants were randomly divided into three groups – namely, *expressive*, *glocal* and *prosumer* – in line with the design directions of the Rhizome Framework.

Each group was given the following exercises:

- *Is craft relevant to sustainability design?* The participants of each group were asked to address this question through concept maps.
- *Systems thinking on the impact of their direction of the Rhizome Framework on the tenets of sustainability*: The participants of each group were asked to address this question through concept maps. Each group was then asked to consider the positive and negative impacts of its direction on the production-to-consumption system from the social, ecological, cultural and economic perspectives. This exercise was designed to enable to participants to critically reflect on the systemic outcome of the directions of the Rhizome Framework.
- *What are the product possibilities for each direction?* The participants and craftspeople of each group were asked to address this question through concept maps, and present the results pictorially, using keywords where required.

All of these questions were formulated in line with Moon's (2004) methods of posing simple, open and leading questions which would stimulate thought and reflection. In order to answer the questions, the groups were asked to follow generic concept-mapping methodology (Saroyan & Amundsen, 2004).
   This included:

- *Brainstorming phase*: Participants were asked to brainstorm individually, and list the emerging facts, terms and ideas succinctly on separate adhesive notes. The relationships, relative importance or redundancy were unimportant; the focus was on creating a comprehensive list.
- *Organizing phase*: Participants were asked to collectively organize all the adhesive notes on a large sheet of paper to create logical groups and subgroups. Some concepts were plotted in multiple groupings.

- *Layout phase:* Participants were asked to collectively arrange the groupings on a sheet of paper in a manner which represented their understanding of priority and interrelationships between the concept groups. Related concept groups were placed next to each other, while more important or meta-concepts were placed above sub-concepts.
- *Linking phase:* Participants were asked to draw arrows to depict the relationships between connected items. Where relevant, the relationship was elaborated upon with a keyword or short phrase.
- *Finalizing the concept map:* Participants worked on the graphic representation of the concept map in order to make it more presentable and easily understandable.

The output of each exercise was shared with the designers and craftspeople, and through interactive sessions. The last exercise, which involved both designers and craftspeople, was designed to enable both factions to see the difference and similarities in their team-members' perceptions vis-à-vis their own, and to learn, bridge and realign their own perceptions where relevant.

Step 3 workshop findings

Relevance of the Rhizome Framework

As one participant was absent, the total number of respondents for this phase was 23. The majority of these participants found the directions developed through the Rhizome Framework relevant for craft evolution; all but one of the others were not sure, and one participant did not find them relevant (Figure 7.15).

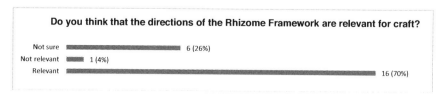

Figure 7.15 Findings from 23 respondents on the relevance of the Rhizome Framework

Product-library workshop

A majority of participants found the product-library somewhat helpful, all but one of the remaining participants found it very helpful and one participant found it barely helpful in understanding the basic level of products and skill available within the craft practice (Figure 7.16).

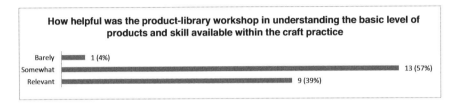

Figure 7.16 Findings from 23 respondents on the efficacy of the product-library workshop

Systems brainstorming exercise

A majority of participants found the brainstorming exercise regarding the systemic effect of their direction very helpful to see the larger picture at a strategic level, all but one of the remaining participants found it somewhat helpful and one participant found it barely helpful (Figure 7.17).

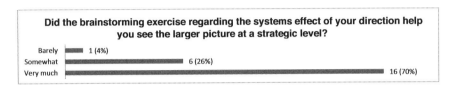

Figure 7.17 Findings from 23 respondents on the efficacy of the systems brainstorming exercise

Designers' group brainstorming exercise

A majority of participants found the designers' brainstorming exercise very helpful in seeing new product possibilities that they would not have considered on their own; all but one of the remaining participants found it somewhat helpful, and one participant found it barely helpful (Figure 7.18).

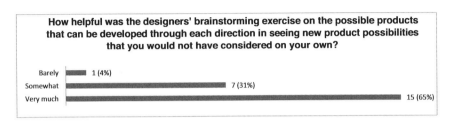

Figure 7.18 Findings from 24 respondents on the efficacy of the designers' brainstorming exercise

Craftspeople's group brainstorming exercise

Sixteen out of 23 participants found the craftspersons' brainstorming exercise helpful in seeing new product possibilities that they would not have considered on their own. However, for six persons the exercise was barely or not helpful (Figure 7.19).

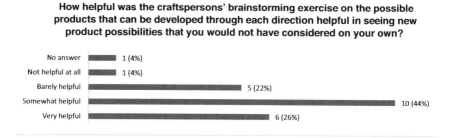

Figure 7.19 Findings from 23 respondents on the efficacy of the craftspeople's brainstorming exercise

Around half of the designers answered that the craftspersons' brainstorming exercise was much more creative than expected, and one-fourth found it much more in touch with the market than they expected (Figure 7.20).

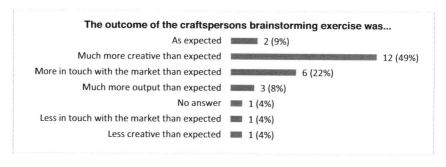

Figure 7.20 Findings from 23 respondents on the outcome of the craftspersons' brainstorming exercise; respondents could select more than one alternative

Most helpful exercise which helped in working towards one strategic goal

Twenty-one of the 23 participants answered this question. A majority of those who answered identified the brainstorming session about the systems impact of each direction exercise the most helpful in working jointly towards one strategic goal (Figure 7.21).

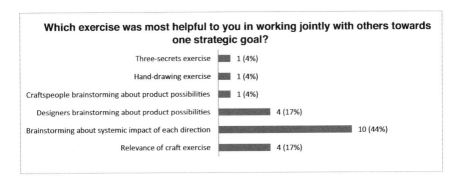

Figure 7.21 Findings from 21 respondents on the most helpful exercise when working towards a strategic goal; participants could mention more than one exercise

7.5   Step 4: articulate sustainability criteria in the design brief

Step 4 of the Rhizome Approach advocates articulating sustainability criteria in the design brief so that it can be factored into the front-end innovation phase.

Step 4 design

Most traditional design briefs are structured in a manner which requires designers to follow linear problem-solving approaches which do not go beyond a product focus. However, to actualize sustainability, designers need to go beyond product design to also look at the design of strategies, systems and services (Brass & Mazarella, 2015). Design briefs need to concretely state and include the elements that designers are expected to shape through sustainability design, including new visions and strategy for sustainability for a cross section of stakeholders (Brass & Mazarella, 2015). Design briefs aiming for sustainability need to be reframed to address a holistic vision of sustainability which includes all of its dimensions – including the ecology, economy, society and culture (Walker, 2011).

Step 4, therefore, focuses on providing designers with a clear brief vis-à-vis sustainability. The brief is supplemented with the Sustainability Checklist to clarify desired decisions and their impact on each tenet of sustainability. The checklist aims to support traditional *T-shaped designers* (Guest, 1991) with broad skill-set bases and single-domain specializations, to transition to being *O-shaped* (Brass & Mazarella, 2015) sustainability designers with systemic and panoptic orientations. Chapters 6 and 9 discuss the first and second iterations of the checklist, respectively.

Step 4 workshop actualization

Clear design brief

The workshop participants were provided with a design brief which clearly indicated expectations vis-à-vis each dimension of sustainability. The design brief was to design a commercially viable (economically sustainable) product made from mature, sustainably harvested bamboo (ecologically sustainable), using local production capacities (socially sustainable) that leverages indigenous knowledge systems (culturally sustainable).

In addition, each group – *expressive, glocal* and *prosumer* – was briefed on which direction of the Rhizome Framework their design direction would center, and what this entailed.

Sustainability checklist

In order to provide clearly stated design expectations (Wurdinger, 2005), and to supplement the design brief, the first iteration of the Sustainability Checklist (discussed in detail in Section 6.2) was shared with the participants. Each point of the checklist was discussed with the design participants, in an interactive session involving the facilitators. Each innovation team was also provided with a copy of the checklist for their reference and use during the design process.

Step 4 workshop findings

Sustainability Checklist

A majority of participants found the checklist very useful in understanding the different sustainability concerns and factors at each stage of the product life cycle (Figure 7.22).

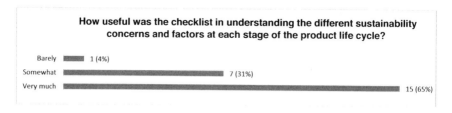

How useful was the checklist in understanding the different sustainability concerns and factors at each stage of the product life cycle?

Barely 1 (4%)
Somewhat 7 (31%)
Very much 15 (65%)

Figure 7.22 Findings from 23 respondents on efficacy of the Sustainability Checklist in helping understand different sustainability concerns and factors over product life cycle

Almost half of the participants answered that they came to know of a lot of new factors relating to sustainability as compared to what they knew of earlier through the checklist; while a little over half came to know of a few factors (Figure 7.23).

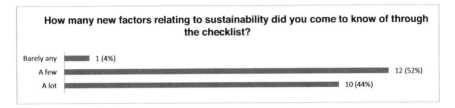

Figure 7.23 Findings from 23 respondents on efficacy of the Sustainability Checklist in helping know about new sustainability-related factors

Most of the participants could not clearly understand the checklist just by reading it. A majority of participants needed each factor explained to them before they could understand the checklist. A few needed just a few factors explained to them after they read it (Figure 7.24).

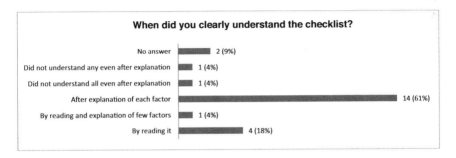

Figure 7.24 Findings from 23 respondents on the understandability of the Sustainability Checklist

A majority of the participants felt a small booklet explaining each factor of the checklist would be very helpful to understand it better, while the remaining felt it would be somewhat helpful or barely helpful (one participant) (Figure 7.25).

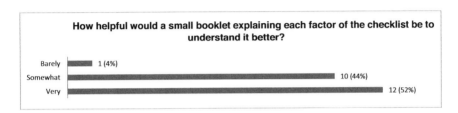

Figure 7.25 Findings from 23 respondents on whether the Sustainability Checklist should be accompanied by an explanatory booklet

A majority of participants referred somewhat to the checklist while designing their products. Because the use of it was below our expectations, the participants were also asked to mention the most important factor that would make them use the checklist (Figure 7.26).

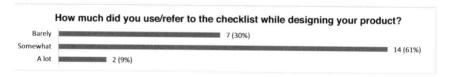

Figure 7.26 Findings from 23 respondents on how much they used the Sustainability Checklist in their design process

Seventeen of the 23 respondents replied to this question, answering that the No. 1 factor cited which would make them more likely to use the checklist more was more time to design. The second-most popular factor was the checklist being explained through an accompanying booklet to make each point clearer (Figure 7.27).

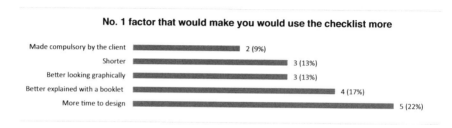

Figure 7.27 Findings from 23 respondents on No.1 factor that would make them use the Sustainability Checklist more

A majority of the participants said they would use the checklist a lot or somewhat when practicing sustainable design in the future (Figure 7.28).

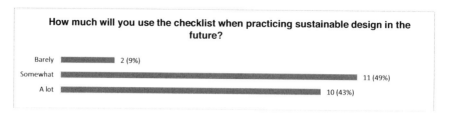

Figure 7.28 Findings from 23 respondents on how much they would use the Sustainability Checklist in the future

7.6   Step 5: collaborative innovation

Step 5 of the Rhizome Approach advocates a collaborative design process, enriched by inputs from different stakeholders of the production-to-consumption system and value chain. Collaborative innovation bridges diverse actors within the organization, shifting the mainstream pipeline design sequence to an integrative and inclusive design process (White et al., 2008).

Step 5 workshop design

Step 5 addresses the need for communication, collaborative decision-making and participatory design. It advocates doing this by encouraging, and actively facilitating, a constant linkage and interaction between the actors, facilitators and enablers of the value chain. The designer is positioned as the facilitator of this participatory design process, coordinating and collaborating with, and between, networks of stakeholders, towards future sustainability scenarios (Brass & Mazarella, 2015).

The workshop design included didactic and hands-on inputs from different stakeholders and experts, in order to funnel diverse inputs to the innovation function. The didactic inputs included presentations by several experts, each of whom offered a different perspective on the production-to-consumption system. Additionally, the facilitators provided hands-on inputs and feedback to the participants throughout the workshop.

Alongside these, inputs from the craftsperson enrich the innovation function. The craftsperson has expert inputs on design based on non-industrial materials and, in this sense, functions as a *barefoot engineer* (Barefoot College, 2016) for the designer. The designer-craftsperson equation is therefore of utmost importance, and needs to be developed and nurtured. This can be done through exercises aimed at icebreaking (to help the team members to get to know one other), team building (to encourage people to bond), and energizing (to facilitate group energy and to liven up a group) (Sixth College, n.d.).

Step 5 actualization

Icebreaking, teambuilding and energizing exercises

Three exercises aimed at icebreaking, team building and energizing were conducted towards facilitating collaborative design during the workshop. These exercises aimed to help the designer-craftsperson teams reach a comfort level where they could easily communicate and collaborate. The exercises used are described below:

- *Animal couples (AEGEE, 2014)*: This exercise was used to randomly divide the participants into designer-craftsperson teams, and also for icebreaking and energizing. The game is based on a common children's party game, and was played by creating two sets of paper chits, each containing the name of the same animal. One set was distributed to the craft participants, and the other to the design participants. Each designer had to find his partner craftsperson and vice-versa, identifying them only through animal sounds. The pair that gets together first wins the game. This game encourages playfulness, reduces inhibitions and helps in teambuilding.

- *Three secrets*: This exercise was aimed at icebreaking and teambuilding, and was developed based on the "My Favorite" exercise. The exercise involved each designer-craftsperson innovation team learning three "secrets" about their team-mate by conversing with them. These secrets could be little-known facts about their team-mate, ranging from their goal in life to their favorite food. The process facilitates discussions and confidence building. Each participant then introduced their partner to the rest of the innovation groups using the three secrets as an introduction point.
- *Hand drawing*: This exercise was aimed at teambuilding, and was adapted from the community-profiling exercises developed by the InHand Abra Foundation in the Philippines. The exercise involved each participant drawing their non-dominant hand. Each participant could be assisted by their teammate, who could help them in any manner, except in the drawing itself. The process allowed the participants to discover the skills of their partner, while encouraging and providing feedback to their partner on improving the drawing; in some cases, this involved encouraging a shy teammate complete the activity. The drawings provided insight into the traits of the artist – a detailed drawing depicted attention to detail, a drawing larger than the actual hand indicated an amplified image of oneself, and a drawing smaller than the actual hand indicated low self-esteem. The drawings were analyzed by the facilitators and the pertinent observations were shared with the group. This helped team-mates have a better insight into the psyche and working style of their partners, and themselves.

Expert presentations

Apart from the exercises described above, the workshop design included inputs from several experts from different nodes of the production-to-consumption system. The intention was that different concerns from across the value-chain were represented, and could be addressed during innovation. These didactic inputs were in the form of digital presentations, followed by informal discussions where the participants interacted with the speakers. The multiple perspectives on the same issue gave the participants food for thought. Several participants began to formulate and discuss their own constructs of concepts like sustainability, craft, space-making elements and development. In addition to the experts, the facilitators provided hands-on inputs in their area of expertise to the participants throughout the workshop.

Step 5 workshop findings

Icebreaking, teambuilding and energizing exercises

A majority of participants found the icebreaking exercises very or somewhat helpful in enabling them to work with their craftsperson as a team towards one strategic goal (Figure 7.29).

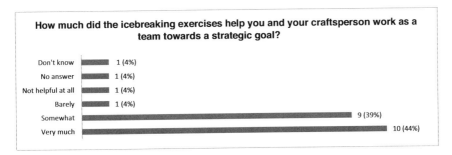

Figure 7.29 Findings from 23 respondents on efficacy of the icebreaking exercises

The least favorite exercise was the hand-drawing exercise, while "finding partner" and "three-secrets exercise" were equally preferred (Figure 7.30).

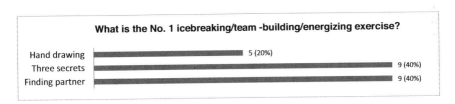

Figure 7.30 Findings from 23 respondents on the No.1 exercise

A majority of participants were somewhat surprised by the three things they found out about their craftsperson partner during the three-secrets exercise (Figure 7.31).

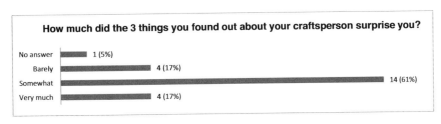

Figure 7.31 Findings from 23 respondents on whether they were surprised at the three things they found out about their craftsperson partner during the three-secrets exercise

Around half of the participants felt their craftsperson team member was somewhat similar to them as compared to what they had expected (Figure 7.32).

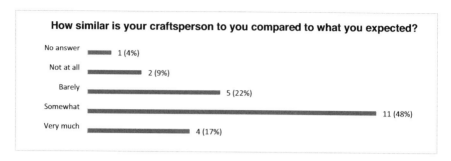

Figure 7.32 Findings from 23 respondents on how similar their craftsperson partner was to them as compared to what they had expected

Expert presentations

A majority of participants answered that the expert input sessions helped them a lot to expand their design concerns to the larger picture (Figure 7.33).

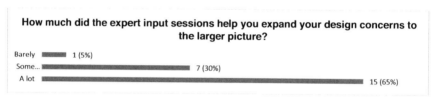

Figure 7.33 Findings from 23 respondents on the efficacy of expert input sessions

Design was the type of input most commonly selected by the respondents as the additional input which could enhance the Rhizome Approach and workshop structure. Technical, sustainability and marketing factors followed a close second. The factor rated No. 1 by a majority of participants was sustainability, followed by design (Figure 7.34).

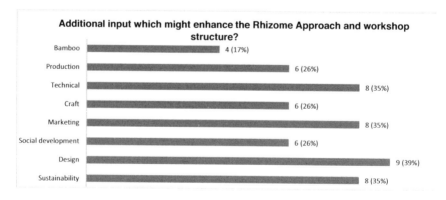

Figure 7.34 Findings from 23 respondents on additional inputs that might enhance the Rhizome Approach and workshop structure; participants could select more than one alternative

All but two of the participants answered that the final product would have been very different or somewhat different without the collaborative process created by the different inputs (Figure 7.35).

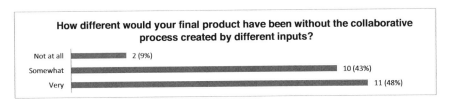

Figure 7.35 Findings from 23 respondents on how different their final product would have been without collaborative process

7.7 Step 6: measuring sustainability

Step 6 centers on increasing the designers' accountability towards sustainability, by quantifying the sustainability their designs have managed to achieve.

Step 6 workshop design

The quantification of sustainability is achieved by evaluating the design against the Sustainability Checklist provided to the participants in Step 4. The evaluators include the designer and two experts. These three sets of data allow for investigator triangulation (Denzin, 1978) as a method of cross-validation of multiple-source data to identify regularities and discrepancies between the data sets. The result yields an indicative *sustainability quotient* of the product. This sustainability quotient can be the benchmark for achieving greater sustainability in the next design iterations, and also make designers aware of the impact of their design decisions on sustainability. The evaluation quantifies this impact, making the *sustainability quotient* of the product clearer. This quantification increases the designers' accountability to make changes and create iterations that make for a more sustainable final product.

The sustainability quotient can also add value to the product via the communication and marketing strategy.

Further information on the next iteration of the scoring method is discussed in Chapter 9, which also discusses how the Sustainability Checklist was adapted and developed for UNIDO.

Step 6 workshop actualization

The products produced by the innovation teams underwent three separate evaluations. The first was a self-evaluation by the designer; the second was by a community development expert, and the third by a design expert. The evaluation was interactive, to increase transparency, and also so the evaluators were able to share detailed feedback with the designers beyond the scoring. Each evaluator scored the product relative to the criteria outlined in each parameter. A score of 1 would indicate *low* or below average, 2 would indicate *medium* or average, and 3, *high* or demonstrably better. The final score per parameter was the triangulated mean of the three grades. This final score was reflected in the ecological, social, cultural and economic sustainability that the parameter impacts. The final scoring was communicated to the design participants.

Step 6 workshop findings

Self-evaluation

Twenty-one out of the 24 participants filled in the final questionnaire. Of these, about half of the participants felt that their design could have been very much improved after the self-evaluation process; the other half felt it could have been somewhat improved (Figure 7.36).

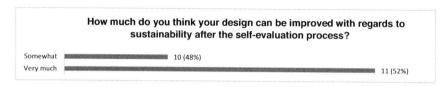

Figure 7.36 Findings from 21 respondents on whether they thought their design can be changed to better address sustainability following the self-evaluation process

A majority of participants answered that they found it somewhat difficult to evaluate themselves against the checklist (Figure 7.37).

Figure 7.37 Findings from 21 respondents on how difficult it was to evaluate themselves against the Sustainability Checklist

External evaluation

A majority of participants found the evaluation process with the two external evaluations very useful in helping them to rethink their design with regards to sustainability (Figure 7.38).

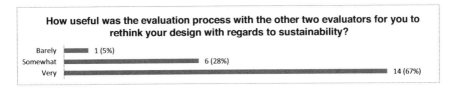

Figure 7.38 Findings from 21 respondents on the usefulness of evaluation process in rethinking design

A majority of participants ranked the inputs from the design expert as No. 1 towards making them consider changes in their product in order to make it more sustainable; this was followed by the self-evaluation, and the evaluation by the community expert (Figure 7.39).

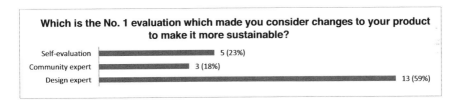

Figure 7.39 Findings from 21 respondents on the No. 1 evaluation which made them consider changes to their product to make it more sustainable

Evaluation process

Of the participants who answered this question, the majority of participants felt the No. 1 way to make evaluation using the Sustainability Checklist easier would be to make it shorter. The second-most popular No.1 factor was that questions should be completely articulated, e.g., "Is your product made from a single material?" instead of the single word, "mono-material." This was followed by the factors "clearer" and "making it digital" (Figure 7.40).

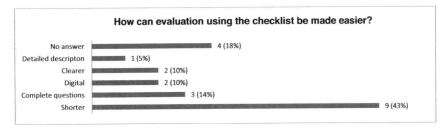

Figure 7.40 Findings from 21 respondents on how the evaluation using the checklist can be made easier

Use of the checklist in the future

A majority of participants said that they would use the checklist in the future to formulate their design briefs and also to evaluate their designs; some would use it just to formulate their design briefs (Figure 7.41).

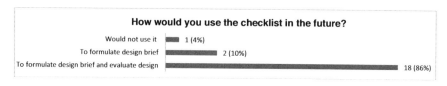

Figure 7.41 Findings from 21 respondents on how they would use the checklist in the future

7.8   Step 7: keep designers in the loop until final product actualization

Step 7 centers on keeping designers in the loop until final product actualization, thereby retaining their responsibility towards making the end product sustainable. This is done by involving the designer in all the iterations of the design, from the prototype stage right up to the final product actualization.

Step 7 workshop design

In the traditional pipeline design sequence, production, costing and marketing revisions often happen in the time-gap between when the product is conceptualized and marketed. By this time, the product-design function is essentially disbanded (White et al., 2008) and the changes in the product are often made without the consent and inputs of the innovator/innovation team. As a result, nobody has a bird's-eye view of the product and the cascading effect of the changes, including vis-à-vis sustainability. The workshop design therefore involved keeping the designers in the loop with regards to the changes made in response to the evaluation of Step 6 – and also as a result of the feedback from the experts across the production-to-consumption chain. The design team is kept in the loop along with the other design collaborators, until the final actualization of the product.

Step 7 workshop actualization

At the end of Step 6, each of the teams had designed and developed a working prototype which had been evaluated. Given the paucity of time, the development and refinement of these prototypes needed to be done after the workshop. Step 7 involved production and marketing experts examining the prototypes post-workshop, and suggesting changes to streamline production, and make the products more appealing and cost-effective. Additional changes post-workshop came from the designers themselves, as a result of the feedback they received during Step 6. Some of the changes required by the designers, production experts and marketing experts translated into radical restructuring of the product's form, construction and joinery. All these changes were examined collaboratively, and the relevant changes were incorporated in the product design, with the consent of, and in agreement with, the original design team. Thus, the design team was involved in the final product actualization even after the duration of the workshop.

Step 7 workshop findings

The process of making changes

None of the participants were comfortable with passing on the prototype to experts who would make changes to complete the prototype without informing them. A majority of participants wanted inputs from experts before deciding on the changes (Figure 7.42).

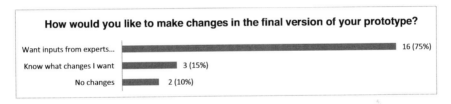

Figure 7.42 Findings from 21 respondents on whether they know what changes they want to make in their final version

7.9   Additional findings

Cross-checking relevance of the barriers which underpin the Rhizome Approach

The Rhizome Approach was developed based on seven barriers to sustainability design which we identified from our literature review. It was important that we cross-checked that these seven barriers – the premise for developing the approach – were relevant to our participants. We did this through a baseline questionnaire wherein we asked respondents to circle the factors which hindered them from designing sustainably. In some cases, more than one question was posed to cover the sub-themes each overall barrier encompassed. Figure 7.43 shows the barrier, the questions posed and the result. Figure 7.44 represents this graphically.

Barrier	Which factors hinder you from designing sustainably?	Participants who felt this factor is a barrier
Lack of knowledge about sustainability	Q1 Lack of training/education in sustainable design	19
	Q2 Lack of access to information on sustainability statistics and data	17
	Q3 Lack of green material suppliers	13
Lack of a holistic overview of the production-to-consumption system	Q1 Lack of holistic overview of the production-to-consumption chain	10
Failure to include sustainability at a strategic level in the overall approach	Q1 Lack of interest in sustainability from the project team, e.g., prototypes, producers, etc.	12
	Q2 Sustainable design means more expensive products	13
Failure to include sustainability criteria in the design brief	Q1 Lack of including sustainability criteria alongside traditional criteria as a design parameter in the design brief	15
Lack of a collaborative design process	Q1 Lack of a collaborative design process	15
Lack of tools to measure holistic sustainability against indicators	Q1 Lack of tools to measure sustainability against indicators	14
Failure to keep the design team in the loop during product actualization	Q1 Lack of control over final product because of limited involvement in the actual product realization	11

Figure 7.43 Empirical validation of the barriers that underpin the Rhizome Approach

Mapping changes in concepts and learnings from pre- to post-workshop

As discussed earlier, the workshop was monitored and documented through videos, photographs and written accounts. The first of the four questionnaires administered served as a baseline of the participants' knowledge and understanding of

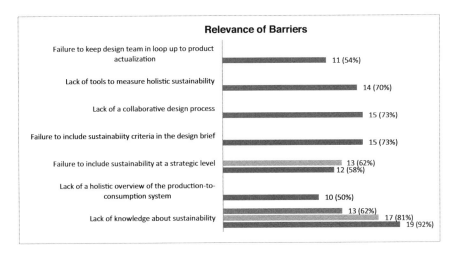

Figure 7.44 Findings from 21 respondents on validating the barriers that underpin the Rhizome Approach; respondents could select more than one option

concepts such as sustainability and craft. The last questionnaire repeated some of the key questions of the first questionnaire, to map the change in these concepts.

Change in knowledge about sustainability

Some of the participants were not familiar with sustainability-related concepts before the workshop. After the workshop, all the participants were familiar with sustainability-related concepts. The number of participants who were somewhat familiar increased significantly. Interestingly, several of the participants who answered that they were very familiar with sustainability-related concepts pre-workshop, answered that they were somewhat familiar post-workshop. This suggests a decline in knowledge on sustainability concepts post-workshop and merits further research. One possibility is that concepts which they were exposed to during the workshop helped them get a realistic picture of their knowledge level (Figure 7.45).

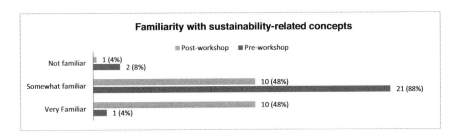

Figure 7.45 Findings from 24 respondents pre-workshop and 21 respondents post-workshop on familiarity with sustainability-related concepts

Change in knowledge about sustainable design

Only a few participants answered that they were very familiar with concepts relating to sustainable design before the workshop. Following the workshop, a majority of participants answered that they were very familiar with concepts relating to sustainable design. This indicates that the workshop helped increase the overall familiarity with concepts relating to sustainable design (Figure 7.46).

Figure 7.46 Findings from 24 respondents pre-workshop and 21 respondents post-workshop on change in their knowledge about sustainable design

Change in knowledge on sustainability models

More than half of the respondents were unfamiliar with sustainability models before the workshop. The remaning were familiar with only one model – Ecodesign. Following the workshop, the knowledge of models had expanded to include the Triple Bottom Line, Four Pillars and Five Capitals models (Figure 7.47).

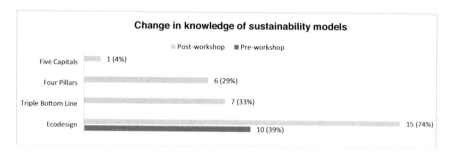

Figure 7.47 Findings from 24 respondents pre-workshop and 21 respondents post-workshop on change in their knowledge about sustainability models; respondents could select more than one alternative

Change in perception of aspects to be considered while designing sustainably

In the baseline questionnaire, the participants felt that ecological, social, cultural, ethical and political aspects should be considered while designing sustainably. Following the workshop, the number of participants who felt these tenets should be considered increased. Participants also felt that the ethical and political tenets which are not yet part of accepted sustainability models, but have been discussed for quite some time now, should be considered (Figure 7.48).

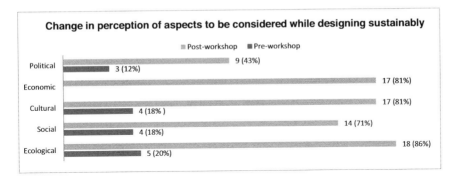

Figure 7.48 Findings from 26 respondents pre-workshop and 21 respondents post-workshop on change in their perception of aspects which need to be considered while designing sustainably before and after the workshop; respondents could select multiple alternatives

7.10   Summary and conclusions

This chapter presented the workshop design to test whether the Rhizome Approach and its constituents helped designers to address sustainability in a more holistic manner through their designs. This was actualized through a workshop in India which explored the efficacy of each step, and the framework as a whole.

While each of the mechanisms and steps overall received a positive response, the Sustainability Checklist received a high level of appreciation vis-à-vis its efficacy as both a brief and as an evaluation tool. A majority of participants also indicated they would use it in the future in their sustainable-design practices. Also relevant were the numerous inputs from the participants on the factors which would make them more likely to use the checklist. Apart from time and a better and clearer checklist itself, the participants cited pressure from clients, the government and peers – which relate to our third question: what mechanisms would support and encourage the use and operationalization of any sustainability design approach that might be developed in response to our second question?

Before we went on to this, we decided to check how relevant our findings were beyond the workshop. The next chapter describes how we solicited this feedback in two different settings.

8 Feedback on the Rhizome Approach

8.1 Towards a new theory: the Rhizome Approach

The previous chapter reported on a workshop conducted in India in 2010 to test the Rhizome Approach and its constituents, including the Rhizome Framework and Sustainability Checklist. The workshop findings indicated that the Rhizome Approach was effective in helping the participating designers to address sustainability in a more holistic manner in the case of the bamboo craft of the Kotwalia community in India. Our next step was to validate these findings, and, if the process revealed scope for improvement, to create a final iteration of the existing version.

It was important to ascertain that the findings from the workshop participants – which were a real-context test group – were applicable and transferable to our wider target problem-class (designers working with MSMEs in developing countries, working with renewable materials). It was also important to check that our findings were valid across treatments, contexts and time (Cook & Campbell, 1979). Every context is unique, and therefore we do not intend the Rhizome Approach to be a grand narrative which provides turnkey solutions across the problem-class (Drechsler, 2015). Our intention is that the Rhizome Approach is adapted to best suit each setting it is used in. Therefore, we focused on checking its relevance in two settings that fall within the wider scope of our problem-class.

- *Vietnam*: Our first setting was a group of Vietnamese sustainable product innovation trainers. We administered two questionnaires to this group in 2011, to check whether the overall response to the Rhizome Approach – and especially the positive response to the Sustainability Checklist and feedback on improving it – were similar in India and Vietnam. This phase and the findings from the questionnaire are discussed in Section 8.2.
- *World*: Our second phase to check the relevance of the Rhizome Approach was conducted by administering a questionnaire by e-mail to 15 designers located across Africa, Australia, Europe, Latin America, Turkey and Southeast Asia in 2016. The questionnaire explored whether the respondents felt there could be complementary, supplementary or alternative steps to the Rhizome Approach to make it more effective and to improve it in general. This phase and the findings thereof are discussed in Section 8.3.

8.2   Feedback from Vietnam

The first phase to check the potential applicability of the Rhizome Approach in a context which was different from our workshop in India was conducted in Vietnam. Vietnam was selected because its developing-country MSME setting was proximally similar (Campbell, 1986) to that of India. It was impossible to exactly replicate the Indian workshop in Vietnam; in any case, attempting such a recreation would have defeated our intention to find out whether the Rhizome Approach was well received in a proximally similar setting. We therefore decided to cross-check what a group of 21 Vietnamese sustainable-innovation trainers thought of the Rhizome Approach. We were especially interested in their views on the Sustainability Checklist, which had received positive feedback and interest in the Indian workshop.

We administered two questionnaires to the trainers at the Sustainable Product Innovation (SPIN) Project's Training of Trainers (ToT) Workshop 2 in Ho Chi Minh City, in May 2011. We selected this group because SPIN's objective – to increase the competitiveness of MSMEs in Vietnam, Laos and Cambodia by developing and producing more sustainable and innovation-centric products for domestic and European markets – resonated with the overall scope of our inquiry. In addition, the trainers were linked to SPIN and had therefore already received inputs in the area of sustainable product innovation in the MSME context from the project. Their potential inputs would therefore be backed by real experience in the area of innovation in the developing world, and also by training on sustainable innovation (Drost, 2011).

The second questionnaire was administered following a digital presentation on the Rhizome Framework and Rhizome Approach, including the Sustainability Checklist. The first questionnaire therefore set a baseline to map concept changes before and after the presentation. With a view to increasing objectivity we were not involved in either making the presentation or administering the questionnaire. The difference in treatment (another facilitator taking inputs before and after presentation rather than during an ongoing hands-on workshop co-facilitated by us), context (asking a group of Vietnamese trainers with expertise in sustainable-design innovation for MSMEs rather than Indian designers) and time (conducting a survey a year after the original results) strengthened our inquiry into transferability to a proximally similar setting within the problem-class.

The key findings of this phase are shared in the following sub-sections.

Relevance of the barriers which underpin the Rhizome Approach

The relevance of the seven barriers which underpin the Rhizome Approach was ascertained by asking the participants whether these barriers hindered them from designing sustainably. Just as in the previous chapter, when required, more than one question was posed to cover the sub-themes each barrier encompassed. This set of questions was identical to the ones posed in the workshop in India. Figure 8.1 shows the barrier, the questions posed and the findings; Figure 8.2

Barrier	Which factors hinder you from designing sustainably?	Participants who feel this factor is a barrier
1. Lack of knowledge about sustainability	Q1 Lack of training/education in sustainable design	17
	Q2 Lack of access to information on sustainability statistics and data	16
	Q3 Lack of green material suppliers	17
2. Lack of a holistic overview of the production-to-consumption system	Q1 Lack of holistic overview of the production-to-consumption chain	11
3. Failure to include sustainability at a strategic level in the overall approach	Q1 Lack of interest in sustainability from the project team, e.g., prototypes, producers, etc.	17
	Q2 Sustainable design means more expensive products	13
4. Failure to include sustainability criteria in the design brief	Q1 Lack of including sustainability criteria alongside traditional criteria as a design parameter in the design brief	13
5. Lack of a collaborative design process	Q1 Lack of collaborative design process	16
6. Lack of tools to measure holistic sustainability against indicators	Q1 Lack of tools to measure sustainability against indicators	14
7. Failure to keep the design team in the loop during product actualization	Q1 Lack of control over final product because on limited involvement in the actual product realization	15

Figure 8.1 Empirical validation of the barriers that underpin the Rhizome Approach with 21 Vietnamese participants

represents this graphically comparing the findings from India and Vietnam. The findings indicate that the barriers which underpin the Rhizome Approach are indeed relevant to the Vietnamese MSME context.

Relevance of Rhizome Framework (Figure 8.3)

A whopping 81% of Vietnamese respondents found the directions outlined by the Rhizome Framework relevant to their context, which indicates that the framework is potentially applicable to craft scenarios in developing countries such as India and Vietnam.

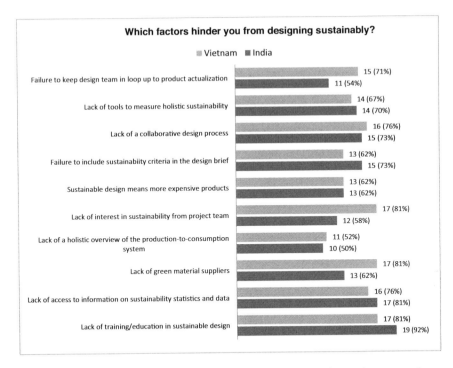

Figure 8.2 Comparison between findings from 21 Vietnamese and 21 Indian respondents on the relevance of the barriers that underpin the Rhizome Approach; respondents could choose more than one alternative

Figure 8.3 Findings from 21 Vietnamese sustainable-innovation trainers on the relevance of the Rhizome Framework

Comparison of findings on the Sustainability Checklist between India and Vietnam

Usefulness of the Sustainability Checklist in understanding sustainability concerns (Figure 8.4)

The findings from India and Vietnam on the usefulness of the Sustainability Checklist in understanding sustainability concerns were very similar. A majority of the respondents in both countries found it very useful.

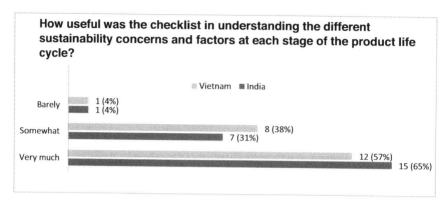

Figure 8.4 Comparison between findings of 21 Vietnamese and 23 Indian respondents on usefulness of the Sustainability Checklist in understanding sustainability concerns

New sustainability-related factors learned through the Sustainability Checklist (Figure 8.5)

More Indian than Vietnamese respondents seem to have learned new sustainability-related factors through the Sustainability Checklist. This may be because the Indian respondents were design students who had little exposure to sustainability and so they had more learning, while the Vietnamese respondents had received several inputs in sustainability already.

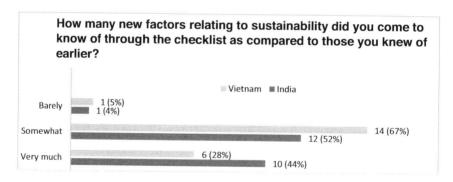

Figure 8.5 Comparison between findings of 21 Vietnamese and 23 Indian respondents on the usefulness of the Sustainability Checklist in creating awareness on different sustainability factors

Understandability of the Sustainability Checklist (Figure 8.6)

Compared to their Indian counterparts, more Vietnamese respondents understood the Sustainability Checklist just by reading it. This may be because the

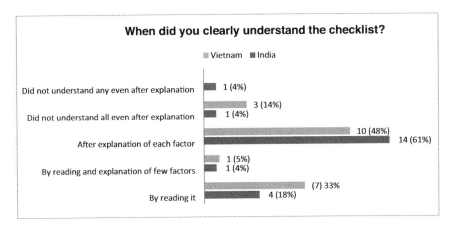

Figure 8.6 Comparison between findings of 21 Vietnamese and 23 Indian respondents on the understandability of the Sustainability Checklist

Indian respondents were design students who had little exposure to sustainability, while the Vietnamese respondents had received several inputs in sustainability already. This possibility is bolstered by the fact that more Indian respondents than Vietnamese respondents could understand the checklist after each factor was explained.

Booklet to explain factors of the Sustainability Checklist (Figure 8.7)

The findings on the usefulness of a booklet to explain the Sustainability Checklist's factors were very similar and positive in both sets of respondents.

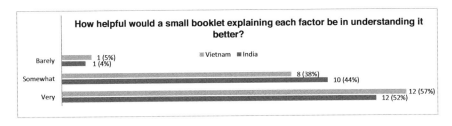

Figure 8.7 Comparison between findings of 21 Vietnamese and 23 Indian respondents on the usefulness of a booklet to understand the factors of the Sustainability Checklist

Use of the Sustainability Checklist in future practice (Figure 8.8)

A little over half of the Vietnamese respondents said they would use the checklist a lot, while only a few said they would not.

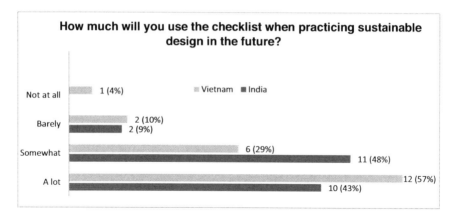

Figure 8.8 Comparison between findings of 21 Vietnamese and 23 Indian respondents on the use of the Sustainability Checklist in future practice

Factors which can increase the use of the Sustainability Checklist (Figure 8.9)

The findings were similar in both India and Vietnam with regards to factors which would increase the use of the Sustainability Checklist. The second-most popular factor in India – "better explained with a booklet" – was the most popular factor in Vietnam.

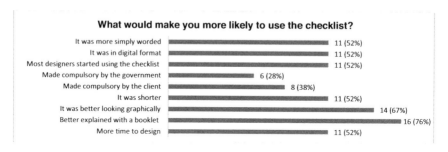

Figure 8.9 Findings from 21 Vietnamese respondents on factors that would make them more likely to use the Sustainability Checklist

Mapping changes in concepts and learnings from pre- to post-presentation

We wanted to check whether sharing the Rhizome Approach through a concise presentation was effective in impacting knowledge and concept changes – especially as compared to the workshop whose duration was 15 days, and which included experiential and hands-on modules. In order to do this, two questionnaires were administered. The first established a baseline of the participants' knowledge and understanding of sustainability-related concepts before the presentation and exposure to the Rhizome Approach, and the second repeated some of the key questions to map the change in these concepts.

Change in knowledge about sustainability (Figure 8.10)

None of the participants remained *unfamiliar* or *barely familiar* about sustainability following the presentation. There was a 10% increase in respondents who were *very familiar* with concepts relating to sustainability following the presentation. This indicates that the Rhizome Approach, even when communicated through a distilled presentation, can still help increase the overall familiarity with concepts relating to sustainability.

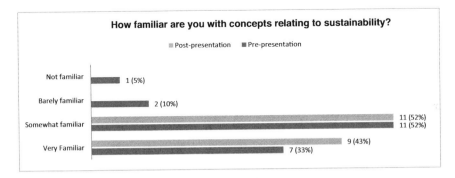

Figure 8.10 Change in knowledge about sustainability among 21 Vietnamese sustainable-innovation trainers, pre-and post-presentation

Change in knowledge about sustainable design (Figure 8.11)

There was a 13% drop in the participants who felt they were very familiar with concepts relating to sustainable design following the presentation. This corresponded with a 19% increase in participants who felt they were barely familiar with concepts relating to sustainable design following the presentation. These findings are surprising and, on the face of it, seem to indicate a knowledge loss following the presentation. One possible explanation is that the inputs from the

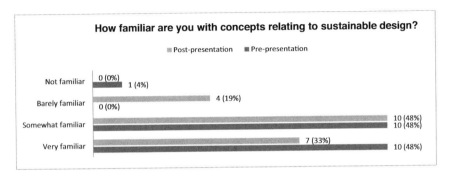

Figure 8.11 Change in knowledge about sustainable design among 21 Vietnamese sustainable-innovation trainers pre-and post-presentation

presentation helped participants evaluate the extent of their knowledge gap with regards to concepts relating to sustainable design.

Change in knowledge on sustainability models (Figure 8.12)

Following the presentation, the knowledge of models had expanded: 9% more respondents knew about Ecodesign, and 5% knew more about the Triple Bottom Line than before the presentation. The percentage of respondents who knew about the Four Pillars and Five Capitals models remained constant.

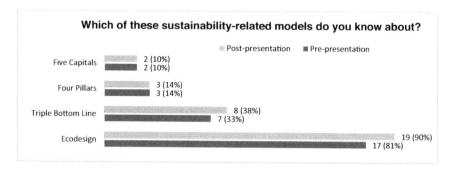

Figure 8.12 Change in knowledge about sustainability models among 21 Vietnamese sustainable-innovation trainers, pre-and post-presentation; respondents could choose multiple options

Change in perception of aspects to be considered while designing sustainably (Figure 8.13)

Following the presentation, the percentage of participants who felt ecological, cultural, economic and political aspects should be considered while designing

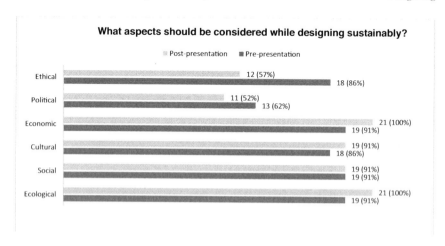

Figure 8.13 Change in perception of aspects to be considered while designing for sustainability among 21 Vietnamese sustainable-innovation trainers, pre-and post-presentation

sustainably increased. The perception on the social factors remained constant, whereas the perception that ethical and economic factors are important to sustainable design, decreased. This seems to indicate the respondents' acceptance of the Four Pillars model.

Change in perception of the aim of sustainable design (Figure 8.14)

Before the presentation, most of the participants cited environment-related factors – preserving the environment and reducing pollution – as aims of sustainable design. The economic factor, or increasing business and sales, was the factor that was cited by the second largest majority. Social factors were cited above cultural factors. Following the presentation, the percentage of respondents who cited each factor dropped, except in the case of reducing pollution, which remained constant. These findings are contradictory to what was expected, and merit future research.

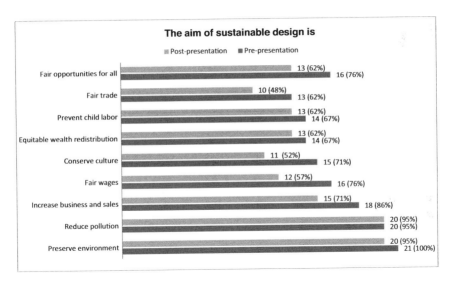

Figure 8.14 Change in perception of the aim of sustainable design among 21 Vietnamese sustainable-innovation trainers, pre-and post-presentation

8.3   Transferability: global

The second exercise to check the transferability of the findings from the workshop in India was conducted by administering a questionnaire to a random cross-section of 15 designers located in different regions around the world – four from Southeast Asia, four from Africa, one from Turkey, one from Australia, three from Europe, and two from Latin America. In order to provide the respondents with the same background information on the Rhizome Approach, we created a 10-minute YouTube video (Reubens, 2016b) explaining the approach. Each of the respondents was sent a link to this video along with the questionnaire, which explored what the respondents thought about the steps of the approach, and whether they felt there could be complementary, supplementary or alternative steps to the Rhizome Approach to make it more effective. The questionnaire was administered in 2016 to check the transferability of the Rhizome Approach. The difference in treatment (taking inputs without a workshop or a presentation, but after a YouTube video), and context (asking a group of designers located around the world rather than Indian or Vietnamese designers) strengthened our inquiry into transferability to a proximally similar setting within the problem-class. The findings of this phase are shared below:

Potential of Rhizome Approach vis-à-vis problem context (Figure 8.15)

Four-fifths of the respondents felt that following the seven steps of the Rhizome Approach would help designers to address sustainability in a holistic manner while working with craft-based MSMEs in the developing world.

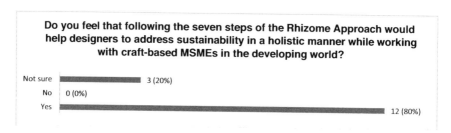

Figure 8.15 Findings on the potential of the Rhizome Approach from 15 designers across the world

Grading of importance of steps of Rhizome Approach (Figure 8.16)

We asked the designers to rate the importance of the steps of the Rhizome Approach vis-à-vis their potential to help designers to address sustainability in a holistic manner, while working with craft-based MSMEs in the developing world. As Figure 8.16 reveals, Step 4 got the highest rank (seven designers), followed by step 3 (four designers). Steps 2, 4, 5 and 7 were rated as the most important step by one designer each.

Additional steps that can make the Rhizome Approach more effective (Figure 8.17)

The majority of respondents were not sure whether there could be additional steps which could make the Rhizome Approach more effective.

Rated	Step 1	Step 2	Step 2	Step 4	Step 5	Step 6	Step 7
#1	7	1	1	5		1	1
#2	1	2	3	3	2	4	1
#3	4	1	6	2	1	2	1
#4	1	1	2	2	3	2	2
#5	1	5	1	2	3	1	
#6	0	3	1		5	3	3
#7	1	2	1	1	1	2	7

Figure 8.16 Hierarchical ranking of the steps of the Rhizome Approach by 15 designers located across the world

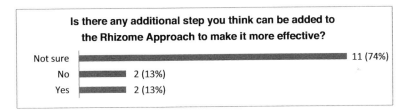

Figure 8.17 Findings on whether additional steps can increase Rhizome Approach's efficacy from 15 designers located across the world

Respondents had the following comments with regards to these topics:

Build upon existing indigenous knowledge

It seems what you are proposing is not building on the indigenous knowledge people have. That should be the starting point to find out about the indigenous knowledge systems craftspeople have and then build the seven steps onto their IKS [Indigenous knowledge systems]. This will make the craft people accept your proposal because it will be an extension of what they already know.

Outline involvement of each member of design team and discursive steps

I think the additional step would be to identify the involvement of each member of the design team throughout the process especially in on their roles in regards of sustainability. Also maybe to view the steps in the discursive nature (can be conducted independently).

Step 1: didactic knowledge through knowledge kit to provide information and knowledge on the core concepts of sustainability

Should Step 1 be part of the Rhizome Approach?

When asked, "Do you feel that Step 1 should be part of an approach towards designers addressing sustainability in a holistic manner through their designs?" all of the 15 respondents answered yes. Specific comments included:

> It should also be addressed to non-designers. Sustainability and the education around it should be easily accessible to not just one group of creative practitioners.
> Yes, but not the first step. Knowledge is something that people will gather once they are triggered.

Is didactic learning through digital presentations and background reading material about sustainability a good way to implement Step 1?

Most of the respondents felt providing designers answered that didactic learning digitally and through background reading material about sustainability was a good way to implement Step 1 (Figure 8.18).

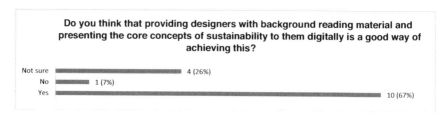

Do you think that providing designers with background reading material and presenting the core concepts of sustainability to them digitally is a good way of achieving this?

Not sure ▬▬▬▬▬▬▬▬ 4 (26%)
No ▬▬▬ 1 (7%)
Yes ▬▬▬▬▬▬▬▬▬▬▬▬▬▬▬▬▬▬ 10 (67%)

Figure 8.18 Findings on the implementation of Step 1 from 15 designers located across the world

Additional points that emerged from the comments included:

Adaptability

It depends on localities in regard to reading cultures and effective usage of the program.

Easy-to-use, engaging format

Most designers are visual learners (my assumption), and they might feel less motivated to read text-heavy information.

I would recommend online courses/e-learning or videos.

PPT (digital presentations using Microsoft PowerPoint) is ok, but human contact and interaction will always trigger people a lot more. A PPT is more for background research. Also, a website where these things are easily findable, locatable is a lot easier. Also, because then it is readily available and a search function easily applied.

Add-on knowledge

Yes, as an introductory phase, but they also need to expand this knowledge along the way (need support in this expansion).

Better ways to actualize Step 1

Four-fifths of the respondents felt there were better ways to realize Step 1 than what the Rhizome Approach proposed (Figure 8.19).

Points that emerged from their comments included:

Nonacademic, visual-rich format

Designers can connect and communicate ideas, philosophies and concepts to a large group of industry practitioners. They speak the language of engineers,

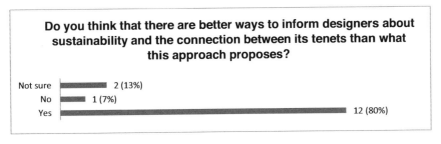

Figure 8.19 Findings on better ways to actualize Step 1 from 15 designers located in different parts of the world

marketers, manufacturers, etc. If the information they receive is very academic, then they will lack the ability to easily digest information specifically developed for the design language.

Visuals are key.

I think a PPT is important, but designers are usually not always very intellectual, they are more practical and like to interact in other ways. So there could be more of a design-thinking approach where you use scenarios and make them learn through those scenarios with design thinking principles. Also other great forms of exploring sustainability is through videos, documentaries, animations, and infographics.

Digital tools

Website/web platform, etc.; sustainability tool kit on CD/DVD.

Providing online tools where you can find the methodology and how to apply it. It could be similar to Invision, but for sustainable design.

Provide tools to introduce different aspects of sustainability for designers to adapt in their project. For example, one project might focus on sustainable material and the other on energy efficiency. Thus the idea and practice of sustainability can be adopted as part of their working culture slowly over time.

Hands-on learning

Approach this through the concept of learning-by-doing. Craft people (sic) are hands-on people and demonstrations using live projects would be more beneficial to them.

Learning by doing training.

In my experience, designers are more "actors" than "readers/listeners." Sustainability should be a mandatory course and design students have to really experience what sustainable design means, what the benefits are, etc. I would not only inform them about what sustainability is, but also let them execute a design project and compare the outcomes per team to indicate differences and why they emerge.

Collaborative learning

Seminars, collaborative meetings with other companies, role-model companies or designers/employees. They can inspire others.

Case studies

Showing videos; demonstrating real-life cases with scenarios.

Show them the concrete outcome of some case studies to inform them how others have contributed to sustainability through design and succeeded. It would be the motivation and inspire designers somehow. (Maybe you already include this in the PPT presentations by experts; I just emphasize it because I think this is important).

Step 2: experiential learning through exposure visits to different nodes of the production-to-consumption system

Should Step 2 be part of the Rhizome Approach?

When asked, "Do you feel that Step 2 should be part of an approach towards designers addressing sustainability in a holistic manner through their designs?" all 15 of the respondents answered yes.

Are exposure visits to different nodes of the production-to-consumption system and value chain a good way to implement Step 2?

Most of the respondents felt exposure visits were a good way to realize Step 2 (Figure 8.20). One additional comment was:

> Exposure visits are important but there should be more things to achieve this step.

Better ways to actualize Step 2

Four of the 15 respondents felt there were better ways to realize Step 2 than what the approach proposed (Figure 8.21).

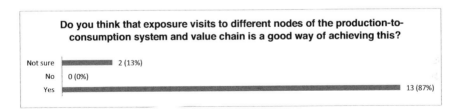

Figure 8.20 Findings on the implementation of Step 2 from 15 designers located in different parts of the world

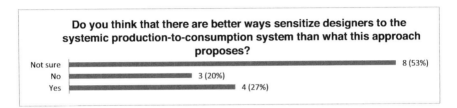

Figure 8.21 Findings on better ways to actualize Step 2 from 15 designers located in different parts of the world

Their comments included:

Seminars/workshops/design clinics

Adopting the design clinic scheme/approach. Seminars/workshops, needs assistants, surveys will help a lot.

Case studies of past experiences; practical workshops.

Background information

In my experience, designers often lack time to do everything they want to. I am not sure if they will make time to visit producers. So, I would provide information about producers as well and advise experiential learning, as I do think that is a better way to learn.

But I think a lot of the lack of knowledge and holistic view is due to design education. So there could a lot be done in education.

To be exposed to value chains from other sectors, especially those who already adopt some sustainability practices within their industry, e.g., the food sector.

Step 3: internalization of sustainablity at a strategic level through discussions and experiential learning

Should Step 3 be part of the Rhizome Approach?

When asked, "Do you thinkthat Step 3 should be part of an approach towards designers addressing sustainability in a holistic manner through their designs?" most of the respondents answered yes (Figure 8.22).

Is internalization through sharing a common framework and concept mapping to understand its relevance a good way to implement Step 3?

Figure 8.23 presents the findings on whether the 15 respondents found the means we applied to implement Step 3 of the Rhizome Approach competent.

One comment was:

I think it is very relevant to have everyone on the same page and work together towards a shared goal.

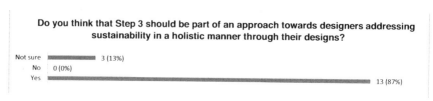

Do you think that Step 3 should be part of an approach towards designers addressing sustainability in a holistic manner through their designs?

Not sure — 3 (13%)
No — 0 (0%)
Yes — 13 (87%)

Figure 8.22 Findings on whether Step 3 should be part of the Rhizome Approach from 15 designers located in different parts of the world

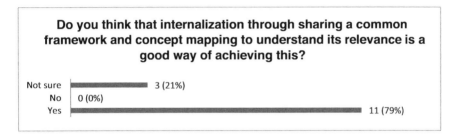

Figure 8.23 Findings on the implementation of Step 3 from 15 designers located in different parts of the world

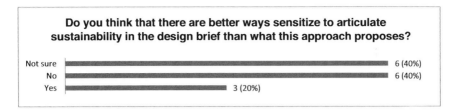

Figure 8.24 Findings on better ways to actualize Step 3 from 15 designers located in different parts of the world

Better ways to actualize Step 3

Around half the respondents were not sure whether there were better ways to realize Step 3 than what the Rhizome Approach proposed (Figure 8.24).

Their comments included:

Ownership

Maybe again add creative techniques. In that way, people feel more ownership of the goal they together created. If it is forced upon you, you are less likely to accept it.

Adaptable and still measureable framework

I definitely agree that there should be a common framework, I did an LCA diploma and we use to talk about how could we be able (sic) to measure and compare one product with the other in terms of sustainable impact if you have evaluated them in different ways? Following the same methodology/framework would really help, but it has to be a methodology that can be tropicalized to the area where it is going to be used; i.e., the economical state of Mexico is not the same to the one of Tanzania, so how do you measure value and price, and how do you measure then what fair trade is?

Enterprise preparedness

I think it is important for companies to be prepared internally, before adopting sustainability practices at a strategic level. Often sustainability will be sacrificed against economic gain (sic) therefore adaptation needs to take this reality into account.

Step 4: clear brief supplemented by the Sustainability Checklist to clarify desired design directions and their impact on each tenet of sustainability

Should Step 4 be part of the Rhizome Approach?

When asked, "Do you feel that Step 4 should be part of an approach towards designers addressing sustainability in a holistic manner through their designs?" all of the 15 respondents answered yes.

Is a clear brief supplemented by the Sustainability Checklist to clarify design directions and their impact on each tenet of sustainability a good way to actualize Step 4?

When asked, "Do you think that a clear brief supplemented by the Sustainability Checklist to clarify desired design directions and their impact on each tenet of sustainability is a good wayof achieving this?" all of the 15 respondents answered yes.

Better ways to actualize Step 4

A few of the respondents felt there were better ways to realize Step 4 than what our approach proposed (Figure 8.25).
    A comment was:

This is a very practical tool which is needed with all the fuzzy other steps.

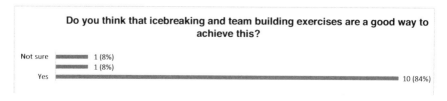

Figure 8.25 Findings on better ways to actualize Step 4 from 15 designers located in different parts of the world

Points emerging from their other comments were:

Dovetail the checklist with other tools

Visit the Life's Principle checklist found in Biomimcry. The checklist can assist the development of the brief in order to ensure a more sustainable outcome.

Ensure that the checklist does not mean complacency

The checklist should not become *just a checklist* which designers use to demonstrate they did the best they could. They should really strive to be *better than the checklist*, be creative in their solutions and therefore also in their requirements. So, maybe attach an exercise to the checklist which makes designers think further, specifically for their project.

Our vision is limited sometimes and somehow. So the design brief that we define at the beginning is not always clear and in the right direction. We need to think about how to put all forces of different nodes of the production-to-consumption system and synthesis them in the design. We have to identify the right questions to find out the problem that we have then we attempt to rephrase the problem to find out the new point of view to solve the problem.

Step 5: constant linkage and interaction with stakeholders of the production-to-consumption system to facilitate collaborative design

Should Step 5 be part of the Rhizome Approach?

When asked, "Do you feel that Step 5 should be part of an approach towards designers addressing sustainability in a holistic manner through their designs?" all of the 15 respondents answered yes.

Are icebreaking and teambuilding exercises a good way to implement step 5?

Figure 8.26 presents the findings on whether the 15 respondents found the means we applied to implement Step 5 of the Rhizome Approach competent.

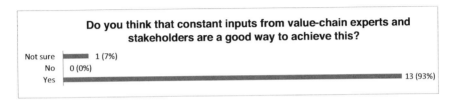

Figure 8.26 Findings on the implementation of Step 5 from 15 designers located in different parts of the world

In addition, their comments reinforced collaborative innovation and were as under:

> Yes, I do believe building shared experiences would enhance the collaboration process in design.
>
> I think it might be good to meet everyone so it is easier to approach everyone, and keep everyone in the loop, but the exercises must not consume too much time.
>
> I think the collaborative-design approach needs to also take into account project objectives and the method that facilitated the process of working together.

Are constant inputs from value-chain experts and stakeholders
a good way to implement Step 5?

Figure 8.27 reflects the findings from 15 respondents.

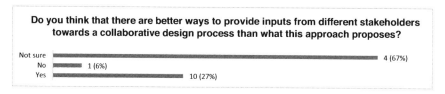

Figure 8.27 Findings on the implementation of Step 5 from 15 designers located in different parts of the world

In addition, one comment was:

> Working across domains is difficult and inputs from one domain might be perceived differently by the others. Therefore, constant inputs without clear objectives might create confusion and stress across stakeholders involved.

Better ways to actualize Step 5

Some of respondents felt there were better ways to realize Step 5 than what the Rhizome Approach proposed (Figure 8.28).

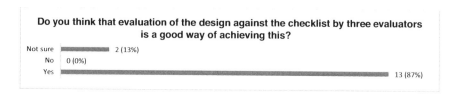

Figure 8.28 Findings on better ways to implement Step 5 from 15 designers located across the world

Their comments included:

Collaborations to empower craftspeople

Clustering craftspeople who are making similar objects.

Experiential learning

By learning from them, by letting them show you what they do and why they do it. Or even do it yourself to experience how it is.

Including market feedback

Such as including front-runner customers. Highly demanding customers, they can boost a company/product to a next level.

Focused inputs

Facilitates the process by having clear objectives why the inputs are required at a certain stage of design process.

Look at existing frameworks and mechanisms

Creating theory of change documents, value-chain track and other tools that add to the teambuilding and ice breaking. Use similar approaches to the tool kit of Human Centered Design.

Design thinking principles, and the 7 Hats principles are also great strategies that can be used together with the icebreaking and teambuilding (exercises). I think brainstorming together at the beginning of a project and then feedbacking each other throughout the process is very crucial.

Step 6: evaluation of design against the Sustainability Checklist by three evaluators

Should Step 6 be part of the Rhizome Approach?

When asked, "Do you feel that Step 6 should be part of an approach towards designers addressing sustainability in a holistic manner through their designs?" 100% of the respondents answered yes.

Is evaluation of the design against the checklist by three evaluators a good way to implement Step 6?

Figure 8.29 presents the findings on whether the 15 respondents found the means we applied to implement Step 6 of the Rhizome Approach competent.

Their comments included:

Yes, for being able to compare projects with each other it is good to have a common measurement standard. However, I think this checklist should be continuously updated and improved upon, based on new insights and I think that designers should be able to add to it.

Yes, especially when external experts evaluate too.

Better ways to actualize Step 6

A little over a quarter of the respondents felt there were better ways to realize Step 6 than what the Rhizome Approach proposed (Figure 8.30).

Their comments included:

Output but also outcome

Maybe the measurement should also be done a year after implementation to check if the design has the expected outcome or not.

Look at other frameworks

Follow up on the LeNSes program that runs through the Politecnic di Milano. It has a developed set of tools and models to assist designers to measure the level of sustainability that they wish to achieve.

Also look at other frameworks.

Carrot instead of stick

Incentives from managers, not necessarily monetary but in the form of other appraisals could also work.

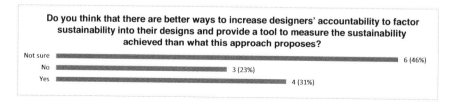

Figure 8.29 Findings on the implementation of Step 6 from 15 designers located across the world

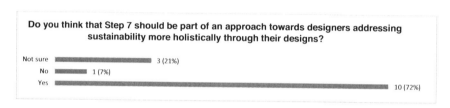

Figure 8.30 Findings on better ways to implement Step 6 from 15 designers located across the world

Link this to Step 1

Maybe this step can be used to support Step 1 (as part of the introductory kit); thus the information and content can be understood and adopted at the earliest stage.

Step 7: involving design team in all iterations of the design up to final product actualization

Should Step 7 be part of the Rhizome Approach?

When asked, "Do you feel that Step 7 should be part of an approach towards designers addressing sustainability in a holistic manner through their designs?" a majority answered yes (Figure 8.31). This was the only step which the participants did not unanimously agree on being part of the Rhizome Approach.

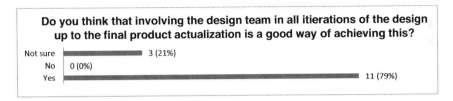

Figure 8.31 Findings on whether Step 7 should be part of the Rhizome Approach from 15 designers located across the world

Additional comments included:

I see the relevance by your example of the glue. Otherwise I would have doubted its relevance, as in my experience designers are always involved until the end. [The glue referred to here is a practical example cited in the YouTube video to better explain how design decisions can evolve without the designer being onboard.]

Is involving the design team in all iterations of the design up to the final product actualization a good way to implement Step 7?

Figure 8.32 presents the findings on whether the 15 respondents found the means we applied to implement Step 7 of the Rhizome Approach competent.
   A single comment was:

At least one designer, yes.

Better ways to actualize Step 7

Three respondents felt there were better ways to realize Step 7 than what our approach proposed (Figure 8.33).

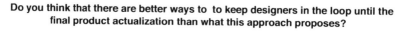

Do you think that there are better ways to to keep designers in the loop until the final product actualization than what this approach proposes?

Figure 8.32 Findings on the implementation of Step 7 from 15 designers located across the world

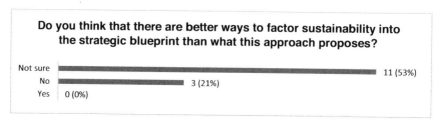

Do you think that there are better ways to factor sustainability into the strategic blueprint than what this approach proposes?

Figure 8.33 Findings on better ways to implement Step 7 from 15 designers located across the world

Points emerging from the comments included:

On how to keep the design team in the loop

Incentives go a long way in motivating team members.
E-mails might be missed, phone calls and visits might be better.
With online tools.

Shared responsibility

Could be better ways, or more ways; it is very connected to the holistic overview (Step 2) Not sure if these two steps should be or are separate steps actually. . . . But that is a whole other discussion!

I just think it is important to have everyone involved from the beginning co-design. To me, it´s the best way you can achieve a successful sustainable product.

I'm not sure on this step because in my experience, designers are not necessarily involved throughout the project (for example they leave after prototypes finished). Therefore, the company has the responsibility (also ownership) to continue (or not) the project according to their own requirements (instead of external partners).

8.4   Summary and conclusions

This chapter explored the transferability of the findings from the workshop to the broader set of those in the problem-class (Venable, 2009) – designers working with developing-country MSMEs with renewable materials. Since the workshop in India centered on a real-time test group, it was important to assess transferability – the extent to which our findings could be generalized to other situations (Merriam, 1998). The prospect of transferability is fundamentally flawed because findings are shaped by the specific contexts in which they occur: claiming that results from one setting can be applicable to another cannot actually be done with certainty (Erlandson, Skipper, Harris, & Allen, 1993). However, transferability is undeniably important, because though each case is unique, it is also an example within a broader group (Stake, 1994; Denscombe, 1998) – such as in the case of our broad problem context, which encompasses all three of the settings from where we derive findings. Assessing transferability is best done by practitioners who can assess the proximal similarity of their situation to that described in the study, and thereby the transferability of the findings to their setting (Bassey, 1981).

We were also concerned with the issue of dependability – whether we would get the same results if we could repeat the experiment exactly (Shenton, 2004). However, as discussed earlier, it is almost impossible to recreate our experiment and that was not our intention, as we designed the Rhizome Approach to be adaptable to changing contexts. We therefore treated our workshop as a prototype model (Shenton, 2004), which can be recreated in a proximally similar manner by future researchers, who may get proximally similar results. This is very much in line with the idea of a prototype that gets refined over subsequent iterations.

The first phase to check transferability was conducted in Vietnam by administering two questionnaires to 21 trainers from the SPIN project. Some of the key conclusions from this phase include:

- The seven barriers to sustainable design, which underpin the Rhizome Approach, are relevant to Vietnamese MSMEs.
- More Vietnamese respondents than Indian could understand the Sustainability Checklist just by reading it. This suggests that Vietnamese respondents understood the checklist more easily at first – possibly because they had already received inputs in sustainable innovation from the SPIN project. However, following the explanation of each factor, more Vietnamese than Indian still couldn't understand the checklist. A possible reason for this could be that the Vietnamese respondents were more unfamiliar with English than the Indian. This hypothesis is supported by the fact that the Vietnamese respondents cited the Sustainability Checklist being supported by an explanatory booklet as the primary factor which would make them more likely to use it. The percentage of Indian respondents who answered the same (17%) is much lower than the Vietnamese respondents (76%).
- Other than the factors in the Sustainability Checklist itself – shorter, digital, better looking, etc. – the most cited factors which would make the respondents likely to use the checklist were peer pressure, client demand and, last, government legislation.
- There was an increase in familiarity with concepts relating to sustainability following the presentation, which indicates that the inputs on the Rhizome Approach were effective even when compressed.

- More respondents answered they were familiar with sustainability before the presentation than after. This is surprising, and seemingly indicates a knowledge loss following the presentation. Only further research could throw light on this; however, one possible explanation is that the inputs from the presentation helped participants realistically and critically evaluate the extent of their knowledge gap with regards to concepts relating to sustainable design. The presentation on the Rhizome Approach helped increase the knowledge of the Ecodesign and Triple Bottom Line sustainability models.
- Following the presentation, there was a rise in the percentage of participants who felt ecological, cultural, economic and political aspects should be considered while designing sustainably. The perception on the social factors remained constant, whereas their perception that the ethical and political factors are important to sustainable design decreased. This seems to indicate the respondents' acceptance of the Four Pillars model.

The second phase, to check transferability, was conducted by administering an e-questionnaire to 15 designers located across Africa, Australia, Europe, Latin America, Turkey and Southeast Asia. Some of the key conclusions from this phase:

- One respondent suggested the Rhizome Approach should build upon existing indigenous knowledge. This was a positive reinforcement, since the Rhizome Approach already does this by documenting and culling out contemporary design markers from indigenous knowledge through the product-library workshop, which is part of Step 4 of the Rhizome Approach.
- Several of the respondents suggested digital tools. In line with this feedback, in the next round of iteration, the Sustainability Checklist was developed into software for ease of operation. This is discussed in the next chapter.
- Providing background information to the designers was suggested as a practical way to provide inputs. This factor is inherent in Step 1, which centers on didactic learning.
- Some of the respondents suggested that hands-on learning/learning by doing would be a good way for designers to learn. Step 2 of the Rhizome Approach addresses this aspect, and centers on experiential learning.
- Collaborative learning was also cited as an important aspect of sustainability innovation. We address this in Step 5 of the Rhizome Approach. Further feedback was to outline the involvement and role of each member of the design team vis-à-vis sustainability and innovation. This is an interesting proposal and could add to the process.
- Some of the respondents suggested a framework that is simultaneously adaptable and measureable. The Rhizome Approach addresses this already through the flexible and adaptable Sustainability Checklist used in Steps 4 and 6. One respondent suggested further flexibility through the possibility of conducting the steps independently. This is in line with our vision of the steps of the Rhizome Approach as being both independent and interdependent.

- The respondents suggested that the increased accountability for the final design if designers were to maintain ownership of the innovation process called for the carrot and the stick – including through incentives, legislation and peer pressure. We address this input in the following chapter.

Based on the feedback on the transferability and expected efficacy of the Rhizome Approach from the phase in Vietnam in 2011, we concluded that we had successfully answered our second question: the Rhizome Approach is a possible sustainability design approach that is mindful of the pros and cons of the existing sustainability design approaches, and which looks at addressing an integrated holistic picture of sustainability in the context of developing country craft-based MSMEs working with renewable materials. This conclusion was supported by the findings from the questionnaire administered to 15 designers around the world in 2016.

We therefore proceeded to answer our final question, which centered on mechanisms which would support and encourage the use and operationalization of the Rhizome Approach. The following chapter discusses our process to answer to this question, and the outputs and findings thereon.

9   Encouraging the use of the Rhizome Approach

9.1   The company: its importance, sustainability journey and sustainability drivers

The previous chapter reported on how we validated the efficacy of the Rhizome Approach and its constituents – especially the Sustainability Checklist – in enabling holistically sustainable design for our problem-class (designers working with non-industrial craft-based MSMEs in developing countries). Our next step was to look at mechanisms which would support and encourage the use and operationalization of the Rhizome Approach.

The Rhizome Approach builds on learning from existing sustainability design approaches and tools. Like most of these – including as LCAs, rules of thumb and checklists – the Rhizome Approach aims to factor sustainability concerns into the product design and development process (Boks, 2006; Bovea & Pérez-Belis, 2012; Brezet & Van Hemel, 1997). The catalysts to operationalize these approaches and tools are designers, who naturally function as brokers between innovation, and the stakeholders linked to the innovation process. Designers introduce new practices in or between individuals, institutions and functions by encouraging and facilitating communication between them (Wenger, 1998). The artifacts they design act as boundary objects, which carry information that can be transferred, translated and transformed in (Wenger, 1998) or between (Hargadon, 2002; Keskin, Diehl, & Molenaar, 2013; Küçüksayraç, 2015; O'Rafferty & O'Connor, 2010) stakeholder communities.

In addition to being ideally positioned as brokers in the innovation process, the increasing scope, role and power of designers around the world, positions them as key players in strategic decisions, which will determine production-to-consumption systems, and thereby, sustainability (British Design Council, 2004; Swedish Design Industry, 2004). However, in order to impact sustainability to their fullest potential, designers need support to be able to navigate, and thereby be able to impact, the complex and interlinked levels of society (Jørgensen, 2012). With adequate support, their scope of design can become increasingly holistic; it can incrementally go from the level of product-technology system to product-service system to socio-technical system to societal system (Joore & Brezet, 2015).

Our inquiry into why, despite seeming ideally positioned to do so, designers do not design sustainably threw up seven barriers. One of these was access to appropriate tools, in response to which we created the Rhizome Approach. However, just because designers have access to sustainable-design tools such as our Rhizome Approach; it does not automatically imply that sustainability will be integrated into the product-development process (Huulgaard, 2015). The lack of tools was just one of the seven barriers to sustainable design we identified. The others centered on the "softer" aspects, such as organizational structures, and systems and competence building. Though these are not obviously and directly linked to the product development-and-design process, they support the implementation and use of sustainable-design tools (Boks, 2006).

The institutional structure within which the designer works – including business/enterprise/company (we will refer to this structure hereafter as the "company") – needs to support sustainable design. As we discussed in Chapter 3, designers often do not practice sustainable design because the companies they work for resist investing in it (Bacon, 2011). We therefore explored (Chapter 3) what could make a company more inclined to investing in sustainable design and identified three main drivers for this: a) regulatory and non-regulatory frameworks, b) market demand and access (Cleff & Rennings, 1999), and c) sustainability as a business opportunity and USP (Rubik & Frankl, 2005). We also discussed in the same chapter how these drivers tend to move from external (stick) to internal (carrot) over the course of a company's sustainability journey (Cleff & Rennings, 1999). The company's initial focus on just meeting the compliance requirements of regulatory and non-regulatory frameworks (external/stick) shifts towards leveraging sustainability to cut costs, to finally using sustainability as a value-addition factor to tap larger markets and increase business opportunities (internal/carrot) (White et al., 2008). This resonates with both, the five stages of a company's sustainability journey (Figure 9.1) outlined by Willard (2002), and also the Scottish Environment Protection Agency's 6C typology for environmental behavior – which classifies regulatees into criminals, chancers, careless, confused, compliant and champions.

9.2   Keeping companies on the sustainability track

In the previous section, we discussed how the company evolves from looking at sustainability as a necessary compliance formality to a potential business edge over its sustainability journey. However, even at an advanced stage, companies are wary of investing in sustainable innovation. This is because the outputs of their investment, including know-how, are leveraged by their competitors at no cost, especially when the know-how is easily accessible, and the eco-innovation is for public good (Beise & Rennings, 2005). This situation is common in the MSME sector, whose low-tech processes, protocols and innovations are relatively easy to copy. Most MSMEs do not have deep pockets; they need all of the investments they make – including in sustainability – to translate into economic value.

STAGE	1 Pre-compliance	2 Compliance	3 Beyond-compliance	4 Integrated strategy	5 Purpose/passion
behaviour	• Actions are unsustainable and illegal	• Actions fulfill bare minimum legal obligations	• Saves money by increasing efficiency to reduce unsustainability	• Includes sustainability in business strategies • Sustainability=business opportunities and competitive advantages	• Uses business as a vehicle to create holistic sustainability to benefit its business opportunities
	EXTERNAL/ STICK				INTERNAL/CARROT

Figure 9.1 The stages of a company's sustainability journey as identified by Willard (2002)

Source: Reubens, 2016c

Hard-regulation instruments	Soft-regulation instruments	Economic instruments	Communicative instruments
Command-and-control or hard instruments focus on policing, controlling and removing activities which are undesirable from the perspective of sustainability (Huulgaard, 2015).	Soft-regulation instruments are used in situations when traditional hard instruments are not necessary. They are more flexible in practice than hard instruments.	Economic instruments are market-based policy devices focus on influencing sustainable behavior through price signals as opposed to policing (Hockenstein, Stavins & Whitehead, 1997). They work on the principle that if the most sustainable product or service is the cheapest, it will be preferred over the more expensive unsustainable one (Winsemius, 1986).	Communicative instruments are non-mandatory or soft instruments (Cleff & Rennings, 1999), which focus on influencing consumer-and company-behavior through information and education (Smink, 2002).
They work on the principle of policing.	They workon the principles of self-regulation and co-regulation, technical standards, recommendations, open methods of coordination and their hybrids (European Commission, n.d.).	They work on the principle of incentives.	They work on the principle of communication.
These create a push for companies to meet minimum compliance, e.g., Ecodesign Directive.	These create a pull for companies to behave sustainably by awarding them legitimacy in a non-mandatory framework.	These create a pull for companies to behave sustainably by incentivizing them, e.g., energy label.	These create a market pull, which motivates companies to behave sustainably to get more business.
Examples of command-and-control instruments include regulations that set specific	Examples of soft instruments include recommendations, technical	Examples of economic instruments include pollution charges, subsidies, deposit–refund	Examples of communicative instruments include eco-labels and voluntary

Figure 9.2 Characteristics of hard, soft, economic and communicative instruments and a comparison between them

Source: Reubens, 2016c

standards for product improvement such as the RoHS (Restriction of Hazardous Substances) Directive (2011/65/ EU).	standards and self-regulation (voluntary standards) to legislation-induced co-regulatory actions (European Commission, n.d.).	systems (Bailey & Ditty, 2009; Sridhar, 2011; United Nations Environment Programme, 2005), taxes and tradable permits (Cleff & Rennings, 1999).	agreements between industry and government (Cleff & Rennings, 1999).
Incentives for improvement disappear once standards are met unless standards are consistently reviewed and raised.	The legitimacy of this system needs to be maintained by addressing issues of transparency, and a credible system to ensure compliance with commitments. Also important is to work out financials to ensure the sustainability of the instrument (European Commission, n.d.).	These can lead to short-term behavioral changes; however, longer-lasting changes need the motivation to come from within the individual and not from an outside force (Pape, Rau, Fahy, & Davies, 2011).	Providing access to accurate information needs to be coupled with incentives in order to create change (Pape et al., 2011).

Figure 9.2 (Continued)

This is why mechanisms which create a push-pull effect, including through regulation (Rennings, 2000), play a vital role in encouraging companies to remain on the sustainability track.

We studied four main types of mechanisms which can help keep MSMEs on the sustainability track: a) hard-regulation instruments, b) soft-regulation instruments, c) economic instruments, and d) communicative instruments. We discuss these mechanisms and compare them side by side in Figure 9.2. As in the case of the companies' sustainability journey, there has been a shift from stick to carrot in the case of the popularity of these instruments. The traction of hard instruments (stick) has been waning since the 1980s, and there has been a subsequent emergence of economic, communicative instruments (Huulgaard, 2015) and soft instruments (carrot).

Figure 9.3 depicts which instruments are most synergistic at the different stages of a company's sustainability journey, and the role of the regulator. This is based

STAGE	**1** Pre-compliance	**2** Compliance	**3** Beyond-compliance	**4** Integrated strategy	**5** Purpose/passion
INSTRUMENTS	Hard-regulation instruments	Economic instruments Hard-regulation instruments	Economic instruments Soft-regulation instruments	Communicative instruments Soft-regulation instruments	Communicative instruments Soft-regulation instruments
ROLE OF REGULATOR	Monitor and prosecute	Set outcomes Educate and advise on sustainability issues Audit performance Enforce incentives where necessary	Set outcomes Audit performance Enforce incentives when necessary	Set outcomes Audit performance Recognize and publicize success	Recognize and publicize success
	EXTERNAL/ STICK	⟵—————————————————⟶			INTERNAL/ CARROT

Figure 9.3 Instruments which are most relevant at the different stages of a company's sustainability journey, based on Willard (2002) and Angus et al.'s (2013) analysis

Source: Reubens, 2016c

on Angus, Booth, Armstrong, and Pollard's (2013) analysis of suitable policy instruments based on firms' characteristics, and our understanding from Figure 9.2.

The Rhizome Approach was designed to facilitate holistically sustainable design for non-industrial craft-based MSMEs working with renewable materials in developing countries. Most of these countries do not prioritize environmental sustainability regulation enforcement, and their ethos of corruption and favoritism allows the bypassing of their nascent legislation systems (Bell & Russel, 2002). The key elements for regulatory instruments to function – including accurate monitoring, a stringent and efficient legal system, and transparency – are largely missing in the developing world (Bell & Russel, 2002). Therefore, for the most part, the driving factor for the developing-world MSMEs to invest in sustainability design is the market, rather than existing legislation or financial incentives.

Accordingly, the developing-world MSMEs that invest in sustainability design and innovation generally fall under the Stages 4 and 5 of Figure 9.3. The corresponding instruments for this stage, which could support and encourage the use and operationalization of the Rhizome Approach, are communicative and soft-regulation instruments.

Rationale to select labeling

We reviewed different types of soft-regulation and communicative instruments (Laurell, 2014) to check which would be a good fit with the Rhizome Approach. These included the numerous forms of self-regulatory instruments which have emerged over the past decade targeting environmental protection – including sectoral guidelines, codes of practice, covenants, environmental management systems, customer and supplier requirements, environmental accounting, environmental auditing, environmental charters, environmental management systems, public reporting requirements and eco-labeling (Andrews, 1998; Borkey, Glachant, & Leveque, 1999; Carmin, Darnall, & Mil-Homens, 2003; Jordan, Wurzel, & Zito, 2005; Mazurek, 2002; Nash & Ehrenfeld, 1997; Sinclair, 1997). Of these, we found labeling to be most synergistic with both developing-country MSMEs and the Rhizome Approach, for four main reasons.

First, labeling spans the categories of both communicative and soft-regulation instruments. It comprises three basic steps: a) standard-setting, b) certification, and c) communicating the results of the assessment (Cassell & Symon, 2006). While Steps a and b align with soft-regulation instruments, Step c aligns with communicative instruments.

Second, labeling spans the range between the mutually exclusive approaches of hard command-and-control regulation, and soft voluntary self-regulation. It can lean towards either, depending on the strictness of the implementation of major aspects of labeling policy – compulsoriness, explicitness and standardization (Mil-Homens Loureio, 2011).

Third, especially in the environmental arena, labeling is a third-generation regulatory instrument which offers the possibility of self-regulation under state supervision. Labeling allows the state to go beyond prescriptive legislation where it would typically punish offenders, to rewarding top performers, thus encouraging them to go beyond compliance (Mil-Homens Loureio, 2011). This promotes a cooperative relationship between the state and businesses (Clinton, 1995).

The fourth reason to select labeling was that it is a management-based mechanism (also known as process-based or systems-based regulation); it encourages firms to self-regulate and plan towards achieving broader societal objectives (Coglianese & Nash, 2004). There are three basic types of regulation: mechanisms–technology-based, performance-based and management-based. Technology-based mechanisms target the manufacturing stage by outlining specific processes or technologies to be used, and performance-based mechanisms target the output stage by specifying outcomes to be met (Coglianese, Nash, & Olmstead, 2003). Management-based mechanisms are more holistic than these, as they target the planning stage (Coglianese & Lazer, 2003), which is in line with our argument for front-end innovation which factors in larger sustainability goals.

Rationale to develop a new certification and labeling initiative

Currently, there are estimated to be more than 400 sustainability-aligned certification and labeling schemes spanning almost every category of consumer products, and this number is projected to be increasing rapidly (Stewart, 2010). We reviewed some of the most recognizable green labels (Stewart, 2010) to check if they would be a good fit with the Rhizome Approach. However, we did not find a single label which addressed sustainability in a holistic manner. Figure 9.4 presents a review of 30 of these labels. All except one of the labels reviewed focused on the ecological dimension, and only four focused on the social and/

Sr. No.	Labelling Scheme	Ecological	Social	Economic	Cultural
1	FSC Certified	●			
2	SCS Certified Cal Compliant	●			
3	Rainforest Alliance Certified	●			
4	Processed Chlorine Free and Totally Chlorine Free	●			
5	Energy Star	●			
6	Dark Sky	●			
7	Lighting Facts	●			
8	Energyguide	●			
9	Watersense	●			
10	LEED	●			
11	BREEAM	●			
12	CRI Green Label and Green Label Plus	●			
13	Smart Certified	●			
14	Floor Score	●			
15	Level	●	●		
16	SCS Certified Indoor Advantage	●			
17	Certified Humane Raised and Handled	●			
18	Fair Trade Certified		●	●	
19	Certified Veliflora Sustainably Grown	●	●		
20	Animal Welfare Approved	●			
21	Whole Trade Guarantee	●	●	●	
22	USDA Organic	●			
23	Leaping Bunny Cruelty free	●			
24	Dolphin Safe	●			
25	SCS Certified Recycled Content	●			
26	UL Environment	●			
27	Ecologoy	●			
28	Green Seal	●			
29	Green E	●			
30	Cradle to Cradle	●			

Figure 9.4 Review of 30 recognizable green labels (Stewart, 2010) vis-à-vis the dimensions of sustainability they address

Source: Reubens, 2016c

or economic dimensions. None of the labels reviewed focused on the cultural dimension.

Most existing sustainability labeling schemes seem to focus on environmental or social aspects (Frankl et al., 2005), with an explicit contradiction between the two foci at times (Harris, 2007). The lack of schemes which integrate the ecological, social and economic dimensions of sustainability and social metrics (Seuring & Muller, 2008) seems to be corroborated by the recent calls from government actors (Baedeker et al., 2005; IEFE & ICEM CEEM, 1998; Mazijn et al., 2004; Sustainable Development Commission, 2008; Teufel et al., 2009) and academics (Eberle, 2001; Eckert, Karg, & Zängler, 2007; Frankl et al., 2005) for current schemes to address multiple dimensions. The parallel call for an overarching meta-sustainability label which integrates the different dimensions of sustainability (Hayn & Eberle, 2006) echoes this sentiment. Dendler (2013) spotlights some existing schemes which look at multiple dimensions, including UK NGO Sustain's (2007) multiple-criteria flower label for food and German retailer REWE's PROPLANET labeling (REWE Group, n.d.) which looks at premium-quality products that are both ecologically and socially sustainable. However, none of these schemes address all four dimensions of sustainability, or the cultural factor that is very important to craft-based MSMEs in the developing world.

The existing labeling schemes specific to the handicraft sector did not address sustainability holistically, either. Several of the schemes, including the Craftmark of the All India Artisans and Craftsworker Welfare Association, looked at the cultural and social dimensions by certifying that the products are genuine and produced in a socially responsible manner (Craftmark, n.d.). Another direction is the labeling of region-specific crafts, such as through India's Geographical Indication (GI) tag for region-specific crafts such as Patan Patola textiles and Chennapatna lacquer toys. The GI tag identifies and attributes a product's quality or distinctive characteristics to its geographical origin thus recognizing and protecting craft's intellectual property (Intellectual Property India, n.d.). In a similar vein, there are several larger and smaller labeling schemes which state the product is *handmade in* a specific region, such as the Laotian local handicraft label "Handmade in Luang Prabang" (International Trade Center Communications, 2013). We found a number of handicraft-sector labeling schemes which were focused on the socio-economic dimension – such as the World Fair Trade Organization's ongoing initiative, which looks at certification, monitoring and labeling scheme for fairtrade labeling of craft (Hall, n.d.). Sometimes, the focus is predominantly social, such as the Good Weave's (2014) label, whereby an NGO certifies that carpets in India are not produced using child labor. Worth noting are some country-level sustainability labeling schemes, as well, such as Morocco's 2013 national handicraft label, which factors in both environmental and social criteria (Sustainable Business Associates, n.d.).

We argue that since craft positively impacts all of sustainability's dimensions, a labeling scheme for the handicraft sector should showcase this holistic impact (Seuring & Muller, 2008). Since holistic sustainability was not targeted in the labeling schemes specific to the handicraft sector, or in eco-labeling schemes in general which we studied, we decided to develop such a scheme. The proposed labeling scheme would be developed by refining the Sustainability Checklist and its evaluation mechanism. Just as in the case of the Rhizome Approach, we sought to develop and test our intervention in a real context (van den Akker, 1999) and improve it iteratively (Plomp, 2009). This real-context sub-set would be representative of our larger audience of craft-based MSMEs in developing countries working with renewable materials, which were linked to designers.

9.3   UNIDO'S branding initiative: the platform for iteration cycle 2

The previous section discussed how we shortlisted communicative and soft-regulation instruments – and labeling in particular – to support and encourage the use and operationalization of the Rhizome Approach. We also discussed how we did not find a labeling system which addressed sustainability holistically, and so decided to create and test one in a real-world setting which would be representative of our client-class.

We selected the United Nations Industrial Development Organization (UNIDO) branding initiative in Vietnam, where we were involved as expert consultants, as this real-world setting. UNIDO had already provided inputs on cleaner production and sustainable product-design to Vietnamese MSMEs from five handicraft value chains – bamboo/rattan, silk, sea grass, handmade paper and lacquerware. We had been involved in product development for three of these five value chains, and had applied the Rhizome Approach for this product development. As a result of UNIDOs efforts, several of these Vietnamese MSMEs could now produce green products. However, it seemed unlikely that these MSMEs would continue to produce these products unless their sustainability efforts and costs translated into economic value. Therefore, UNIDO aimed to put in place a branding initiative which would help differentiate the value of these sustainable products from their mainstream counterparts: this would make it economically viable for the MSMEs to remain on the sustainability track. This backdrop fitted well with our objective – to develop a labeling system which would increase the possibility of the Rhizome Approach being used – because it translated the additional costs incurred for sustainable design into realizable economic value.

Underpinning the branding initiative with a labeling scheme

We decided to underpin the branding initiative with a labeling scheme, because, as previously discussed, labeling schemes are among the most prominent measures to facilitate sustainable production and consumption (Dendler, 2012), which was both our goal and UNIDO's. Labeling would also provide legitimacy to the proposed brand, which was required because of existing consumer skepticism about *green* or *sustainable* products, given the plethora of spurious sustainable products in the market (Golden, 2010).

The highest degree of success in green or environmental branding has been with non-durable, frequently used, and highly visible consumer goods (Gallastegui, 2002) – such as food, whose standardized manufacturing processes are relatively easy to examine and measure. The comparatively informal nature of the handicraft sector is not conducive to similar scrutiny, making it difficult to transfer the experience from the industrial sector to craft-based MSMEs (Reubens, 2013b). Therefore, we decided to work towards a transparent, accountable and inclusive labeling scheme, specifically for the handicraft sector, which would instill rather than undermine confidence and credibility of the brand to be developed. At the highest level, the brand would align with Vietnam's national branding initiative *Value from Vietnam*, adding further credibility to the brand.

The labeling scheme comprised three basic steps:

- Standard-setting, or identifying criteria to be met.
- Certification, or assessing to which level that standard is being met.
- Labeling, or communicating the results of the assessment, including the assessment criteria with or on the product.

(Cassell & Symon, 2006)

Standard-setting is the first step of most certification and labeling schemes, ranging from seal-of-approval programs to ISO-Type II eco-labels, to ISO-Type III product-declaration labels (Dendler, 2012). Step 2, certification, is also an inherent part of most product-labeling schemes. Communicating the results of Step 2, on or with the product, distinguishes product-labeling from certification schemes (Dendler, 2012).

9.4   Assessing the suitability of using the Sustainability Checklist for UNIDO's labeling scheme

We did not want to force the use of the Sustainability Checklist for UNIDO's labeling scheme. We, therefore, checked whether the Sustainability Checklist was a suitable starting point for developing criteria for the Vietnamese handicraft sector in a participatory manner. We did this by collecting feedback from two Vietnamese groups – officials and representatives, and value-chain actors – after we presented the checklist and evaluation method to them. Details of the exercise with the two groups and the findings thereof follow.

Group 1: officials and representatives from Vietnam's handicraft sector

Our first group included 19 officials and representatives from across the Vietnamese handicraft-sector value chain at UNIDO's Branding Workshop in Hanoi, in March 2012. The workshop comprised several activities, including our presentation on the Sustainability Checklist and the evaluation mechanism. Following the presentation, the participants discussed the viability of using the checklist as sustainability assessment criteria and evaluation mechanism for Vietnam's handicraft sector, and of developing a visual representation of the assessment through a branding and labeling scheme. We documented their inputs through notes and a questionnaire. The findings of this questionnaire are presented in Figures 9.5–9.9, alongside the comparative findings from the second group.

Group 2: value-chain actors from the handicraft sector

Our second group included 25 random value-chain actors of the Vietnamese craft sector – including craftspeople, buyers, wholesalers, MSME owners and institutional representatives. We solicited their input through the same questionnaire used with the first group. The questionnaire was administered in September 2012 by the Vietnamese UNIDO team to increase objectivity, and also due to the language barrier.

Comparative findings

Usefulness of the checklist in understanding sustainability concerns

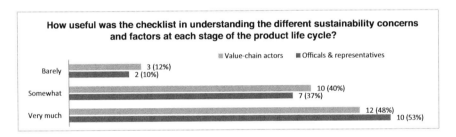

Figure 9.5 Comparison between findings from 19 respondents from Group 1 and 25 respondents from Group 2 on the usefulness of the checklist in understanding sustainability concerns

New sustainability-related factors learned through the checklist

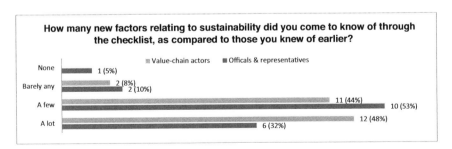

Figure 9.6 Comparison between findings from 19 respondents from Group 1 and 25 respondents from Group 2 on the usefulness of the checklist in creating awareness on different sustainability factors

Improving the checklist

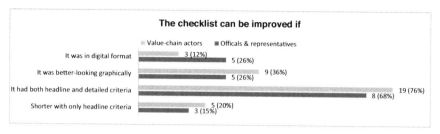

Figure 9.7 Comparison between findings 19 respondents from Group 1 and 25 respondents from Group 2 on improving the checklist

360-degree evaluation

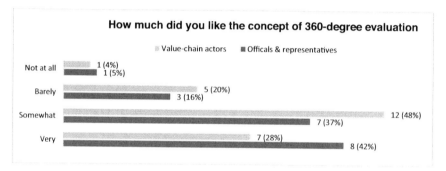

Figure 9.8 Comparison between findings 19 respondents from Group 1 and 25 respondents from Group 2 on the 360-degree evaluation

Sustainability landscape

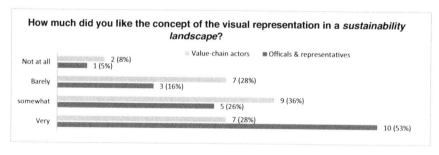

Figure 9.9 Comparison between findings 19 respondents from Group 1 and 25 respondents from Group 2 on visual representation in a sustainability landscape

Least-liked

We asked the respondents, "In your own words, please tell us which part of the entire system you liked least and why." We clustered their comments thematically as follows:

Criteria are difficult to understand

So difficult to understand.

Difficult to understand because of many specialized words.

In my opinion, I would like to criteria of this more clear and simple to understand because almost the Vietnamese enterprises has low education (sic).

I like the checklist concept that helps things to be clearer.

Quite complicated criteria system, some criteria are unclear in terms of measurement/ assessment.

Definition of criteria should be provided, bullet points should be reconsidered.

Criteria can be more simple.

Adapt to local conditions

Needs to be adapted to local context.

End-of-life handling considerations are not practical for Vietnamese procedures.

Some questions are not realistic.

Needs to be further studied to be suitable for Vietnamese context.

Localized and adaptable to local condition and handicraft features.

The evaluation system can be easily manipulated

The evaluation system proposed is too simple, easy to be distorted (sic) by corrupt evaluators, depending on persons rather than a concrete and transparent system.

Some criteria are more important than others/weightage

Distribution consideration because it is somewhat not very relevant (sic).

Material and production: these criteria should be more detailed and measureable.

The entire system is ok, customer consideration: should be more detailed.

Weight factors should be applied.

The checklist of criteria should be more simple and easier to use. There should be a system of weighting the relevant importance of each criteria concerning each sector studied. (Not all criteria are equally important to each sector.) (sic).

I think that it should involve different proportions between the different criteria.

Organize criteria into larger groups

Group certain criteria, e.g., under production once could have several sub-headings (working condition/emp/CP etc. could be grouped, packaging could be grouped also).

Explain current rating and provide directions on improving rating

Furthermore, add a column in which you provide a short description. E.g. Packaging can be more sustaining (sic) if it uses recycled material, less material, biodegradable . . .). Add a column in which you explain the rating given.

Learn from and dovetail with existing labeling systems

There are some green label systems such as eco cotton. We should learn from these case study (sic).

VIRI HRPC is a member of WFTO (Fair trade). We have 10 criteria to follow and it is already a lot of assessment and compromise!

Clearer representation of the results

I like the concept but the proposition with the dots is a bit confusing (colors of dots and numbers of dots).

Findings from Part 2 of the questionnaire

The questionnaire administered to the second group had an additional set of questions, on branding and operationalizing of the label. The questions explored what value-chain actors from the Vietnamese handicraft sector felt about sustainability and about a national brand for handicrafts underpinned by sustainability. The questions also explored practical issues such as who should own the brand and how the assessment should be carried out, and also their thoughts on aligning this brand to Vietnam's national brand. The questions presented ahead are translations from the Vietnamese originals. The findings from these questions (see figure 9.10 – 9.16) are as follows:

Importance of sustainability

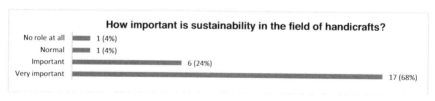

Figure 9.10 Findings from 25 Vietnamese value-chain actors on the importance of sustainability

Importance of sustainability brand value

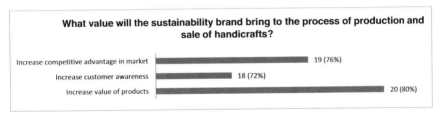

Figure 9.11 Findings from 25 Vietnamese value-chain actors on the importance of sustainability brand value; respondents could select more than one option

Most important stage of the life cycle for a sustainability brand

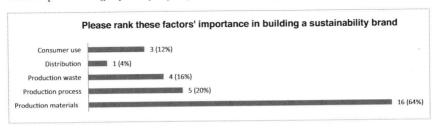

Figure 9.12 Findings from 25 Vietnamese value-chain actors on the most important stage of the life cycle for a sustainability brand

Who should be assessed?

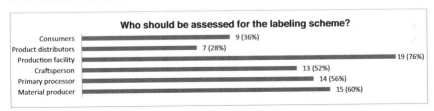

Figure 9.13 Findings from 25 Vietnamese value-chain actors on who should be assessed for the labeling scheme

Brand-building

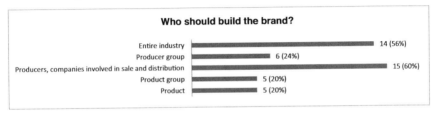

Figure 9.14 Findings from 25 Vietnamese value-chain actors on who should build the brand

Brand ownership

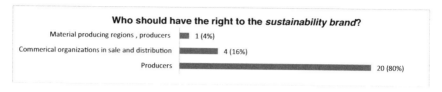

Figure 9.15 Findings from 25 Vietnamese value-chain actors on who should own the brand

Sustainability brand linked to national brand

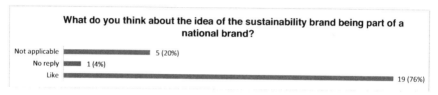

Figure 9.16 Findings from 25 Vietnamese companies on whether the sustainability brand should be part of the national brand

9.5 Revising the checklist based on feedback and getting feedback from another group

Based on the feedback from the two groups, we revised the criteria of the checklist as in Figure 9.17. The criteria in bold are the ones which were added (represented by a "+" sign) or subtracted (represented by a "−" sign).

We presented the new checklist to a group of 14 different actors from the Vietnamese handicraft-sector value chain at a UNIDO workshop in Hanoi on November 21, 2012, and solicited their feedback through a questionnaire and through focus-group discussions. The aim of this workshop was to discuss the refined checklist, and how it would work vis-à-vis the assessment. We noted the key points from the discussion. They are as follows:

Minimal compliance criteria

The respondents agreed with our suggestion that there should be some minimal compliance criteria which were non-negotiable. The respondents suggested these criteria to be:

- Minimally treated.
- No child and/or forced labor.
- Safe for users' health.

PCS	Sustainability Checklist	Sustainability Checklist Version 2
MATERIAL CONSIDERATIONS	Renewable	Uses renewable materials
	Minimally treated	Minimally treated
	Recyclable	Uses recyable materials
	Recycled	Uses recycled materials
	Local materials	Uses local materials
	Fair traded	Uses fairly traded materials
		Uses certified materials (+)
		Uses non-toxic materials (+)
		Avoids materials from intensive agriculture (+)
PRODUCTION CONSIDERATIONS	Minimum material	Uses minimum material
	Minimum production steps	Has minimum production steps possible
	Renewable energy	Renewable energy used for production
		Minimal energy used for production (+)
	Less emissions	Uses low emission techniques
		Production effluents and waste are properly managed (+)
	Less waste generated	Reduce production waste
	Waste reused	Resues production waste
		Reduce rejects (+)
	Indigenous treatments and processes	Uses indigenous treatments and processes
	Indigenous representation in decision making	Consults indigenous communities on production issues that affects them
	Healthy and safe work environment	Safe and healthy work environment
	Fair wages and benefits to producers	Fair wages and benefits to producers
	No child labor	No child labor
	No forced labor	No forced labor
		Fair working hours (+)
	Capacity building of producers (–)	
		Allows freedom of association and collective bargaining (+)
	No discrimination	No discrimination
		Gender neutral (+)
	Respect for human rights	
		Provides local employment opportunities (+)
DISTRIBUTION CONSIDERATIONS	Minimum distribution volume	Minimum product volume
	Minimum distribution weight	Minimum distribution weight
	Energy efficient transport	Uses minimum and clean transport
	Localized production to consumption system	Most of the PCS is local
	Minimum packaging	Minimum packaging
	Reusable packaging	Reusable packaging
	Recyclable packaging	Recyclable packaging
	Packaging made from reused/ recycled material	Packaging made from low impact materials
CONSUMER USE CONSIDERATIONS	Low/ clean energy consumption during usage	Uses minimum and clean energy
	Reduced and clean consumables during use	Uses minimum consumables
	Safe for users health	Safe to use
	Customizable	Customizable
	User friendly (–)	
	Affordable (–)	
	Easily upgradeable	Easily upgradeable
	Classic design	Classic design
	Promote a strong-user product relationship	Promotes user-product relationship
	Locally repairable and maintainable	Minimum and local maintenance and repair
END-OF-LIFE HANDLING CONSIDERATIONS	Mono-material	Mono-material
		Biodegradable (+)
	Designed for disassembly	Easy to disassemble
		Reusable (+)
	Recyclable packaging	Recyclable packaging
	End-of-life dissasembly facilitates employment for local communities	End-of-life phase facilitates local employment

Figure 9.17 Revised checklist criteria

Source: Reubens, 2013b

In addition, the respondents suggested that in order to qualify for the label, there should be a minimum score required in each of the four tenets – ecological, social, economic and cultural.

Remove criteria

The respondents suggesting removing some of the criteria as follows:

- Indigenous representation in decision-making.
- Localized production and distribution systems to reduce physical production and delivery gap.
- End-of-life handling facilitates employment for local communities through recycling.

Club criteria

The respondents suggested clubbing some of the criteria as follows:

- Recyclable and recycled, as both have to do with recycling.
- Reusable packaging and recyclable packaging.
- Customizable and user-friendly.
- All the criteria on packaging.
- All the consumer criteria.

Evaluation

The respondents had suggestions on the evaluation as follows:

- There should be evaluators from consumer protection agencies.
- While a self-evaluation from the company is an important exercise, it should not be included in the scoring.
- There should be knowledgeable, independent evaluators.
- Sector associations can be involved in evaluation.

Weightage

The respondents agreed collectively on the need for weightage for the different criteria for use in different value chains and sectors.

9.6   Summary and conclusions

This chapter discussed how we used the Sustainability Checklist and evaluation mechanism of the Rhizome Approach as the starting point to develop the Holistic Sustainability System. As in the case of our development of the Rhizome Approach, we developed this mechanism iteratively, against the backdrop of a real-world context, which represented the larger problem-class of our domain-craft-based MSMEs in developing countries working with renewable materials, linked to designers. Figure 9.18 represents how the Rhizome Framework, Rhizome Approach and Holistic Sustainability System work independently and interdependently. The Rhizome Framework outlines our desired end with regards to craft-design collaboration that can impact sustainability holistically – it shows what we want to do. The Rhizome Approach is the means to that end – it shows how we can actualize the Rhizome Framework. Finally, the Holistic Sustainability System outlines the justification for craft-design initiatives to be underpinned by both the Rhizome Framework and the Rhizome Approach – it centers on how labeling adds value, thus providing the justification for craft-based MSMEs in the developing world to remain on the sustainability track.

We began the process of developing this system as a way to make sustainability commercially viable for MSMEs. We explored carrot and stick approaches to keep these enterprises on the sustainability track, and concluded that in the long run, the driver for the company to stay on the sustainability track needs to come from an internal, and not external, motivation (Pape et al., 2011). Hard regulation and economic instruments can force or incentivize sustainable behavior, respectively: they can also force the premature end of a company's sustainability journey, because these MSMEs are generally less able to absorb the cost of legislation compared to larger businesses (Angus et al., 2013). Internal drivers such as the possibility to increase competitive edge (Bey, Hauschild, & McAloone, 2013) by

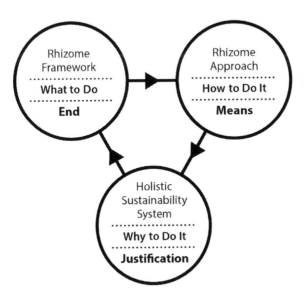

Figure 9.18 How the Rhizome Framework, the Rhizome Approach and the Holistic Sustainability Framework fit together

Source: Reubens

tapping innovation opportunities and through better product quality – thereby increasing the market share – are stronger drivers than regulation (van Hemel & Cramer, 2002). We therefore concluded that the carrot – soft regulation and labeling – offered the best solution to our client-class. We tried to identify pre-existing sustainability labeling schemes and labeling schemes in the handicraft sector which could help operationalize and underpin the Rhizome Approach. However, the schemes we reviewed did not address the dimensions of sustainability holistically. Therefore, we decided to develop such a mechanism against the backdrop of UNIDO's Branding Initiative in Vietnam.

The initiative was looking for a way to keep the MSMEs it had supported with inputs on sustainability on the track to sustainability, by adding value to, and creating differentiation for, their products through branding. The suitability of using the Sustainability Checklist for this initiative was ascertained in a participatory manner, from two groups of stakeholders. Using this feedback, we refined the checklist and evaluation, and ran the second iteration by a group of stakeholders from the Vietnamese handicraft sector.

Finally, we developed the last iteration of our design, known as the Holistic Sustainability System, which would work as the mechanism to support and encourage the use and operationalization of the Rhizome Approach and its constituents. We present the Holistic Sustainability System in the following chapter.

10 The Holistic Sustainability System

10.1 Design of the final iteration: standard-setting

In the previous chapter, we discussed how we solicited feedback from different focus groups and stakeholders of the Vietnamese handicraft value chain, towards developing the final iteration of the labeling scheme. We offer our final design of this labeling system for UNIDO, called the Holistic Sustainability System, in this chapter. This labeling scheme will potentially encourage the use of the Rhizome Approach, and sustainability design in general, by translating sustainability achievements into market value. The Holistic Sustainability System will include three components, namely: standard-setting, certification and labeling. We discuss the first component in this section, and the remaining two in the following sections.

Standard-setting: the Holistic Sustainability Checklist

We refined our Sustainability Checklist to develop the Holistic Sustainability Checklist based on feedback. The checklist was graphically improved (Figure 10.1) and icons were developed to indicate the key dimensions, in response to the findings which indicated that participants would be more likely to use it if it looked better graphically.

The Holistic Sustainability Checklist draws on different frameworks such as the D4S rules of thumb by UNEP and Delft University of Technology, the Business for Social Compliance (BSCI) code of conduct of the Foreign Trade Association (FTA) and the conventions of the International Labour Organization (ILO). The checklist therefore functions as a theoretically integrative framework that supports the policies, standards and compliance methodologies of different institutions working towards sustainability at different nodes of the production-to-consumption system.

The Holistic Sustainability Checklist illustrates the generic production-to-consumption system (Figure 10.2) for product-material selection, production, distribution, use and end-of-life handling, and the Design for Sustainability (D4S) parameters relevant at each stage.

HOLISTIC SUSTAINABILITY CHECKLIST		ECOLOGICAL	SOCIAL	CULTURAL	ECONOMIC
MATERIAL CONSIDERATIONS	1 Renewable materials	·			
	2 Minimally treated materials	·			·
	3 Recyclable materials	·			·
	4 Recycled materials	·			
	5 Local materials	·	·	·	·
	6 Fairly traded materials		·		
	7 Ecologically certified materials	·			
	8 Non-toxic materials	·	·		
	9 Less/no materials from intensive agriculture	·			
PRODUCTION CONSIDERATIONS	10 Minimum materials	·			·
	11 Minimum production steps	·			·
	12 Renewable energy for production	·			
	13 Minimal energy for production	·			·
	14 Low-emission techniques	·	·		
	15 Proper management of production effluents and waste	·	·		
	16 Reduce/reuse production waste	·			·
	17 Indigenous treatments and processes	·	·	·	
	18 Consulting indigenous communities on production issues that affect them		·	·	
	19 Safe and healthy work environment		·		·
	20 Fair wages and benefits to producers		·		·
	21 No child labor		·		·
	22 No forced labor		·		
	23 Fair working hours		·		
	24 Freedom of association and collective bargaining		·		
	25 No discrimination			·	
	26 Local employment opportunities		·	·	·
DISTRIBUTION CONSIDERATIONS	27 Minimum product volume and weight	·			·
	28 Minimum and clean transport	·			·
	29 Local PCS	·	·		
	30 Minimum packaging	·			·
	31 Reusable packaging	·		·	
	32 Recyclable packaging	·			
	33 Packaging made from low-impact materials	·			·
CONSUMER USE CONSIDERATIONS	34 Minimum/clean energy during usage	·			·
	35 Minimum consumables	·			
	36 Safe to use		·		
	37 Customizable	·		·	
	38 Easily upgradable	·		·	
	39 Classic design	·		·	
	40 Minimum and local maintenance and repair	·	·	·	
END-OF-LIFE HANDLING CONSIDERATIONS	41 Reduced material complexity	·			
	42 Biodegradable	·			
	43 Easy to disassemble	·			·
	44 Reusable			·	
	45 Recyclable	·			·
	46 Promotes/uses local recycling systems	·	·	·	·

Figure 10.1 Holistic Sustainability Checklist

Figure 10.2 Generic production-to-consumption system
Source: Reubens, 2013a

The checklist indicates the social, cultural, ecological and economic tenets of sustainability strongly influenced by each parameter. This supports the designer in understanding the potential and desired criteria that can make a product more holistically sustainable at each node of the production-to-consumption system. The checklist can be used as a guideline during the product development or innovation stage, or as a standard during product redesign. Newly developed and existing products can be evaluated against the same checklist, making it an indicator of sustainability factors achieved.

Each criterion of the Holistic Sustainability Checklist is discussed in detail below:

Material selection

Traditional material selection parameters include function, appearance, reliability, service life, environment, compatibility, production viability and cost (Chitale & Gupta, 2007). The Sustainability Checklist proposes the following supplementary parameters towards sustainability.

1. RENEWABLE MATERIALS

Materials from the biosphere (that grow on Earth), such as bamboo or sea grass, are renewed more quickly than those from the lithosphere (under the surface of Earth), such as coal. Among these, some biosphere materials get renewed faster than others – for example, bamboo gets renewed faster than wood. Materials that are more renewable should be used, and exhaustible materials should be substituted as far as possible (Crul & Diehl, 2006).

2. MINIMALLY TREATED MATERIALS

Minimizing the treatments required to prepare raw materials reduces emissions and energy consumption, thereby impacting ecological sustainability. Minimizing treatments also positively impacts economic sustainability, as reducing the processes reduces the overall cost.

3. RECYCLABLE MATERIALS

Recyclable materials positively impact ecological sustainability by reducing the burden of disposal, and inputting existing material into a fresh life cycle.

Recyclable materials are valued economically as inputs into another material life cycle, even after their original use, and so also positively impact economic sustainability. To facilitate easy recyclability, the product should be made of a single material as far as possible (Crul & Diehl, 2006). If this is not possible, materials with similar end-of-life paths, such as biodegradable materials, should be used. Materials that are difficult to separate, including compound materials, laminates, fillers, fire retardants and fiberglass reinforcements should be avoided (Crul & Diehl, 2006). Add-on elements like stickers, which complicate the recycling process, should also be avoided (Crul & Diehl, 2006).

4. RECYCLED MATERIALS

The use of recycled input materials positively impacts ecological sustainability, since they reduce the need to harvest fresh materials for production. Wherever possible, virgin materials should be replaced by recycled materials, especially in functions that do not require materials with high standards with regards to mechanical ability, hygiene or tolerance (Crul & Diehl, 2006).

5. LOCAL MATERIALS

Using local input materials positively impacts the social, economic, cultural and ecological tenets of sustainability. Supplying local materials gives indigenous and local communities a source of livelihood (economic sustainability), and therefore the opportunity to sustain their social and cultural practices. Since environmental degradation caused by unsustainable practices such as over-extraction directly affects local communities, they tend to be more conscientious and, therefore, ecologically sustainable.

6. FAIRLY TRADED MATERIALS

Trade is *fair* when a grower/producer is guaranteed a just price for their produce over a guaranteed term (Roddick, 2001). Fairly traded materials build direct connections between the buyer and seller, and between origin and destination – much like the personal interaction and relationship of exchange in the craft production-to-consumption system. This increases social accountability, and thus, positively impacts social sustainability.

7. ECOLOGICALLY CERTIFIED MATERIALS

Eco-certified materials include those with certifications for chain of custody, reduced pollutants and environmental impacts, use of renewable energy, post-consumer recycling or organic/best management practices bio-based materials and reclaimed materials – all of which positively impact ecological sustainability.

8.   NON-TOXIC MATERIALS

Replacing toxic materials with non-toxic materials minimizes environmental damage, thus positively impacting ecological sustainability. Materials or additives that are prohibited due to their toxicity – such as polychlorinated biphenyls, polychlorinated terphenyls, lead, cadmium and mercury – should not be used (Crul & Diehl, 2006). Highly toxic materials,including those that deplete the ozone layer – such as chlorine, fluorine, bromine, methyl bromide, halons and aerosols, foams, refrigerants and solvents that contain CFCs – or release harmful emissions during processing should also be avoided (Crul & Diehl, 2006).

9.   LESS/NO MATERIALS FROM INTENSIVE AGRICULTURE

Intensive agriculture is characterized by a low fallow ratio, capital-intensive inputs and the heavy use of pesticides and chemical fertilizers relative to land area. Intensive agriculture enables a substantial increase in production, however, it also causes environmental degradation through increased erosion and water pollution due to agricultural chemicals such as fertilizers and pesticides. Materials produced through intensive agriculture should be avoided, as they negatively impact ecological sustainability.

Production considerations

Traditional production-selection parameters include geometry or form, material constraints and potentials, and the production-volume requirement (Chitale & Gupta, 2007). The Sustainability Checklist proposes the following supplementary parameters towards sustainability.

10.   MINIMUM MATERIAL

Minimizing material input positively impacts ecological sustainability. It also cuts costs, facilitating economic sustainability. Input materials can be minimized by efficient production and insistence on *minimum materials* at the product-development stage (Crul & Diehl, 2006).

11.   MINIMUM PRODUCTION STEPS

Minimizing production steps cuts emissions, energy consumption and overall costs, aiding ecological and economic sustainability. Combining multiple functions into one component, and using materials that do not need additional treatments, can help reduce production steps (Crul & Diehl, 2006).

12.   RENEWABLE ENERGY FOR PRODUCTION

Using renewable energy which is fueled by wind, water and solar power positively impacts ecological sustainability (Crul & Diehl, 2006). Renewable energy sources such as low-sulphur coal and natural gas should be substituted for fossil fuels wherever possible (Crul & Diehl, 2006).

13. MINIMAL ENERGY FOR PRODUCTION

Materials that require less energy to process positively impact both ecological and economic sustainability. Low energy requirements translate into lower energy costs, and thereby reduced environmental impact and increased economic sustainability.

14. LOW EMISSION TECHNIQUES

Cleaner production processes with minimal emissions positively impact both the micro environment (society), and the macro environment (ecology). Emissions should be in compliance with statutory laws and regulations (BSCI, 2004). Further steps to minimize emissions can include replacing techniques like joining and soldering with techniques like bending (Crul & Diehl, 2006).

15. PROPER MANAGEMENT OF PRODUCTION EFFLUENTS AND WASTE

Properly managing production effluents and waste positively impacts the producer and the ecology – the micro and macro environments, respectively. Effluents should be treated, and waste should be managed and disposed of, as per statutory laws and regulations (BSCI, 2004).

16. REDUCE/REUSE PRODUCTION WASTE

Reducing and reusing production waste helps to curb ecologically harmful waste streams. Reducing the waste generated during the production process, recycling production residues and maintaining production standards (which, in turn, decrease the amount of rejected products) all help in reducing the waste (Crul & Diehl, 2006). Less waste also translates into lower material and processing costs, thus positively impacting economic sustainability.

17. INDIGENOUS TREATMENTS AND PROCESSES

Incorporating indigenous treatments and processes into the production process helps preserve the inherent ecological, social and cultural sustainability embedded within the indigenous and traditional craft practice.

18. CONSULTING INDIGENOUS COMMUNITIES ON PRODUCTION ISSUES
THAT AFFECT THEM

Decision-making in large private sector corporations is primarily profit-driven, with the structure of shareholding distancing accountability from ownership

(Thorpe, 2007). Involving local indigenous communities in decision-making sustains the culture of accountability and social sustainability in the production-to-consumption system. This is especially true if the indigenous communities constitute the workforce. The ILO92 requires that indigenous and tribal peoples are consulted on issues that affect them, and that they are able to engage in free, prior and informed participation in policies and development processes that affect them.

19. SAFE AND HEALTHY WORK ENVIRONMENT

A healthy and safe working environment positively impacts social sustainability, which, in turn, leads to increased productivity, thus positively impacting economic sustainability. The International Labour Organization (ILO) estimates that 4% of the global annual GDP is lost due to accidents and occupational disease. The suffering and social unsustainability caused by these is incalculable. These losses can be averted through a healthy and safe work environment. Such an environment would be hygienic and well lit, with proper ventilation and lighting to offer the best possible protection for employees' health and safety (BSCI, 2004). Employees should have access to clean areas for eating and cooking, as well as clean, lockable and gender-specific toilets and washing and changing facilities. ILO articles 16–19 state that workers should have access to protective gear such as gloves, earplugs and goggles, and should also be urged to use this equipment. Sufficient fire-fighting equipment should be installed and maintained (ILO, 2017). In addition, proper signage should indicate high-voltage junctions, hazardous chemical and biological substances (ILO, 2017) and electric installations and cables (BSCI, 2004). Employees should have access to – and basic training in – first aid (ILO, 2017). Exits and escape routes should be conspicuously marked and kept clear of incendiary devices such as steam boilers (BSCI, 2004). A majority of craftspeople and traditional producers work as family units (Jaitley, 2001) in their own homes or as apprentices to mastercraftspeople. However, the widespread poverty in the craft sector often means that these families do not have access to potable water or basic healthcare facilities. Efforts for a safe and healthy work environment also need to include these craftspeople/traditional producers, when they are suppliers to the company.

20. FAIR WAGES AND BENEFITS TO PRODUCERS

UNESCO defines a fair wage as that which recognizes the value of the work and is proportionate to the retail price received for the completed product. Large corporations which outsource production to the cheapest labor in *sweatshops* often do not pay workers a fair wage, despite increasing revenues, leading to economic and social unsustainability. Employees should receive at least the statutory minimum wage, required overtime supplements, paid leave, statutory contribution for social insurance funds (health insurance, accident insurance, etc.) and statutory maternity benefits (BSCI, 2007). The ILO advises at least 14 weeks of paid maternity leave for workers. The rate for overtime should not be less than 125% of the regular rate. Employees should be provided with written and transparent information on wages and terms of payment on employment, and a written pay slip indicating the amount in the official currency (BSCI, 2004). Wages should be paid regularly, as prescribed by law, under a collective agreement, or fixed by an arbitration award (ILO, 2017). With traditional socio-economic systems of exchange and subsistence breaking down, most traditional craftspeople now live hand to mouth, with wage parities and minor benefits (Jaitley, 2001). Fair wages should be paid to these self-employed craftspeople – who do not pay their family members a wage, and under-cost their own labor (Jaitley, 2005) – leading to depressed costing of products.

21. NO CHILD LABOR

The ILO website (2017) states, "Child labour perpetuates poverty across generations by keeping children of the poor out of school and limiting their prospects for upward social mobility." Thus, child labor damages both social sustainability and long-term economic sustainability. Children have long been involved in craft and industry production, generally, as part of the family unit, as apprentices and as hired labor between families and mastercraftspeople (Roy, 2001). The change from social contract to unregulated labor market happened when family-based production evolved into formalized workshops, which employed surplus labor, including child labour from impoverished zones (Roy, 2001). Thus, the fundamental difference in the two formats was the shift in context of the child laborer, from within the master-apprentice system as a student, to the child laborer as cheap and vulnerable labor (Roy, 2001). While the former situation helped the child-apprentices to acquire skills which would contribute to their social and economic sustainability, the latter preys on existing social and economic unsustainability of child laborers. To avoid such exploitation of children, it is essential to ensure that workers are above the statutory minimum age for employment, by checking their relevant documents (BSCI, 2004).

22. NO FORCED LABOR

The ILO defines forced labor as any type of work or service engaged in involuntarily, under some implied coercion or manifest threat of penalty or oppressive measure. There are many forms of forced labor, including debt bondage and sweatshop or farm workers forced to work through illegal tactics (ILO, 2017), all of which negatively impact social sustainability. Generally, victims of forced labor comprise vulnerable and marginalized groups such as women and migrants. Companies that do not indulge in forced labor allow employees to leave the factory premises after work, and return employees' original documents, such as identification cards, passports and birth certificates after hiring is complete (BSCI, 2004). Employees are also free of monetary deposits to the company, which could constitute bonded labor, which is a form of forced labor existing mainly in Asian and agricultural societies (Iftikar, 2012). The ILO also states that allowing employees to work more than 56 hours a week is also akin to forced labor.

23.   FAIR WORKING HOURS

Fair working hours are part of fair labor practices, and so positively impact social sustainability. Employees should not be compelled to work beyond the statutary number of working hours per week defined by national law. In general, the maximum working hours of the workforce should not exceed 48 hours of regular working time, plus 12 hours of overtime per week (BSCI, 2004). In addition to this, employees should be given one weekly holiday, i.e., one free day following six consecutive days of work (ILO, 2017). Every worker with one year's service should be entitled to three weeks of paid annual leave in addition to sick leave, casual leave and maternity/paternity leave (BSCI, 2004).

24.   FREEDOM OF ASSOCIATION AND COLLECTIVE BARGAINING

The right of workers and employers to freely form and join organizations of their choice is integral to social sustainability (ILO, 2017). Within the legal framework, employees should not need permission from their employers to join and take action in or form worker's organizations, including unions (BSCI, 2004). Representatives of worker's unions should have access to members in the workplace within the legal framework (BSCI, 2004). In addition to this, employees should be allowed to bargain collectively and complain anonymously in line with statutory legal regulations (BSCI, 2004).

25.   NO DISCRIMINATION

Discrimination against producers negatively impacts social and cultural sustainability. There should be no distinction, exclusion or preference (ILO, 2017a) in the areas of compensation (ILO, 2017b), benefits, hiring procedure, job assignment, retirement provisions, access to services, etc. (BSCI, 2004), based on age, caste, disability, ethnic ornational origin, gender, political affiliation, race, religion, sexual orientation, pregnancy or parenthood, social background, indigenousness, membership in workers' organizations including unions or other personal characteristics (ILO, 2017a). All employees should be treated with dignity and respect, and there should be no sexual harassment (BSCI, 2004).

26.   LOCAL EMPLOYMENT OPPORTUNITIES

Localized employment positively impacts social, cultural and economic sustainability. When employment is localized, the impacts of the PCS – including ecological, social, cultural and economic unsustainability – are apparent to local inhabitants who can act on them. This feedback loop makes systemic unsustainabilities – such as child labor or resource depletion – easier to detect and, therefore, to monitor and regulate (Thorpe, 2007).

Distribution considerations

Distribution considerations such as packaging, warehousing, promotional strategies and distribution systems impact the overall sustainability of a product's production-to-consumption system (Chitale & Gupta, 2007). The Holistic Sustainability Checklist proposes the following supplementary parameters towards sustainability.

27. MINIMUM PRODUCT VOLUME AND WEIGHT

A product which is light and compact after it is packaged needs less packaging material and less energy to transport it, thus positively impacting ecological sustainability. This, in turn, translates into reduced costs, facilitating economic sustainability. Nesting, knockdown, modular and folding products all have lower distribution volumes (Crul & Diehl, 2006). Products with good design and well worked out construction details can cancel the need for over-dimensioning, which would again mean reduced volume and weight (Crul & Diehl, 2006).

28. MINIMUM AND CLEAN TRANSPORT

While all forms of transport consume energy, some – such as trains and ships – are more ecologically sustainable because they optimize energy (Crul & Diehl, 2006). These modes should be preferred over transport by air or road as far as possible. Minimum transport saves energy and simultaneously cuts costs, thereby positively impacting both ecological and economic sustainability.

29. LOCAL PRODUCTION-TO-CONSUMPTION SYSTEMS

Local production and distribution systems are economically sustainable because they are simple, cost-effective and time-effective. When the locations of production and consumers are closer geographically, the need for complicated packaging and energy for transport, impacting ecological sustainability is reduced. The local PCS supports local livelihoods, and is therefore economically and socially sustainable as well.

30. MINIMUM PACKAGING

Packaging serves both a utilitarian and aesthetic purpose. It protects the product, making it easier to distribute, and increases the perceived value of the product, supporting the marketing function. Lean design achieves both ends, and can also indicate a returnable packaging system (Crul & Diehl, 2006). Another strategy is to minimize packaging or dispense with it altogether, thus positively impacting both ecological and economic sustainability. Distribution considerations such as packaging, warehousing, promotional strategies and distribution systems impact a product's sustainability (Crul & Diehl, 2006).

31. REUSABLE PACKAGING

Reusable packaging positively impacts ecological sustainability, since it reduces the amount of fresh material inputs required to make new packaging materials. By encouraging the user to reuse, it also positively impacts the culture of consumption and facilitates cultural sustainability. Bulk packaging for transport can be made reusable by tying it to strategies like a return system or a monetary deposit (Crul & Diehl, 2006).

32. RECYCLABLE PACKAGING

Packaging that is made from recyclable materials positively impacts both ecological and economic sustainability. The recyclability of the material translates into reduced pressure on Earth's resources. Since the packaging can be recycled into another product, it continues to have commercial value, making it economically sustainable, as well.

33. PACKAGING MADE FROM LOW-IMPACT MATERIALS

Materials that are organic, not highly toxic, which do not deplete the ozone layer, do not contain hydrocarbons or release harmful emissions, have a low impact on the environment. Packaging made from such low-impact materials positively impacts ecological sustainability.

Consumer user considerations

Consumer use considerations such as easy maintenance, reliability, safety and user friendliness (Chitale & Gupta, 2007) impact a product's sustainability. The Holistic Sustainability Checklist proposes the following supplementary parameters towards sustainability.

34. MINIMUM/CLEAN ENERGY CONSUMPTION DURING USAGE

Products whose usage requires minimal or no energy positively impact ecological and economic sustainability, as they translate into lower energy costs, and also have lower environmental impacts. Products should aim to use as little energy as possible while being used, and no energy when idle (Crul & Diehl, 2006). Factors like minimum weight if the product needs energy to move it and well insulated components help in lowering energy consumption during use (Crul & Diehl, 2006). Products should ideally use clean energy, sourced from harnessed wind, water and the sun, and low-sulphur energy sources such as natural gas and low-sulphur coal (Crul & Diehl, 2006). Built-in features can help advocate the culture of sustainable consumption and use. For example, a built-in battery charger (Crul & Diehl, 2006) can help promote the idea that disposable energy sources – such as batteries – need not be used. Products that require clean energy for their usage educate the consumer on sustainability, thus impacting the culture of consumption, and, in turn, cultural sustainability.

35.   MINIMUM CONSUMABLES

Products that use minimal consumables save materials and energy used to manufacture the consumables, thus aiding both ecological and economic sustainability. Consumables can be minimized by product semantics which direct usage; for example, calibration marks or measures that encourage the use of precise amounts of auxiliary materials (Crul & Diehl, 2006). Making the most sustainable state the default state – for example, a default overdrive setting in automatic transmission cars – helps efficient use of consumables as well (Crul & Diehl, 2006).

36.   SAFE-TO-USE PRODUCTS

Products that have no/minimal negative impact on the users' health (Crul & Diehl, 2006) and safety, positively impact social sustainability and the user's sense of well-being. Poorly designed products violate health and safety norms, and in some cases, even cause fatalities. For example, emissions from several common household products – such as those containing formaldehyde – can degrade indoor air quality.

37.   CUSTOMIZABLE

Customized products allow the user to avoid superfluous features, making the product cost-effective and positively impacting economic sustainability. Customization extends the life of the product (ecological sustainability), since it allows the user to be part of the innovation process, thereby creating a stronger user-product bond. This affects the culture of consumption, and thus positively impacts cultural sustainability.

38.   EASILY UPGRADABLE

Products which are easy to upgrade or repair have an extended product life, thus contributing to ecological sustainability. They also encourage the culture of sustainable consumption, contributing to cultural sustainability.

39.   CLASSIC DESIGN

The aesthetic life of classic products is at least as long as their technical life (Crul & Diehl, 2006). This extended life of the product positively impacts ecological sustainability. The classic design makes this sustainable product desirable to the consumer, thereby positively impacting cultural sustainability.

40. MINIMUM AND LOCAL MAINTENANCE AND REPAIR

Locally repairable and maintainable products positively impact the social, cultural, economic and ecological tenets of sustainability. They are ecological because they negate the necessity to buy a new product, and therefore reduce material flows. Since the repair network is local, the products needing to be repaired do not need to be transported over long distances, making it an energy-efficient system. The repair activity is a source of livelihood for local communities, thereby facilitating social sustainability. When the user repairs and maintains the product instead of discarding it, it contradicts the prevalent "use-and-throw" mindset (Taylor-Hough, 2011) and contributes to cultural sustainability.

End-of-life handling considerations

End-of-life handling considerations are often overlooked. The Holistic Sustainability Checklist proposes the following supplementary parameters towards sustainability.

41. REDUCED MATERIAL COMPLEXITY

Products made from a single material, or as few materials as possible, are easier to deal with in the end-of-life phase than composite products. While natural materials degrade, other materials such as technical nutrients can be recycled into another product life cycle, thus eliminating waste and positively impacting ecological sustainability.

42. BIODEGRADABLE

Biodegradable materials include those that can be broken down chemically using bacteria and other biological means. Products made from organic matter, or artificial materials that can be broken down by micro-organisms, positively impact ecological sustainability, since they do not damage the environment at the disposal stage.

43. EASY TO DISASSEMBLE

Most products are made from several components. If these components are dismantleable at the end of the product's life, each component can be treated differently. Some can be cleaned and/or repaired before being used as inputs into other products, whereas others may need to be disposed of. Making products easy to take apart reduces the burden of disposal, and inputs existing material into a fresh life cycle, thus impacting ecological sustainability in a positive manner. The disassembled parts can be repurposed or reused. They are not waste. They retain economic value in their new life cycles, thereby positively impacting economic sustainability as well. Products with easily accessible, standardized mechanical joineries which can be dismantled with universal tools allow for better disassembly than welded, glued or soldered connections (Crul & Diehl, 2006).

44. REUSABLE PRODUCTS

Products that are designed for reuse positively impact ecological sustainability, since they reduce the amount of fresh material inputs needed to make new products. They also help avoid down-cycling – the process of converting waste materials or useless products into new materials or products of lesser quality and reduced functionality. Products designed for reuse affect the culture of sustainable consumption by encouraging the user to reuse them, thus combating planned or perceived obsolescence. This, in turn, positively impacts cultural sustainability.

45. RECYCLABLE PRODUCTS

Recyclable products positively impact both ecological and economic sustainability. The recyclability of the material translates into reduced pressure on Earth's resources. Since the product material can be recycled into another product, it continues to have economic value, making it economically sustainable, as well. Products made from materials that facilitate primary recycling – where the recycled material goes back into the same product line – are better than those which need secondary recycling – where the material is used in some other end product – or tertiary recycling – where the material is broken down into its original constituents.Recyclable products need to be easy to disassemble, especially if they include toxic materials that need to be isolated (Crul & Diehl, 2006).

46. PROMOTES/USES LOCAL RECYCLING SYSTEMS

Most waste goes into landfills, while the remaining is recycled, composted or incinerated. Landfills are designed to isolate the waste from groundwater and air – so most waste in landfills does not decompose, making landfills a less-than-ideal waste-disposal solution. Products which can be easily sorted in local collection and recycling systems (Crul & Diehl, 2006) – such as by indicating recyclable components in the product, and making it easy to disassemble – reduce waste in landfills. These products impact all the tenets of sustainability. They provide livelihoods to communities that collect and sort the waste, thus enhancing economic and social sustainability. They also help safeguard the ecology, thus enhancing ecological sustainability. In addition, the culture of sorting and recycling waste impacts the culture of disposal, thus positively impacting cultural sustainability.

10.2   Design of the final iteration: certification

We finalized the design of the final iteration of the certification process – the Holistic Sustainability Assessment – based on the feedback we collected. In an ideal situation, each product should be separately assessed for sustainability. However, this may not be possible, especially in the initial start-up phase of labeling programs, when the requisite resources, support and infrastructure to implement the labeling scheme may not be in place. Therefore, the Holistic Sustainability Assessment system advocates that each country/sectoral institution decide for itself whether the assessment should be at the level of the product, company or sector, depending on existing logistical infrastructure.

Evaluators

Once the implementing agency decides the level at which to conduct the evaluation, a minimum of three evaluators will score the product/company/sector against the Holistic Sustainability Checklist. While the criteria for selecting an evaluator will vary in each context, it is suggested that they be chosen from reputed institutions to increase the legitimacy of the evaluation (Dendler, 2012). Institutions can also function as evaluators, and can delegate a member of their team to conduct the evaluation. It is recommended that the evaluators reflect the groupings of institutional subordinates, peers and supervisors in order to facilitate a well-rounded evaluation. This is in line with the idea of 360-degree feedback, where feedback comes from sources other than the traditional manager or supervisor. Including feedback from different nodes of the value chain and production-to-consumption system – including self-evaluation – helps to incorporate cross-cutting perspectives into the evaluation, and helps future performance. The goal of this approach is to improve future sustainability performance, alongside evaluating current performance.

Evaluation method

Each evaluator scores the product relative to the criteria outlined in each parameter. A score of 1 would indicate *low* or below average, 2 would indicate *medium* or average, and 3, *high* or demonstrably better. The final score per parameter will be the triangulated mean of the three grades. Scores from 0 to 1 will be considered low, from 1.1 to 2 will be considered medium, and from 2.1 to 3 will be considered high. This final score will be reflected in the ecological, social, cultural and economic sustainability that the parameter affects (Figure 10.3).

Take, for example, a scenario whereby a product is being evaluated against Parameter 1 – renewable materials – by evaluators A, B and C. Supposing the scores given by the three evaluators are 2, 2 and 3, respectively, the overall score for this parameter would be 2 + 2 + 3 divided by 3, so 7/3 or 2.33. If the same product is being evaluated against Parameter 2 – "minimally treated materials" – and evaluators A, B and C rate it 2, 3 and 3, respectively, the overall score for this

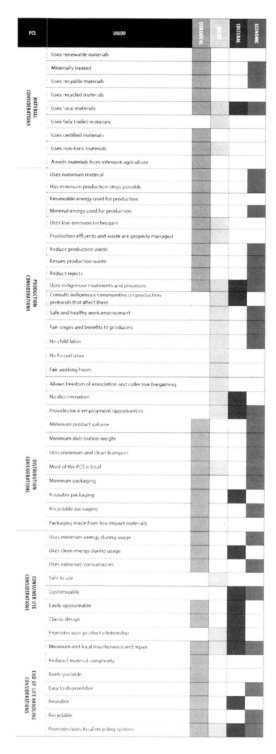

Figure 10.3 Depiction of the tenets that each parameter impacts

Source: Reubens, 2016 (c)

parameter will be 2 + 3 + 3 divided by 3, or 8/3, which is 2.67. The score for Parameter 1 will reflect in ecological sustainability, as this is the tenet it impacts. The score for Parameter 2, i.e., "minimally treated materials", will reflect in both ecological and economic sustainability as it impacts both of these tenets.

Scoring

Such a scoring system is mindful of the reality that meeting or not meeting criteria is often not a black or white absolute, and so works better than a basic minimum-requirement approach. The scoring system acknowledges that criteria can be met to varying degrees, and reflects both negative and positive aspects of meeting criteria. A negative score can motivate better performance, as low-score areas are communicated to both the consumer and the producer. Scoring also offers the possibility to strategically compensate for low scores in certain criteria with higher scores in other criteria (Scheer & Rubik, 2005). This reflects the reality of trade-offs between sustainability's social, cultural, economic and ecological aspects.

Benchmarks

This labeling scheme has been designed as a flexible framework, which can be adapted to several regions and countries. Labels such as that of Fair Trade and EU Eco-label have been criticized for their insufficient adaptability to local conditions, whereas labeling organizations such as the Marine Stewardship Council and EU Energy have been criticized for inconsistent interpretation of criteria (Dendler, 2012). Being mindful of these critiques – and considering that the system may be used in several developing countries with vastly different contexts and resources to implement this labeling – the Holistic Sustainability Assessment first defines cross-cutting and generic standards, and then goes on to describe the sustainable ideals and unsustainable practices clearly. It does so in a manner that is flexible enough to allow for regional and geographical variability in the interpretation and definition of these standards (Dendler, 2012). The scoring is therefore relative to outlined criteria in each parameter, described earlier in the Holistic Sustainability Checklist.

Stringency

While assessment should ideally be as stringent as possible, the method of scoring takes into account variations in infrastructure and resources, and hence allows the country/sectoral institution flexibility in terms of stringency. The respective country/sectoral institution can identify the criteria it deems non-negotiable, based on statutory legislation and international norms. Some parameters (including user safety, no child and/or forced labor) and statutory compliance measures (including proper disposal of effluents) may be scored more stringently than others due to their inherent non-negotiability. Some parameters which already have existing high standards may also be rated more stringently – for example, using recycled materials for a sector that can more easily use, and which does already routinely use, recycled materials such as the paper industry.

The stringency of evaluation should be increased at regular intervals based on reviews, as the labeling scheme becomes more mature, and those being assessed become more familiar and comfortable with the assessment procedure. This is in line with the ISO-Type I labels, which review and tighten their standards regularly (Dendler, 2012).

Minimum compliance criteria

Different labeling schemes prioritize different criteria. However, compliance with some criteria – such as user safety, no child and/or forced labor – and statutory compliance measures – such as proper disposal of effluents – are non-negotiable. Each country/sectoral institution will identify the criteria which are non-negotiable, based on statutory legislation and international norms. These criteria will comprise the minimum compliance criteria, and those products/organizations failing to comply with these may not be part of the labeling scheme until they meet these criteria.

Software

In line with the feedback from the respondents from the SPIN group in Vietnam and the Indian respondents who indicated that the checklist would be easier to use and implement if it were digital, we developed a web-based software for UNIDO, to make the Holistic Sustainability Assessment easy to implement. Its features support the creation of a database of companies, products, evaluators and evaluations. Thus, while evaluating a product or company, evaluators can be selected from the database based on their professional expertise or institutional profile.

The sustainability landscape of each sector is different, and therefore, the assessment mechanism needs to be mindful of this difference. This is why the software also allows customization of the master Holistic Sustainability Checklist by adding or deleting criteria. In addition, the weightage of each criterion can be customized. For example, "made from recycled materials" could be given very high importance in a checklist customized for the handmade paper or glass sector, but comparatively low for a sector which uses few processed natural materials such as sea grass. This is in line with the discussion on stringency and minimum compliance criteria in the subheadings above.

10.3   Communication: the Holistic Sustainability Label

Communicating the score in an easy-to-understand manner is central to the success of a labeling scheme. To ensure easy communication – especially when the audience ranges from household consumers to tourists to import companies – the best approach seems to be to condense the score into a single level of grading (Banerjee & Solomon, 2003; Truffer, Markard, & Wustenhagen, 2001). Such highly condensed information makes communication simple and clear; however, the lack of details also reduces the decision-making capacity of an informed audience (Teisl & Roe, 2005). We therefore tried to create a label with sufficient and still easy-to-understand information.

We explored various options to graphically represent the sustainability score. The final version – the four-ring Holistic Sustainability Graphic (Figure 10.4) – was shortlisted from amongst other options, based on feedback from stakeholders across the value chain, and questionnaires randomly administered to visitors at UNIDO's booth at the LifeStyle Vietnam fair in 2013. Considering that the right amount of information needs to be communicated simply, the Holistic Sustainability Label shows four sub-level grades – one each for the ecological, social, cultural and economic aspects. These scores are then communicated through a single Holistic Sustainability Graphic that encompasses the four sub-level scores. The four sub-level grades are aggregated into a single holistic sustainability grading, indicated by the stars.

The final Holistic Sustainability Label communicates the scoring through an easy-to-understand graphic, supported by a legend. The design elements which comprise the label are elaborated upon below.

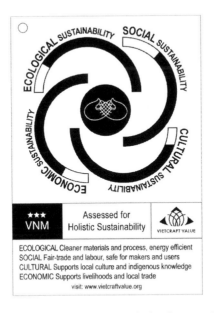

Figure 10.4 The Holistic Sustainability Label with the four-ring Holistic Sustainability Graphic

Source: Reubens, 2013b

The four-ring Holistic Sustainability Graphic

The final graphic comprises four rings, each of which represents one of the tenets of sustainability. The rings are interlinked, to represent the complete and cohesive system formed by the ecological, social, cultural and economic tenets of society. The rings were chosen over linear elements to represent the holistic, 360-degree circular ethos of the assessment and labeling system.

Each ring functions as a *meter* (Figure 10.5) to communicate the single-level grade of the social, ecological, economic and cultural tenet of sustainability. The rings in the actual label are color-coded to enable easy and intuitive understanding of the tenet they represent (House of Commons Environmental Audit Committee, 2009). The ring for ecological sustainability is green, the one for economic sustainability is blue, the ring for social sustainability is brown and the one for cultural sustainability is yellow. In addition to color, the tenet each ring represents is clearly communicated by text – *ecological sustainability, social sustainability, cultural sustainability, economic sustainability* – placed around the ring.

Sector icon

At the center of the four rings is a circle containing an icon, representing the sector domain of the Holistic Sustainability Label. Since the labeling scheme is for the handicraft sector, the icon has two hands intertwined to represent the handicraft sector. The Holistic Sustainability Label was designed to be extendable to sectors other than handicrafts. In each case, relevant icons for that sector will replace the handicraft-sector icon.

Country code

Since this labeling scheme is designed to be extended to different geographies and regions, a country code – consisting of the key letters in the country name – was included below the star rating. This was also necessary because as discussed earlier, the level of stringency of assessment may differ from country to country, so the country in which the labeling scheme is being implemented needs to be

Figure 10.5 Each ring functions as a meter depicting 0% sustainability (left), 50% sustainability (center) and 100% sustainability (right)

clearly communicated on the label. The three-letter country codes used in the label allow for easy visual communication of names of countries. It is recommended that the country codes used are as defined in ISO 3166–1 standardized by the International Organization for Standardization 3166 Maintenance Agency (ISO 3166/MA) (ISO, n.d.).

Legend

A legend included at the bottom of the graphic uses keywords to clearly communicate the key areas covered by the four rings. These keywords were arrived at by choosing phrases that are popularly used in sustainability frameworks, including in educational and marketing frameworks. Using keywords that are easily understandable and that have an association with other common frameworks, increases the legitimacy of each sub-grade.

10.4 Summary and conclusions

The last chapter talked about how we began to develop the Holistic Sustainability System based on the feedback received from different focusgroups and individuals, against the backdrop of UNIDO's Branding Initiative in Vietnam. This chapter offered the final iteration of our design, known as the Holistic Sustainability System, which would work as the mechanism to support and encourage the use and operationalization of the Rhizome Approach and its constituents. The Holistic Sustainability System includes the Holistic Sustainability Checklist and the Holistic Sustainability Label as tangible outputs. We examine the criteria included in the Holistic Sustainability Checklist in comparison to the frameworks on which it draws in Figure 10.6.

Various options were explored for the graphic representation of the Holistic Sustainability Label and the Holistic Sustainability Checklist. These were evaluated through discussions with stakeholders in Vietnam, and also through the feedback of visitors at UNIDO's booth at the LifeStyle Vietnam fair.

The Holistic Sustainability System we developed for UNIDO's branding and labeling initiative leveraged the additional time and cost investment in a holistic sustainability-aligned design process as value-addition and product differentiation. The outputs of the Holistic Sustainability Checklist were quantified and communicated, thus legitimizing sustainability efforts as credentials. Both of these showed how the investment in sustainability is worthwhile for companies, thus creating a pull for designers to practice sustainability holistically by using the Rhizome Approach.

UNIDO's beneficiary, Vietcraft, was selected to operationalize the Holistic Sustainability System by the Vietnamese Ministry of Industry and Commerce in August 2015. The system is online on their website (Vietcraft Excellence, 2015) which indicates that the Holistic Sustainability System and the branding and labeling scheme were well received by the Vietnamese handicraft sector, which is representative of handicraft sector MSMEs in developing countries. Additional

	D4S	BSCI	ILO
MATERIAL CONSIDERATIONS			
1 Renewable materials	•		
2 Minimally treated materials	•		
3 Recyclable materials	•		
4 Recycled materials	•		
5 Local materials	•		
6 Fairly traded materials	•		•
7 Ecologically certified materials	•		
8 Non-toxic materials	•		•
9 Less/no materials from intensive agriculture	•		
PRODUCTION CONSIDERATIONS			
10 Minimum materials	•		
11 Minimum production steps	•		
12 Renewable energy for production	•		
13 Minimal energy for production	•		
14 Low-emission techniques	•		•
15 Proper management of production effluents and waste	•		
16 Reduce/reuse production waste	•		
17 Indigenous treatments and processes			
18 Consulting indigenous communities on production issues that affect them			•
19 Safe and healthy work environment	•	•	•
20 Fair wages and benefits to producers		•	•
21 No child labor		•	•
22 No forced labor		•	•
23 Fair working hours		•	•
24 Freedom of association and collective bargaining		•	•
25 No discrimination		•	•
26 Local employment opportunities	•		
DISTRIBUTION CONSIDERATIONS			
27 Minimum product volume and weight	•		
28 Minimum and clean transport	•		
29 Local PCS	•		
30 Minimum packaging	•		
31 Reusable packaging	•		
32 Recyclable packaging			
33 Packaging made from low-impact materials			
CONSUMER USE CONSIDERATIONS			
34 Minimum/clean energy during usage	•		
35 Minimum consumables	•		
36 Safe to use	•		
37 Customizable	•		
38 Easily upgradable	•		
39 Classic design	•		
40 Minimum and local maintenance and repair	•		
END-OF-LIFE HANDLING CONSIDERATIONS			
41 Reduced material complexity	•		
42 Biodegradable	•		
43 Easy to disassemble	•		
44 Reusable	•		
45 Recyclable	•		
46 Promotes/uses local recycling systems	•		

Figure 10.6 Criteria covered by the Holistic Sustainability Checklist vis-à-vis those from the frameworks it draws on

validation for the efficacy of the Holistic Sustainability System are that two other institutions working with handicraft MSMEs in Vietnam – the Sustainable Product Innovation (SPIN) Project and the Centre for Promotion of Imports from Developing Countries (CBI) – also showed interest in it. Of this, SPIN used the Holistic Sustainability Assessment, including the Holistic Sustainability Checklist, for its assessments (Jin, 2015). It was heartening to learn that Shauna Jin, a Ph.D. researcher at Delft University of Technology, linked to the SPIN project, adapted and used the Holistic Sustainability Assessment to evaluate the outcome of her collaborative design project for Vietnamese MSMEs. This indicates that our intention that this system can be tweaked and adapted to different contexts, thereby being a map and not a tracing, was realized. Overall, the interest in the Holistic Sustainability System, and the usage into which it has translated, indicates that it is applicable to the larger client-class. Further observations and conclusions on the Holistic Sustainability System are offered in the following, final chapter of this book.

11   Insights and conclusions

11.1   Background

This final chapter offers insights and conclusions towards reflectively and coherently tying together the pertinent learning that emerged in the preceding chapters. We started this book with the assumption that design for and in developing countries can be instrumental in realizing development that is holistically sustainable – which looks not only at ecological and economic aspects, but also social and cultural aspects. This is especially so in the case of design for and with MSMEs in developing countries which work with renewable materials – such as bamboo, cork and hemp. These materials are abundantly available in the developing world, and can potentially be a viable and sustainable resource base; their processing can provide employment to some part of the developing world's huge labor force. The resultant products can leverage growing sustainability-aligned markets around the world, which are increasingly looking beyond ecological considerations to a wider spectrum of sustainability criteria (Potts et al., 2010). The spin-offs from the production of these products in the developing world – including employment generation and the resultant income security, poverty reduction, food security, access to healthcare and education – can create a holistically sustainable counter trajectory to the currently unsustainable development of the developing world.

There has been a steady emergence of *green* products, which address the ecological dimension of sustainability, in response to the global market demand for sustainable products and systems (Potts et al., 2010). The material sourcing and production of these products are often done in the developing world, where renewable materials are abundant and the cost of production is low. Often, the designers of these aforementioned *green* products recontextualize renewable material through industrial techniques and technologies, resulting in ecologically sustainable products with commercial viability. However, a narrow ecological and economic design focus (Reubens, 2013a) keeps these products from being the basis for production-to-consumption systems that address a compound picture of sustainability. This picture would include the social and cultural dimensions – both of which are very important for developing countries, reeling under the issues of poverty, unemployment and increasing consumption.

Most renewable materials in the developing world are already part of languishing craft production-to-consumption systems, whose decline causes unsustainability at several levels. The lack of economic or productive skills, assets and options has led craftspeople to distress migrate to urban areas in search of wage labor (Society for Rural, Urban and Tribal Initiatives, 1995). This distress migration, together with unprecedented urbanization (Akubue, 2000; Craft Revival Trust, 2006) causes: a) tremendous socio-economic unsustainability, and b) the loss of cultural capital due to vanishing crafts. If designers were to build upon traditional production-to-consumption systems – by leveraging the craft and all it encompasses for their designs – they could create products whose production-to-consumption systems that address sustainability in a holistic manner. They would be made from renewable materials (ecologically sustainable), crafted in a labor-intensive manner (socially sustainable), build on craft traditions and indigenous knowledge (culturally sustainable) and target viable sustainability-aligned markets (economically sustainable).

In order to address the many layers of sustainability in the context of developing countries, design needs to facilitate production-to-consumption systems that are underpinned by technologies which have a high potential for employment, are not capital intensive and are highly adaptable to social and cultural environments (Jequier & Blanc, 1983). To do this, design needs to challenge mainstream, technology intensive, industrial design approaches, which do not address the concept of sustainability in a holistic manner (Maxwell et al., 2003). This is easier said than done, as the design-industrialization bond is deeply rooted; the discipline of design emerged as a result of the process of industrialization, and therefore inherently aligns to industrial logic and philosophies. This book, therefore, focuses on the relatively unexplored area of alternatives to mainstream design approaches (Maxwell et al., 2003)

Mapping the intersection of craft, design and sustainability

We constructed a diagram (Figure 11.1) to illustrate the different components of the scenario previously discussed – including existing and tentatively proposed actors, causal chains and directions. Juxtaposing these components created a systems picture which illustrated the complexity of the sustainabilitydesign scenario – especially vis-à-vis craft-based MSMEs in developing countries.

Narrative explanation of diagram

1 Sustainability is depicted on top of production-to-consumption systems, representing the fact that sustainability rests on production-to-consumption systems.
2 The diagram also depicts the four tenets – ecological, economic, cultural and social – outlined in our construct of holistic sustainability.
3 In order to convey that the tenets of sustainability – though depicted separately for visual coherence in Figure 11.1 – are interlinked and inseparable, we have circumscribed a square with diagonals within the sustainability circle.

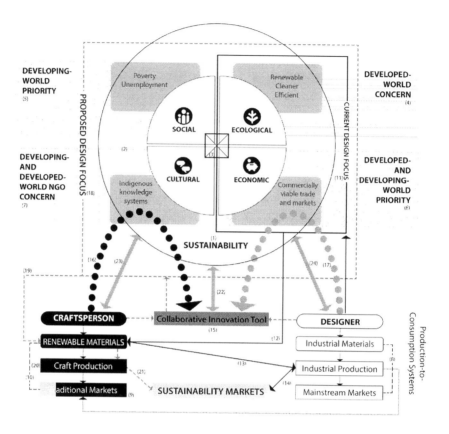

Figure 11.1 Diagrammatic representation of the existing and proposed design focus in the developing world with regards to craft, design and sustainability

Source: Reubens, 2019

4   The developed world is concerned with the ecological aspect of sustainability, which it prioritizes for global action – including through the use of renewable materials, and cleaner and more efficient production-to-consumption systems.

5   The developing world prioritizes socio-economic issues, such as poverty and unemployment, over ecological issues.

6   Economic development takes precedence in both the developed and developing worlds.

7   The issue of cultural sustainability has only recently been highlighted by not-for-profit organizations, development-sector institutions and scholars. However, it has received comparatively less attention than the other tenets, in the agendas of both developed and developing countries.

Black dotted lines and arrows: The black dotted lines and arrows in the bottom half of Figure 11.1 represent existing production-to-consumption chains.

8   A generic industrial production-to-consumption system includes design by a designer, and the industrial processing of industrial materials, the output of which is sold in mainstream markets.

9   Industrial products have penetrated and captured a substantial share of the traditional market segment – as indicated by the darker color in the tra-ditionalmarkets box; simultaneously, the market share of craft products in traditional markets is shrinking – as depicted by the lighter color.

10 A generic craft production-to-consumption system includes design by a craftsperson, the use of renewable materials (in most cases), which are crafted – generally in a labor-intensive manner; the resulting products are sold in traditional markets.

Black lines and arrows: The black lines and arrows in Figure 11.1 represent existing scenarios and causal production-to-consumption chains orchestrated by design efforts towards facilitating sustainability.

11 Current design efforts towards sustainability focus predominantly on the ecological and economic aspects of sustainability.

12 Sustainable-design efforts include leveraging renewable materials that are traditionally used in non-industrial value chains.

13 These renewable materials are industrially processed.

14 Finally, they are pushed into emerging markets for sustainable products and systems.

Gray dashed lines and arrows: The gray dashed lines and arrows in Figure 11.1 rep-resent our expected and proposed scenarios and causal chains, orchestrated by design efforts towards sustainability.

15 We propose collaborative innovation which will leverage both design and craft expertise.

16 The craftsperson will bring expertise on the indigenous knowledge systems repositoried in craft to the collaboration.

17 The designer will bring expertise on commercially viable markets and trade to the collaboration.

18 The joint inputs of the craftsperson and the designer will lead to collabora-tive innovation, whose focus will be on a holistic picture of sustainability – including its ecological, economic, cultural and social aspects.

19 We propose to use renewable materials, traditionally used in non-industrial value chains, for these collaborations.

20 MSMEs will process these renewable materials in labor-intensive craft set-ups.

21 Finally, the holistically sustainable products will be marketed in emerging segments which demand and desire sustainable products and systems.

Broad gray arrows: The broad gray arrows in Figure 11.1 represent our expected outcome vis-à-vis holistic sustainability.

22 The proposed collaborative innovation tool will holistically impact all of the dimensions of sustainability, and will be informed by all of sustainability's dimensions.
23 Craftspeople will be better equipped to sustain their livelihoods and lives, and will thereby be better positioned to affect sustainability positively; the poor are both victims and agents of unsustainability.
24 Designers will be better equipped to address sustainability holistically; their designs will be better informed by a holistic picture of sustainability.

Our inquiry

We decided to explore alternatives to mainstream design approaches against the background of the scenario represented in (Figure 11.1). We asked:What could be a possible sustainability design approach that is: a) mindful of the pros and cons of the existing sustainability design approaches, and b) which looks at addressing a holistic picture of sustainability – including its ecological, social, economic and cultural dimensions – in the context of non-industrial craft-based MSMEs working with renewable materials in developing countries? In order to avoid presupposing that existing design approaches do not address sustainability holistically in the context we defined, we decided to explore literature which could throw light on the extent to which design addresses sustainability in a holistic manner. We acknowledge that design approaches do not work in vacuum, and simply providing a mechanism will likely not bring about the change we envisaged. In order to be useful, the mechanism needs to be used; therefore, we asked: what mechanisms would support and encourage the use and operationalization of a holistic sustainabilitydesign approach that might be identified or developed?

We had some expectations of what findings our inquiry would potentially achieve. These propositions are outlined in Figure 11.2.

We proposed that the output of our inquiry would:

Proposition 1: Provide direction to the means and ends of design-craft collaboration, aimed at facilitating the development of holistically sustainable products and production-to-consumption systems.
Proposition 2: Provide a methodology towards collaborative innovation.
Proposition 3: Facilitate designers' access to sustainable-design knowledge and greater clarity on the holistic impact of design decisions on sustainability.
Proposition 4: Allow for a holistic assessment of design decisions' impacts on sustainability, including at the front-end innovation stage.
Proposition 5: Function as a driver for sustainability design and marketing; and for craft-based MSMEs to remain on the sustainability track

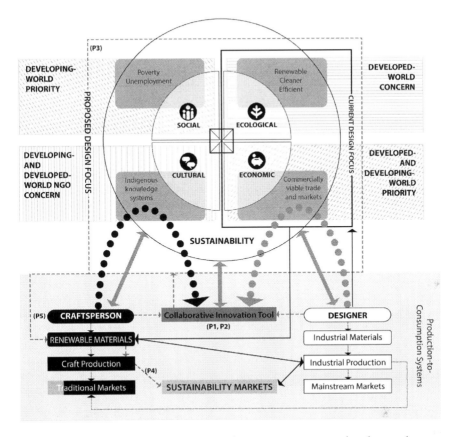

Figure 11.2 Diagrammatic representation of our propositions on the change that our inquiry could potentially effect

Source: Reubens, 2019

11.2 Main conclusions

Our main conclusions are as follows.

There is no single understanding of sustainability

The concept of *holistic sustainability* is a key underpinning of this book. We argue that *holistic* is a pleonasm for sustainability; sustainability is inherently a holistic construct which includes the sum of all of its conceptual sub-sets including ecological sustainability, social sustainability, cultural sustainability and economic sustainability. *Sustainability* has no single commonly accepted definition; there have been several interpretations of this concept, given that human understanding of sustainability and its dimensions is expanding (Mann, 2011). Over time, the social (people), ecological (planet) and economic (profit) dimensions of sustainability have been supplemented by culture as a vital tenet (Duxbury & Gillette, 2007).

In order to anchor our inquiry, we defined sustainability in Chapter 2 as:

> A continual process of actualizing "the possibility that humans and other life will flourish on the Earth forever" (Ehrenfeld, 2008, p. 49) by maintaining the balance between different dimensions, including ecological, cultural, social and economic ones.

Our broad-based, inclusive and holistic definition of sustainability is underpinned by the Four Pillars model of sustainability, because its ecological, social, cultural and economic pillars encompass the broad themes contained in current and emerging discussions on holistic sustainability. The Four Pillars are also congruent with the set of 17 UN Sustainable Development Goals, which outline the need for sustainable development to be holistic and balanced (Le Blanc et al., 2012).

Sustainability rests on sustainable development

In order to understand where, when and how the sustainability problem began, we attempted to trace the beginning of unsustainability through literature (Chapter 2). We found that while the beginning of unsustainability is commonly traced back to the industrial revolution, the conditions for the industrial revolution's full-blown *take-off* (Rostow, 1960) were created over the course of human development, and by the production-to-consumption systems that underpinned this process. The current state of unsustainability cannot therefore be attributed to the industrial revolution, or any isolated phenomenon (Rostow, 1960). It is the cumulative result of the development process. Development resulted in secure production-to-consumption systems, which resulted in population growth, which called for more resources and which, in turn, prompted more development (Nkechinyere, 2010). Thus, through the ages, development has been both the cause and effect of incremental development, and simultaneous incremental unsustainability.

Each production-to-consumption system that emerged and evolved over the development process had significant direct and indirect impact on the world and its systems. The tiniest change in each production-to-consumption system affected each of the world's complex, interlinked and dynamic systems to differing degrees. Sustainability – or the lack thereof, i.e., unsustainability – is, therefore, the emergent property of the collective production-to-consumption systems that underpin development (Nkechinyere, 2010). This interconnectedness points to the fact that efforts to cultivate and maintain sustainable development must rest on a holistic concept of sustainability, which is mindful of multiple dimensions. This sentiment has been reiterated through different global forums and platforms, including the recent UN Sustainable Development Goals that outline the need for sustainable development to address all of sustainability's dimensions and their interlinkages in a balanced manner (Le Blanc et al., 2012).

Design shapes development by shaping the production-to-consumption systems which underpin it

Design – "the act of deliberately moving from an existing situation to a preferred one by professional designers or others applying design knowingly or unknowingly" (Fuad-Luke, 2009, p. 5) – shapes production-to-consumption systems and, thereby, sustainability (Section 3.2). Design decisions orchestrate production-to-consumption systems, including material production and processing, fabrication, distribution, use, repair and maintenance, and end-of-life handling (Waage, 2005) – and thereby determine the flow of materials and human resources (White et al., 2008). Production-to-consumption systems in part and in whole, and their collateral effects – including environmental, social (White et al., 2008) and cultural spin-offs – shape sustainability. The possibility of shaping production-to-consumption systems towards sustainability, challenges designers to create a counter-narrative (Fuad-Luke, 2009) that seeks to proactively actualize holistic sustainability; it calls for designers to step out from their traditionally values-agnostic orientation (White et al., 2008) into the role of an activist (Thorpe, 2007). This possibility is more realizable than ever before, since the increasing scope, role and power of designers positions them as key players in strategic decisions which determine production-to-consumption systems, and thereby sustainability, around the world (British Design Council, 2004; Swedish Design Industry, 2004).

Design does not currently address sustainability in a holistic manner

In order to understand the extent to which design addresses sustainability holistically, we looked at two aspects: a) design practice (Section 3.5), and b) the existing approaches and assessment methods which position themselves as sustainability-aligned, and whose frameworks and tools provide scaffolding for designers working towards sustainability (Section 3.4).

Our investigation into sustainability practice revealed that the interest in sustainability and sustainable design (Fuad-Luke, 2009) has not translated into frequent practice by designers in either developed (Aye, 2003; Kang et al., 2008; Kang & Guerin, 2009; Mate, 2006) or developing countries (Hankinson & Breytenbach, 2012). The approaches and assessment systems we studied prioritized the economic and ecological aspects of sustainability – with the exception of BoP and SLCS, which prioritized the social dimension. None looked at sustainability in a holistic manner. However, the fact that the newer and hybridized frameworks and assessment systems, including D4S, LCSA and EVR, increasingly recognize and attempt to address multiple factors, despite retaining their economic and ecological precedence, confirms the need and gap for a holistic sustainability approach and assessment system.

Craft-design collaborations can address sustainability – but currently do not

We studied the decline of flourishing craft production-to-consumption systems in the developing world, first due to the industrial revolution – which created low-cost, high-volume industrialized goods – and the subsequent information revolution which facilitated their penetration into previously inaccessible markets and, more importantly, into the psyche of consumers (Section 4.1). Over the past few decades, craftspeople in developing countries have found themselves disconnected from their consumers, unable to cater to distant markets and, therefore, with no takers for their products (Jaitley, 2001). Several crafts have vanished or are declining (Jaitley, 2001), and the low-cost craft available comes with hidden costs – including environmental degradation, unsafe and unhealthy working conditions, and unfair wages (Chotiratanapinun, 2013).

We also outlined the opportunity that the information revolution offers to craftspeople to dovetail with its growing *knowledge class* (Humbert, 2007). The information revolution replaces capital and labor – the key factors of production of the industrial revolution – with knowledge and information (Humbert, 2007). This creates a new development paradigm that links the economy and culture; and acknowledges that creativity, knowledge and access to information are powerful engines for economic growth and development in a globalizing world (United Nations Conference on Trade and Development, 2008). If craft dovetails with the creative economy, it can flourish. If not – if craft's indigenous knowledge is not recognized or leveraged, the perilous situation of craftspeople will grow even more untenable, due to their lack of formal education and formalized knowledge (Bhaduri, 2016).

Craft offers a potential platform to address sustainability (Section 4.2), especially in our context of developing-country MSMEs working with renewable materials, because many overarching concepts of sustainability – for instance, environmental responsibility, social justice, cultural diversity and economic inclusion (Borges, 2013) – underpin craft practice (Rees, 1997). Craft has a huge potential to contribute to sustainable development in developing countries. It is labor-intensive, it comprises a substantial part of the economic fabric of developing countries, and it has the potential to dovetail with the information revolution's knowledge and creative economy, to access new and lucrative sustainability-aligned markets. For these reasons, it provides developing countries with the opportunity to potentially side-step the generic development paradigm, provided it can dovetail with the innovation-led, value-added and manufacturing-oriented paradigm, through design inputs.

There has been a surge of interest in craft over the past 15 years (Ferris, 2009) from the developed world and urban areas in the developing world. Consumers in these segments have higher incomes which allow them to look beyond meeting basic needs to purchasing differentiated hand-crafted products with an ethnic identity (United Nations Development Organization, 2002). Both of these parallel realities – the decline of rural craft markets and the growth of urban ones – indicate the need and potential to reposition the place, purpose and relevance of craft in post-industrial societies (Ferris, 2009). Recent academic discourse (Plymouth College of Art, n.d.) touches upon the need to reposition craft more closely with contemporary economic, social, cultural and ecological needs, including sustainability concerns.

Most traditional craftspeople are unable to access these lucrative markets for sustainable products (Potts et al., 2010), because of the information gap.

> While the "know-how" (how to make things – knowledge and skills) exists abundantly in the traditional crafts sector, there is a severe shortfall in the "know-what" (what to make – strategies and designs) that curtails the ability of crafts communities to survive intense competition or, better still, develop value-added solutions in the complex economic and social matrix in which they exist.
>
> (Panchal & Ranjan, 1993, p. 14).

A synergistic collaboration between craft and design that centers on innovation, responding to contemporary needs, and sustainability issues seems to offer a way forward (Greenlees, 2013).

The prevailing design-craft interactions which we studied (Section 4.4) leave craftspeople very vulnerable because they lack an equal exchange, continuity and respect for the local culture (Intellect, n.d.). Our literature review revealed several examples of top-down designer-led approaches in the craft sector, which failed to contribute to sustainability's social tenet – including the sustainability of craft communities, in terms of their income or social status (Frater, 2009). Some of these interactions were criticized for eroding the cultural capital of communities (Frater, 2009), and the ecological dimension was not addressed in most of the interactions. We concluded that there is a paucity of models where craft capital has been successfully leveraged through craft-design collaborations, towards tapping sustainability markets, and thus influencing sustainable development. This points to an urgent need for mechanisms which can actualize craft's potential for value-added manufacturing, within the context of sustainability and sustainable development (Greenlees, 2013).

Design for and with developing-country MSMEs does not currently address sustainability holistically

Our first question asked whether design addresses sustainability holistically – considering simultaneously all of its dimensions, including social, economic, ecological and cultural ones – while working with non-industrial craft-based MSMEs working with renewable materials in developing countries. Our study of literature answers this question: Existing sustainability design approaches and assessment systems, practice and craft-design interactions in the developing-country context do not currently address sustainability holistically. Existing sustainability design praxis in general focuses on the ecological and economic dimensions. However, encouragingly, it appears to be expanding its purview to encompass social and cultural dimensions. In the case of craft-based MSMEs, the design focus and impact seem to be primarily on the economic dimension. Although social and cultural priorities are cited, the extent to which they have been achieved and the means of achieving them are questionable. Existing design practice does not contain examples whereby design, craft and sustainability have been successfully harnessed together for holistic sustainability. Emerging scholarship and discourse is beginning to recognize design's potential and intention to position craft as a methodological framework (Ferris, 2009), through which to impact and leverage social, economic, cultural and economic sustainability (Borges, 2013). However, this potential is yet to be realized, and the proposed means to realize this are few and far between.

The Rhizome Approach builds on existing sustainability approaches and addresses sustainability holistically for design for and with developing-country MSMEs

The answer to our first question pointed to the need to develop a sustainability design approach which addressed sustainability holistically in our problem context. We developed the seven-step Rhizome Approach (Section 6.2) and the mechanisms to operationalize it – including the Rhizome Framework and the Sustainability Checklist – based on seven recurrent themes in literature with regards to the barriers to sustainable-design practice (Section 3.5). The barriers to sustainability design, the corresponding steps of the Rhizome Approach and the proposed methods to actualize these steps are depicted in Figure 11.3.

We tested whether the Rhizome Approach helped designers to address sustainability in a more holistic manner through their designs. The platform for this was the Bamboo Space Making Craft Workshop (Chapter 7) held in India in 2011, which involved the creation of sustainable bamboo products through a craft-design collaboration between 24 Indian designers and 24 Kotwalia craftspeople (who represented the overall client-class). At the end of the 15-day workshop, each designer-craftsperson team designed and developed a working prototype which was evaluated by three experts. While each of the sub-mechanisms of the Rhizome Approach and all of its seven steps were well received by the workshop participants, the Sustainability Checklist (Chapter 6) received a high level of interest from the participants, both as the basis of a design and as an evaluation tool. A majority of participants also indicated they would use it in the future in their sustainable-design practice.

The potential transferability of these findings was assessed through the feedback of two groups who represented the client-class: a) Vietnamese MSMEs, and b) designers around the world (Chapter 8). The positive findings from these exercises indicated the answer to our second question: The Rhizome Approach addresses

Step	Barrier	Aim	Method
1	Lack of knowledge about sustainability	Inform designers about sustainability, and the connections between its tenets	Provision of background reading material covering the connections between sustainability, design, material and the production-to-consumption system
2	Lack of a holistic overview of the production-to-consumption system	Sensitize designers to the systemic production-to-consumption system	Exposure visits to stakeholders of the different nodes of the value chain and production-to-consumption system
3	Failure to include sustainability at a strategic level in the overall approach	Factor sustainability into the strategic blueprint of the enterprise	Introducing a blueprint, towards which all the participants of the collaborative design process will work together collectively
4	Failure to include sustainability criteria in the design brief	Articulate sustainability criteria in the design brief so that it can be factored into the front-end design phase	Clear brief supplemented by the Sustainability Checklist to clarify desired design and their impact on each tenet of sustainability
5	Lack of a collaborative design process	Provide inputs from different stakeholders towards a collaborative design process	Constant linkage and interaction with stakeholders of the production-to-consumption system during the design process
6	Lack of tools to measure holistic sustainability against indicators	Increase designers' accountability to factor sustainability into their designs and provide a tool to measure the sustainability achieved	Evaluation of the design against the Sustainability Checklist by the designer and two external evaluators
7	Failure to keep the design team in the loop during product actualization	Keep designers in the loop until final product actualization thereby retaining their responsibility for the product's sustainability	Involving the design team in all iterations of the design, up to final product actualization

Figure 11.3 Overview of the Rhizome Approach

Source: Reubens, 2019

sustainability holistically in the context of non-industrial craft-based MSMEs working with renewable materials in developing countries, and it is mindful of the pros and cons of existing sustainability design approaches.

Designers can lead the change, but they need to be supported

Just because tools which aim to address sustainability – such as the Rhizome Approach – exist, it does not automatically mean that sustainability factors will be integrated into the product-development process (Huulgaard, 2015). Designers need support to navigate, and thereby be able to impact, the complex and interlinked levels of society (Jørgensen, 2012). The immediate outside envelope which impacts designers' practice of sustainability design, and from where support needs to come, is the company or organizational framework within which the designer works. Most organizations resist investing in sustainability design because, while the company pays to develop the innovation, the fruits of this investment are also leveraged by their competitors, especially if the know-how is easily accessible and if the eco-innovation is for the public good (Beise & Rennings, 2005). This reality is felt keenly by the MSME sector, whose low-tech processes, protocols and innovations are relatively easy to copy, and who do not have deep pockets and therefore need to capitalize upon all of the investments they make – including those for sustainability. Mechanisms that create push-and-pull effects – including through regulation (Rennings, 2000) – can play a vital role in encouraging companies to remain on the sustainability track. This led to our third question, which centers on mechanisms which can support and encourage the use and operationalization of the Rhizome Approach, and its constituents.

Existing regulatory mechanisms do not resonate with our domain

We found four main types of mechanisms – hard-regulation instruments, soft-regulation instruments, economic instruments and communicative instruments – which keep companies on the sustainability track (Section 9.2). Hard regulation and economic regulation are not suited for developing-world situations, which lack some of the key elements for regulatory instruments to function – including accurate monitoring, a working legal system and transparency (Bell & Russel, 2002). The driver for the developing-world MSMEs in our problem-class to invest in sustainability design is therefore, in most cases, not existing legislation or financial incentives, but the market. The instruments which create a market pull are communicative and soft-regulation instruments.

We reviewed different types of soft-regulation and communicative instruments (Laurell, 2014), and selected labeling from among these, because it consists of three basic steps: a) standard-setting, b) certification, and c) communicating the results of the assessment (Cassell & Symon, 2006). These steps allow it to span the categories of both communicative and soft-regulation instruments and the range between hard command-and-control regulation and soft voluntary self-regulation depending on the strictness of the implementation. Labeling is a third-generation regulatory instrument, which promotes cooperative state-business relationships (Clinton, 1995) because, instead of punishing wrong-doers, it encourages top performers (Mil-Homens Loureio, 2011). Labeling targets the planning stage (Coglianese & Lazer, 2003), in line with our argument for front-end innovation which factors in larger sustainability goals (3.2).

Currently, there are estimated to be more than 400 sustainability-aligned certification and labeling schemes spanning almost every category of consumer products, and this number is projected to be increasing rapidly (Stewart, 2010). We reviewed some of the most recognizable of these (Stewart, 2010) to check if they could provide an answer to our third question. We found that most sustainability labeling schemes seem to focus on environmental or social aspects (Frankl et al., 2005). Schemes which integrate the ecological, social and economic dimensions of sustainability and social metrics are rare (Seuring & Muller, 2008) and we couldn't find any schemes which also included the cultural dimension.

A scheme focusing on holistic sustainability is very important to showcase the achievements of the handicraft sector, which impacts all four dimensions significantly. Therefore, we proceeded to develop a labeling scheme and the mechanisms to underpin it, through a second cycle of design and development.

The Holistic Sustainability System can support and encourage the use and operationalization of the Rhizome Approach

We developed our Sustainability Checklist and evaluation system into the Holistic Sustainability System in a real-time scenario – UNIDO's branding and labeling initiative for Vietnamese handicraft MSMEs – through a participatory and iterative design process (Chapter 9). We solicited feedback from two Vietnamese groups (Section 9.4) – a) officials and representatives, and b) value-chain actors – to develop the system and also ran the final version by a third group of actors from the Vietnamese handicraft-sectorvalue chain (Section 9.5).

We offered the final version of our design, known as the Holistic Sustainability System (Chapter 10), towards a mechanism to support and encourage the use and operationalization of the Rhizome Approach and its constituents. Various options were designed for the graphic representation of the Holistic Sustainability Label and the Holistic Sustainability Checklist. We shortlisted the final optionthrough discussions with stakeholders in Vietnam, and also by administering random questionnaires to visitors at UNIDO's booth at the Life-Style Vietnam fair.

The Holistic Sustainability System leverages the additional time and cost investment in a holistic sustainability-aligned design process as value addition and product differentiation. This added value demonstrates how the outputs of the

Holistic Sustainability Assessment could be quantified and communicated, thus legitimizing sustainability efforts as credentials make the investment in sustainability worthwhile for companies. When companies see value in sustainability, they are interested in operationalizing it. This interest from companies creates a pull for designers to practice sustainability holistically by using the Rhizome Approach, thereby answering our third question.

It was heartening to see UNIDO's beneficiary, Vietcraft, begin to operationalize the Holistic Sustainability Assessment System through a branding and labeling scheme, under the aegis of the Vietnamese Ministry of Industry and Commerce in 2015 (Vietcraft Excellence, 2015). The Centre for Promotion of Imports from Developing Countries (Centrum tot Bevordering van de Import uit Ontwikkelingslanden – CBI) approached us to explore the potential of using the Holistic Sustainability System as a certification scheme for Vietnamese exports.

The Sustainable Product Innovation (SPIN) Project used the Holistic Sustainability Assessment for its programmatic and overall assessments in 2015 (Jin, 2015). Additionally, Shauna Jin, a Ph.D. researcher at Delft University of Technology, linked to the SPIN project, adapted and used the Holistic Sustainability Checklist and used the Holistic Sustainability Assessment to evaluate the outcome of her collaborative design project for Vietnamese MSMEs (Jin, 2015). This interest, and the usage into which it has already translated, seems to indicate that the Holistic Sustainability System answers our third question.

11.3   Key findings and reflections thereon

We juxtaposed our key findings with the contextual scenario we mapped earlier (Figure 11.1) in Figure 11.4 below.

Narrative explanation of diagram (Figure 11.4)

- Holistic design's focus expands to encompass all of the elements in the diagram. Design traditionally looks at production, design and marketing, all of which are in inverted commas to emphasize their mainstream understanding and scope. Design also factors in all of the dimensions of sustainability.
- The Rhizome Approach, and Rhizome Framework and the Holistic Sustainability Labeling Scheme are depicted in the dotted lined boxes, and their sub-elements are represented in the dark and light gray boxes.
- The diagram depicts how inputs from the craftsperson and the designer are the basis for what is traditionally considered the design function, and how this design is crafted using renewable materials in line with the directions outlined by the Rhizome Framework.
- The final products are assessed, and the results are communicated through the Holistic Sustainability Labeling Scheme.

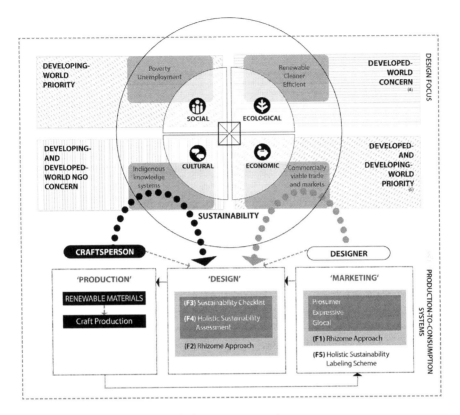

Figure 11.4 Juxtaposition of key findings in contextual scenario
Source: Reubens, 2019

Summary of key findings

In the context of non-industrial craft-based MSMEs in developing countries working with renewable materials:

- *F1*: A framework which provides direction to the ends and means of actualizing design-craft collaboration towards holistic sustainability – in this case, the Rhizome Framework, which identifies three viable directions and means of realizing them for traditional craft-facilitates the development of holistically sustainable products and production-to-consumption systems.
- *F2*: A flexible, step-by-step approach based on collaborative innovation – in this case, the Rhizome Approach – can empower designers to leverage craft production-to-consumption systems in developing countries for sustainability design, while simultaneously addressing sustainability's dimensions holistically.

- *F3*: An adaptable checklist which maps a life-cycle analysis to a FourPillarsapproach – in this case, the Holistic Sustainability Checklist – is an efficient and appropriate design tool to clarify desired design decisions, and their impact on each tenet of sustainability, from the front-end innovation onwards in the design process.
- *F4*: A relative sustainability evaluation method – in this case, the Holistic Sustainability Assessment – which evaluates against an adaptable checklist, which maps a life-cycle analysis to a FourPillarsapproach, is an efficient and appropriate tool to assess holistic sustainability.
- *F5*: A labeling scheme which communicates the result of the Holistic Sustainability Assessment in an easy-to-understand manner – in this case, the Holistic Sustainability Label – is a driver for sustainability design and marketing and for sustainable production-to-consumption systems to remain on the sustainability track.

11.4   Intersections

This book spanned several diverse and discrete variables – including craft, sustainability, design and developing countries. Such a broad-based field of inquiry was necessary because the interconnections between the variables were as important as the variables themselves, owing to the panoptic nature of the inquiry. The sub-sets of our client-class and the scenarios and elements they encompassed – including the handicraft and sectors in Vietnam and India, the developing world, and bamboo craft – anchored our research. We believe these findings from these scenarios can be potentially extended to the wider domains of sustainability, design, renewable materials and sustainable development. This is especially so because the mechanisms that underpinned our findings were designed to be flexible and adaptable. We were also mindful of the mechanisms being able to function independently as well as independently; we therefore hope they complement and supplement other sustainability design and design methodology approaches.

This book also drew on the domain of collaborative innovation, which could therefore be an avenue to explore potential synergies. Collaborative innovation is commonly practiced by businesses, especially in the field of information and communication technology (Emden, Calatone, & Droge, 2006), but research on the intersection of collaboration and social innovation is limited (Christensen, Baumann, Ruggles, & Sadtler, 2006). We agree with the emerging scholarship, such as the work of Halme (2015), Bhaduri (2016), Ranjan (n.d.) and Gupta (2009), which talks about the value of which non-traditional innovation partners from the developing world can bring to developed-developing partner co-creation. We also concur with Fulgencio (2012), who states that collaborative innovation has a role in addressing societal issues, and also with Cisneros (Technology Innovation Hub, n.d.), who argues that the collaborative innovation process has a social value of its own and is the means to a fulfilling life. We discussed how craftspeople are often vulnerable in design-craft exchanges, and we therefore outlined the unique and important contribution that both designers and craftspeople bring to the innovation process, leading to the development of the Rhizome Approach to maximize each party's contribution. This is in line with Brass et al's (2004) social exchange theory which argues for a fair bi-directional exchange so that, over time, mutually rewarding transactions and interdependent relationships can develop (Cropanzano & Mitchell, 2005).

11.5   Closing thoughts

The sustainability playing field is a great leveler. Given the limited and evolving knowledge on sustainability – and the urgent need to act immediately despite the knowledge gap – every potential solution and solution-provider needs to be considered. This situation has thrown up unlikely potential heroes and champions. The unlikely champions of this book have been craftspeople, who have insofar generally been viewed as potential recipients of hand-holding and handouts from urban value-chain supporters, including designers from the developing and developed worlds. However, sustainability design is a new discipline: its dynamic pool of knowledge still in flux. Against this backdrop, craftspeople emerge as actors whose roles extend beyond being knowledge recipients – they emerge as potential sustainability knowledge repository sharers. Craftspeople have an edge on innovation towards sustainability on two counts: a) they are often inherently better at systems thinking and seeing the compound picture because they come from a background which is still not completely globalized, and therefore not yet subjected to division of labor and fragmented roles; and b) by virtue of constantly needing to almost instantaneously and tirelessly evolve a quick and dirty Plan B (or C, or D . . .) for the several instances when their social and state systems fail them, they often possess the ability to quickly internalize and respond to crises in flux – which is exactly what the sustainability crisis requires.

Craftspeople are the keepers of indigenous systems, which have much to offer to sustainability praxis by way of a localized knowledge base and systems which have proven over time to be more sustainable than not. This book has worked to devise a way to include them, and their knowledge, into the sustainability-centric innovation process. Throughout this process, we have been mindful of Aristotle's wisdom in noting that the worst form of inequality is to try and make unequal things equal. Therefore, this research has not focused on comparing or attempting to equalize craft and design. Instead, it has centered on finding an equitable path to ensure that craft and design both have their own contribution, due and place to work together towards sustainability.

Also on the note of forcing equality between unequals is the demand of developing countries to rightfully pursue the development trajectory of developed countries, and the expectation of developed countries that developing countries comply with sustainability compliance frameworks developed in the context of developed countries. In our opinion, both sets of expectations and demands are unfair and unrealistic. The adage of thinking globally and acting locally seems to offer a way forward – systems need to be adaptable locally, but adhere to minimum global compliance in their essence and key criteria.

Hearteningly, our journey in this book seems to indicate that designers can practice sustainability design – even holistic sustainability design – if exposed to why and how. Through disruptive innovation, design can create and highlight spaces for change, in that which it cannot change yet. However, design can only do so much; designers function in an ecosystem like the rest of the world. Design needs a facilitating environment and support from agencies, including those in the field of policy, legislation and education. At the end of the day, everybody needs to be on board. Everybody counts.

The call for design is therefore not to change the world single-handedly. It is to realize that whether or not it is obvious yet, each designer – just like every other actor in the world – changes and shapes the world and its sustainability by their choices and actions. The real question therefore is not whether or not you will make a change, but whether or not you will author it and own your agency – whether you will be the change you want to see.

Bibliography

Acemoglu, D., Simon, J., & James, A. R. (2001). The colonial origins of comparative development: An empirical investigation. *American Economic Review*, 2001(91): 1369–1401.

Adams, W. M. (2006, January 31). *The future of sustainability: Re-thinking environment and development in the twenty-first century* (Report of the IUCN Renowned Thinkers Meeting). Retrieved from http://cmsdata.iucn.org/downloads/iucn_future_of_sustanability.pdf

Adamson, G., Cooke, E. S., & Harrod, T. (2008). Editorial introduction. *The Journal of Modern Craft*, 1(1): 5–12.

Afacan, S. (n.d.). *Iranian craft industries in the age of factorization: Large-scale industrialization and small scale industries during the 1930s*. International Society for Iranian Studies. Retrieved from http://iranianstudies.com/content/iranian-craft-industries-age-factorization-large-scale-industrialization-and-small-scale-ind

Agarwal, A., Annadorai, P., Bedekar, T., Chhabra, P., Edakhe, A., Deb Burman, K., Gupta, S., Joshi, S., Kawadkar, P., Mahajan, C., & Mehta, P. (2018). *Deconstructing Craft*. Specialization Studio 2, Building Crafts, Monsoon 2018. Faculty of Design, Centre of Planning and Technology (CEPT): Ahmedabad.

Akubue, A. (2000). Appropriate technology for socioeconomic development in third world countries. *The Journal of Technology Studies*, 26(1): 33–43.

Alvarez, A., & Rogers, J. (2006). Going 'out there': Learning about sustainability in place. *International Journal of Sustainability in Higher Education*, 7(2): 176–188.

Amelung, B., & Martens, P. (2008). Wankele Wieg. *Milieude-fensie Magazine*, 5, 28–29.

Anand, S., & Sen, A. (2000). Human development and economic sustainability. *World Development*, 28(12): 2029–2049.

Andrews, R. (1998). Environmental regulation and business 'self-regulation'. *Policy Sciences*, 31(3): 177–197.

Angus, A., Booth, C., Armstrong, G., & Pollard, S. J. T. (2013). *Better evidence for regulatory reform: Rapid evidence appraisals* (Contract report ERG117 prepared for the Department for Environment, Food and Rural Affairs (Defra) by the Centre for Environmental Risks and Futures, Cranfield University). Bedfordshire: Defra.

Arrow. K., Daily, G., Dasgupta, P., Ehrlich, P., Goulder, L., Heal, G., Levin, S., Maler, K., Schneider, S., Starrett, D., & Walker, B. (2004). Are we consuming too much? *Journal of Economic Perspectives*, 18(3): 147–172.

Asheim, G., Buchholz, W., & Tungodden, B. (2001). Justifying sustainability. *Journal of Environmental Economics and Management*, 41(3): 252–268.

Association des Etats Generaux des Etudiants de l'Europe (AEGEE). (2014). *Eco-games.* Retrieved from www.projects.aegee.org/suct/su2014/files/cooperations/Eco-Games.pdf

Atwater, J., Kannan, V., & Stephens, A. (2008). Cultivating systemic thinking in the next generation of business leaders. *Academy of Management Learning & Education,* 7(1): 9–25.

Austa, S. (2015, April 15). *From a roadside tea stall to the Mitticool success story: How Manshuk Lal Prajapati did it all.* Retrieved from https://yourstory.com/2015/04/manshuk-lal-prajapati-mitticool/

Aye, E. (2003). *Taking the pulse: Sustainability and the interior design practice.* Retrieved from http//www.greenbuildingservices.com/news/releases/2003_13_55_pulse.pdf

Bacon, L. (2011). *Interior designer's attitudes towards sustainable interior design practices and barriers encountered when using sustainable interior design practices* (Master's Thesis, Paper 104). Lincoln: University of Nebraska-Lincoln.

Baedeker, C., Liedtke, C., & Welfens, J. M., et al. (2005). *Analyse vorhandener Konzepte zur Messung des nachhaltigen Konsums in Deutschland einschließlich der Grundzüge eines Entwicklungskonzepts: Abschlussbericht zur gleichnamigen Vorstudie im Auftrag der Bundesanstalt für Landwirtschaft und Ernährung als Projektträger und dem Bundesministerium für Verbraucherschutz, Ernährung und Landwirtschaft.* Berlin: Federal Minstry of Consumer Protection, Food and Agriculture.

Bagheri, A., & Hjorth, P. (2007). Planning for sustainable development: A paradigm shirt towards a process-based approach. *Sustainable Development,* 15(2): 83–96.

Bailey, I., & Ditty, C. (2009). Energy markets, capital inertia and economic instrument impacts. *Climate Policy,* 9(1): 22–39.

Baille, J., & Ravich, W. (1993). On endoscopic training and procedural competence. *Annals of Internal Medicine,* 118(1): 73–74.

Bailly, O. (2010). *Fair trade sustainable trade? Fair trade and the environment* [Brochure]. Brussels: BTC Belgian Development Agency.

Bakker, C. A., & den Hollander, M. (n.d.). *Six design strategies for longer lasting products in circular economy.* Retrieved from www.theguardian.com/sustainable-business/six-design-strategies-longer-lasting-products

Bakker, C. A., Wever, R., Teoh, Ch., & De Clercq, S. (2010). Designing cradle-to-cradle products: A reality check. *International Journal of Sustainable Engineering,* 3(1): 2–8, First Published on: 09 November 2009 (iFirst).

Bakshi, S. R. (1987). *Gandhi and ideology of swadeshi.* New Delhi: Reliance Publishing House.

Balooni, K. (2002). Participatory forest management in India: An analysis of policy trends amidst management change. *Policy Trend Report*: 88–113.

Banerjee, A., & Solomon, B. D. (2003). Eco-labeling for energy efficiency and sustainability: A meta evaluation of US programs. *Energy Policy,* 31(2): 109–123.

Barash, D. P., & Webel, C. P. (2002). *Peace and conflict studies.* London: Sage Publications.

Barbier, E. B. (1987). The concept of Sustainable Economic Development. *Environmental Conservation* 12(02): 101–110.

Barefoot College (2016). *A path to development led by communities.* Retrieved from www.barefootcollege.org/barefoot-approach/

Bartelmus, P. (1999). *Economic growth and patterns of sustainability* (Wuppertal Papers No. 98). Wuppertal: Wuppertal-Institut für Klima, Umwelt, Energie.

Bassey, M. (1981). Pedagogic research: On the relative merits of search for generalization and study of single events. *Oxford Review of Education,* 7(1): 73–93.

Baumeister, D., Tocke, R., Dwyer, J., Ritter, S., & Benyus, J. (2013). *Biomimicry resource handbook: A seed bank of best practices.* First Public Print ed. Missoula: Biomimicry 3.8.

Beise, M., & Rennings, K. (2005). Lead markets and regulation: A framework for analyzing the international diffusion of environmental innovations. *Ecological Economics*, 52(1): 5–17.

Belcher, B. M. (1998). A production-to-consumption systems approach: Lessons from the bamboo and rattan sectors in Asia. In E. Wollenberg & A. Ingles (Eds.), *Incomes from the forest: Methods for the development and conservation of forest products for local communities* (pp. 59–84). Bogor: Center for International Forestry Research Bogor.

Bell, R. G., & Russel, C. (2002). Environmental policy for developing countries. *Issues in Science and Technology*,18(3): 63–70.

Ben Letaifa, S., & Reynoso, J. (2015). Toward a service ecosystem perspective at the base of the pyramid. *Journal of Service Management*, 26(5): 684–705.

Benyus, J. M. (1997). *Biomimicry: Innovation inspired by Nature.* New York: William Morrow & Co.

Benyus, J. M. (2002). *Biomimicry: Innovation inspired by nature.* New York: William Morrow Paperbacks.

Berkeley, J. (2011). Welcome to the Anthropocene. *The Economist.* Retrieved from www.economist.com/node/18744401

Bersalona, C. (2002). *The industrialized handicraft (in-hand) philosophy: The Abra experience.* Manila: In-Hand Abra.

Bey, N., Hauschild, M. Z., & McAloone, T. C. (2013). Drivers and barriers for implementation of environmental strategies in manufacturing companies. *CIRP Annals: Manufacturing Technology*, 62: 43–46.

Bhaduri, S. (2016). *Frugal innovation by 'the small and the marginal': An alternative discourse on innovation and development* [PDF]. Retrieved from http://static1.1.sqspcdn.com/static/f/1215623/27046515/1464344610367/3977+1051+Prince+Claus+Chair+Lecture_WEB.pdf?token=ihiWoqGLev2wcLlfxDEhvqOILLI%3D

Bhamra, T., Lilley, D., & Tang, T. (2008, July). *Sustainable use: Changing consumer behaviour through product design.* Paper presented at Changing the Change: Design Visions, Proposals and Tools, Turin.

Bhamra, T., Lilley, D., & Tang, T. (2011). Design for sustainable behavior: Using products to change consumer behavior. *The Design Journal*, 14(4), 427–445.

Bhamra, T., & Lofthouse, V. (2003). Using information/inspiration as a sustainable design tool. *Design and Manufacture for Sustainable Development*, 133–143.

Biomimicry Institute (2015). *What is biomimicry?* Retrieved from www.biomimicry.org

Biomimicry Institute (2018). *Solutions to global problems are all around.* Retrieved from https://biomimicry.org/biomimicry-examples/

Bjørn, A., & Hauschild, M. Z. (2013). Absolute versus relative environmental sustainability. *Journal of Industrial Ecology*, 17(2): 321–332.

Blaszczyk, R. L. (2011). *Producing fashion: Commerce, culture and consumers.* Philadelphia: University of Pennsylvania Press.

Blau, P. M. (1964). *Exchange and power in social life.* New York: John Wiley.

Boks, C. (2006). The soft side of ecodesign. *Journal of Cleaner Production*, 14(1516): 1346–1356.

Bonsiepe, G. (2011). *Design, cultura e sociedade.* Sao Paulo: Blucher.

Borges, A. (2013). Craft revitalization as a change agent in Latin America. *Making Futures Journal*, 3: 11–15.

Borkey, P., Glachant, M., & Leveque, F. (1999). *Voluntary approaches for environmental policy: An assessment.* Paris: OECD.

Bovea, M. D., & Pérez-Belis, V. (2012). A taxonomy of ecodesign tools for integrating environmental requirements into the product design process. *Journal of Cleaner Production*, 20(1): 61–71.

Brass, C., & Mazarella, F. (2015, September). *Are we asking the right questions? Rethinkingpostgraduate education towards sustainable visions for the future.* IN: Proceedings of the 17th International Conference on Engineering and Product Design Education, E&PDE 2015: Great Expectations: Design Teaching, Research & Enterprise, University of Loughborough, UK.

Brass, D. J., Galaskiewicz, J., Greve, H. R., & Tsai, W. (2004). Taking stock of networks and organizations: A multilevel perspective. *Academy of Management Journal*, 47: 795–817.

Brezet, H. (1997). Dynamics in ecodesign practice. *Industry and Environment*, 20(1–2): 21–24.

Brezet, H., & van Hemel, C. (1997). Industry and environment. In H. Bottcher & R. Clarke (Eds.), *Ecodesign: A promising approach to sustainable production and consumption.* Paris: United Nations Environment Programme, Industry and Environment.

Brezet, J. C., Horst, T. v. d., & Riele, H. T. (1994). *PROMISE:Handleiding voor milieugerichte productontwikkeling.* Den Haag: NOTA/SDU.

British Design Council (2004). *Theimpact of design on stock market performance* (An Analysis of UK Quoted Companies 1994–2003). London: British Design Council.

Brumfiel, E. (2003). It's a material world: History, artifacts, and anthropology. *Annual Review of Anthropology*, 32: 205–223.

Brundtland, G. H. (1987). *Our common future.* Oxford: Oxford University Press.

Business for Social Responsibility (2007). *Perspectives on information management in supply chains.* Retrieved from www.yooyahcloud.com/MOSSCOMMUNICATIONS/ZNjZ2b/BSR_Info-Management-Supply-Chains.pdf

Business Social Compliance Initiative (BSCI) (2004). *BSCI: Self-assessment, foreign trade association: Brussels, global sustainable management cologne.* Migros-Genossenschafts-Bund, zürich, Systain Consulting GmbHHamburg.

BSCI (2007). BSCI System: Rules and Functioning. Retrieved from http://www.allyservice.com/photo/2009111613209.pdf

Campbell, D. T. (1986). Relabeling internal and external validity for applied social scientists. In, W. M. K. Trochim (Ed.), *Advances in quasi-experimental design analysis: New directions for program evaluation* (Vol. 31, pp. 67–77). San Francisco: Jossey-Bass.

Carmin, J., Darnall, N., & Mil-Homens, J. (2003). Stakeholder involvement in the design of U.S. voluntary environmental programs: Does sponsorship matter? *Policy Studies Journal*, 31(4): 527–543.

Carney, D. (1999). *Social capital: Key sheets for sustainable livelihoods, policy planning and implementation.* London: DFID/ODI.

Cassell, C., & Symon, G. (Eds.) (2006). *Essential guide to qualitative methods in organizational research.* London: Sage Publications.

Castillo, L. G., Diehl, J. C., & Brezet, J. C. (2012, May). *Design considerations for base of the pyramid (BoP) projects.* Paper presented at Cumulus, Helsinki.

Ceschin, G.,& Gaziulusoy, I. (2016). Evolution of design for sustainability: From product design to design for system innovations and transitions. *Design Studies*, 47: 118–163.

Chakrabarti, R., & Mason, K. (2014). Designing better markets for people at the bottom of the pyramid: Bottom-up market design. In S. Geiger, D. Harrison, H. Kjellberg, & A. Mallard (Eds.), *Concerned markets: Economic ordering for multiple values.* Cheltenham: Edward Elgar Publishing.

Chapman, J., & Gant, N. (Eds.) (2007). *Designers, visionaries and other stories.* London: Routledge.

Charter, M. (2001). Managing ecodesign. In M. Charter, & U. Tischner (Eds.), *Sustainable solutions: Developing products and services for the future* (pp. 220–242). Sheffield: Greenleaf Publishing.

Chatterjee, A. (2014). *Can our future be handmade?* (Fifth Kamaladevi Chattopadhyay Memorial Lecture). New Delhi: Centre for Cultural Resources and Training.

Chaudhary, S. V. (2010). *Understanding the urban and rural consumer*. Retrieved from www.indianmba.com/Faculty_Column/FC1111/fc1111.html

Checkland, P. B. (1997). *Systems thinking, systems practice*. Chichester: John Wiley & Sons. Ltd.

Chitale, A. K., & Gupta, R. C. (2007). *Product design and manufacturing* (3rd edition). New Delhi: PHI learning Pvt. Ltd.

Chotiratanapinun, T. (2013). The emergence and existence of sustainable craft practices: Case studies from Indonesia and Thailand. *Making Futures Journal*, 3: 8–18.

Christensen, C. M., Baumann, H., Ruggles, R., & Sadtler, T. M. (2006). Disruptive innovation for social change. *Harvard Business Review*, 84(12): 94–101.

Christiaans, H. H. C. M., & Diehl, J. C. (2007). The necessity of design research into cultural aspects. In S. Poggenpohl (Ed.), *IASDR07 proceedings: Emerging trends in design research* (pp. 1–18). Hong Kong: The Hong Kong Polytechnic University.

Ciriacy-Wantrup, S. V. (1952). *Resource conservation: Economics and policies*. Berkeley: University of California Press.

Ciroth, A., Finkbeiner, M., Hildenbrand, J., Klöpffer, W., Mazijn, B., Prakash, S., Sonnemann, G., Traverso, M., Ugaya, C., Valdivia, S., & Vickery-Niederman, G. (2011). In S. Valdivia, M. L. Cássia, G. Sonnemann, & J. Hildenbrand (Eds.), *Towards a life cycle sustainability assessment: Making informed choices on products*. Paris: UNEP/SETAC Life Cycle Initiative.

Clark, G., Kosoris, J., Hong, L. N., & Crul, M. (2009). Design for sustainability: Current trends in sustainable product design and development. *Sustainability*, 1: 409–424.

Cleff, T., & Rennings, K. (1999). Determinants of environmental product and process innovation. *European Environment*, 9(5): 191–201.

Clift, R. (2014, November). *Social life cycle assessment: What are we trying to do?* Paper presented at the International Seminar on Social LCA, Montpellier.

Clinton, B. (1995). *Reinventing environmental regulation* (State of the Union Address). Retrieved from http://govinfo.library.unt.edu/npr/library/rsreport/251a.html

Coglianese, C., & Lazer, D. (2003). Management-based regulation: Prescribing private management to achieve public goals. *Law and Society Review*, 37(4): 691–730.

Coglianese, C., & Nash, J. (2004). *Leveraging the private sector: Management-based strategies for improving environmental performance* (Regulatory Policy Program Report RPP-06-2004). Cambridge, MA: Center for Business and Government, John F. Kennedy School of Government & Harvard University.

Coglianese, C., Nash, J., & Olmstead, T. (2003). Performance-based regulation: Prospects and limitations in health, safety and environmental protection. *Administrative Law Review*, 55(4): 705–728.

Colantonio, A. (2008, November). Traditional and emerging prospects in social sustainability. *Measuring Social Sustainability: Best Practice from Urban Renewal in the EU, 2006/02: EIBURS Working Paper Series*. Oxford, UK: Oxford Institute for Sustainable Development (OISD).

Committee on Culture of the World Association of United Cities and Local Governments (UCLG) (2015). *Culture 21: Agenda 21 for culture*. Barcelona: UCLG.

Conservation International (2018). *Nature is Speaking*. Retrieved from www.conservation.org/nature-is-speaking/Pages/About.aspx

Cook, T. D., & Campbell, D. T. (1979). *Quasi-experimentation: Design and analysis issues for field settings*. Boston, MA: Houghton Mifflin Company.

Costanza, R. (1991). *Ecological economics: The science and management of sustainability*. New York: Columbia University Press.

Costanza, R. (2000). Social goals and the valuation of ecosystem services. *Ecosystems*, 3(1): 4–10.

Craft+Design Enquiry (n.d.). *About c+de*. Retrieved from http://craftdesignenquiry.blogspot.in/

Craftmark (n.d.). *About us*. Retrieved from www.craftmark.org/

Craft Revival Trust (2006). *Designers meet artisans*. New Delhi: Grass Root Publications Pvt. Ltd.

Díaz-García, C., González-Moreno, A., & Sáez-Martínez F. J. (2015). Eco-innovation: Insights from a literature review. *Innovation: Management, Policy & Practice*, 17(1): 6–23.

Cropanzano, R., & Mitchell, M. S. (2005). Social exchange theory: An interdisciplinary review. *Journal of Management*, 31(6): 874–900.

Crul, M. R. M., & Diehl, J. C. (2006). *Design for sustainability: A practical approach for developing economies*. Paris: United Nations Environment Programme.

Cuginotti, A., Miller, K. M., & van der Pluijm, F. (2008). *Design and decision making: Backcasting using principles to implement cradle-to-cradle* (Master's Thesis). Karlskrona: Blekinge Institute of Technology.

Cusumano, M. A. (1991). *From craft production to flexible systems and software factories* (Sloan School of Management, Working Paper 3325-91/BPS). Massachusetts: Massachusetts Institute of Technology.

Cuthill, M. (2010). Strengthening the 'social' in sustainable development: Developing a conceptual framework for sustainability in rapid urban growth region in Australia. *Sustainable Development*, 18: 362–373.

Daly, H. E. (1996). *Beyond growth: The economics of sustainable development*. Boston: Beacon Press.

Davis, A. (2001). *Barriers to building green*. Retrieved from www.architectureweek.com/2001/0822/environment_1-1.html

Davis, K., Öncel, P., & Yang, Q. (2010). *An innovation approach for sustainable product and product-service system development* (Master's Thesis). Karlskrona: Blekinge Institute of Technology.

De Déa Roglio, K., & Light, G. (2009). Executive MBA programs: The development of the reflective executive. *Academy of Management Learning & Education*, 8(2): 156–173.

Deleuze, G., & Guattari, F. (1987). *A thousand plateaus: Capitalism and schizophrenia*. Minnesota: University of Minnesota.

de Man, R., & Brezet, H. (2016). Cradle to cradle: A utopia that is misleading politics and business. To be published (in Dutch) in the *Tijdschrift voor Milieu*, VVM, The Netherlands.

Demirel, P., & Kesidou, E. (2011). Stimulating different types of eco-innovation in the UK: Government policies and firm motivations. *Ecological Economics*, 70: 1546–1557.

Dendler, L. (2012, June). *Sustainable meta-labelling: An effective measure to facilitate more sustainable consumption and production?* Paper presented at Global Research Forum on Sustainable Consumption and Production Workshop, Rio de Janeiro.

Dendler, L. (2013). *Sustainability meta labelling: Prospects and potential challenges for institutionalization* (PhD Thesis). Manchester: Manchester Business School.

Denscombe, M. (1998). *The good research guide for small-scale social research projects.* Buckingham: Open University Press.

Denzin, N. K. (1978). *Sociological methods.* New York: McGraw-Hill.

Department for Culture, Media & Sport (2016). *Creative industries: Focus on employment.* Retrieved from https://assets.publishing.service.gov.uk/government/uploads/system/uploads/attachment_data/file/534305/Focus_on_Employment_revised_040716.pdf

Design (2018). *OxfordDictionaries.com.* Retrieved from http://oxforddictionaries.com/definition/design

Design Innovation and Craft Resource Center (2013). *Bamboo craft: Space making craft workshop.* Ahmedabad: DICRC.

De Waal, E. (2002). Altogether elsewhere: The figuring of ethnicity. In P. Greenhalgh (Ed.), *The persistence of craft: The applied arts today* (pp. 188–189). London: A & C Black.

Dewulf, K. (2013). Sustainable product innovation: The importance of the front-end stage in the innovation process. In D. A. Coelho (Ed.), *Advances in industrial design engineering* (pp. 139–166). New York: Intech.

Díaz-García, C., González-Moreno, A. & Sáez-Martínez, F. J. (2015). Eco-innovation: insights from a literature review, *Innovation*, 17(1): 6–23.

Diehl, J. C. (2010). *Product innovation knowledge for developing economies towards a systematic transfer approach* (PhD Thesis). Delft: Delft University of Technology.

Diehl, J. C., & Christiaans, H. (2015, October 17). Product service systems: The future for designers? The changing role of the industrial designer. *International design congress.* Gwangju, Korea.

Diez, T. (2013). The Fab City. *Making Futures Journal*, 3: 16–22.

Domask, J. J. (2007). Achieving goals in higher education: An experiential approach to sustainability studies. *International Journal of Sustainability in Higher Education*, 8(1): 53–68.

Dormer, P. (1997). The Salon de refuse? In P. Dormer (Ed.), *Theculture of craft* (pp. 2–16). Manchester: Manchester University Press.

Dovie, D. B. K., Witkowski, E. T. F., & Shackleton, C. M. (2008). Knowledge of plant resource use based on location, gender and generation. *Applied Geography*, 28(4): 311–322.

Drechsler, A. (2015, May). *A postmodern perspective on socio-technical design science research.* Paper presented at 10th International Conference, DESRIST 2015, Dublin.

Drost, E. A. (2011). Validity and reliability in social science research. *Education Research and Perspectives*, 38(1): 105–123.

Dunham-Jones, E. (2007). Post-industrial landscape. In K. Tanzer & R. Longoria (Eds.), *The green braid: Towards an architecture of ecology, economy and equity* (pp. 44–59). London: Routledge.

Duxbury, N., & Gillette, E. (2007). *Culture as a key dimension of sustainability: Exploring concepts, themes, and models.* Vancouver: Centre of Expertise on Culture and Communities and Simon Fraser University.

Dworkin, R. (1981). What is equality? Part 2: Equality of resources. *Philosophy and Public Affairs*, 10: 283–345.

Eberle, U. (2001). *Das Nachhaltigkeitszeichen: Ein Instrument zur Umsetzung einer nachhaltigen Entwicklung?* (PhDDissertation). Freiburg: Justus-Liebig-Universität Gießen.

Eckert, S., Karg, G., & Zängler, T. (2007). Nachhaltiger Konsum aus Sicht der Verbraucher. In F. M. Belz, G. Karg, & D. Witt (Eds.), *Nachhaltiger Konsum und Verbraucherpolitik im 21 Jahrhundert* (pp. 53–77). Metropolis: Marburg.

The Economist (2015, March 26). The 169 commandments. Retrieved from www.economist.com/leaders/2015/03/26/the-169-commandments

The Economist (2017, March 23). The sustainability summit 2017. Retrieved from https://events.economist.com/events-conferences/emea/sustainability-summit-2017/

Edwards, A. R. (2005). *The sustainability revolution: Portrait of a paradigm shift.* Gabriola Island: New Society Publishers.

Ehrenfeld, J. R. (2008). *Sustainability by design: A subversive strategy for transforming our consumer culture.* New Haven: Yale University Press.

Ekins, P., Simon, S., Deutsch, L., Folke, C., & De Groot, R. (2003). A framework for the practical application of the concepts of critical natural capital and strong sustainability. *Ecological Economics*, 44(2): 165–185.

Elkington, J. (1998). *Cannibals with forks: The triple bottom line of 21st century business.* Gabriola Island: New Society Publishers.

Ellen MacArthur Foundation (2013). *Towards the circular economy: An economic and business rationale for an accelerated transition.* Isle of Wight: Ellen MacArthur Foundation.

Ellen MacArthur Foundation (2017). *Case studies.* Retrieved from www.ellenmacarthur-foundation.org/case-studies/selling-light-as-a-service

Emden, Z., Calatone, R. J., & Droge, C. (2006). Collaborating for new product development: Selecting the partner with maximum potential to create value. *Journal of Product Innovation Management*, 23: 330–341.

Emory, C. W., & Cooper, D. R. (1991). *Business research methods* (4th edition). Boston: Irwin.

Erlandson, D. A., Skipper, E. L., Harris, B. L., & Allen, S. D. (1993). *Doing naturalistic inquiry: A guide to methods.* London: Sage Publications.

European Commission (2007). *Communication from the commission to the European Parliament, the Council, the European economic and social committee and the committee of the regions on a European agenda for culture in a globalizing world.* Retrieved from http://eur-lex.europa.eu/LexUriServ/LexUriServ.do?uri=COM%3A2007%3A0242%3AFIN%3AEN%3AHTML

European Commission (n.d.). *Better regulation: Tool #15: The choice of policy instruments.* Retrieved from http://ec.europa.eu/smart-regulation/guidelines/tool_15_en.htm

European Task Force on Culture and Development (1997). *In from the margins: A contribution to the debate on culture and development in Europe.* Strasbourg: Council of Europe.

Fanchette, S., & Stedman, S. (2010). *Discovering craft villages in Vietnam: Ten itineraries around Ha Noi.* Hanoi: Research Institute for Development (IRD).

Ferris, M. (2009). The crafts in the context of emerging global sustainability agendas (Keynote Address). *Making Futures Journal*, 1.

Finkbeiner, M., Schau, E. M., Lehmann, A., & Traverso, M. (2010). Towards life cycle sustainability assessment. *Sustainability*, 2010(2): 3309–3322.

Fisher, I. (1906). *The nature of capital and income.* New York: Macmillan.

Frankl, P., Pietroni, L., Scheer, D., Rubik, F., StØ, E., & Montcada, E. (2005). Recommendations. In F. Rubik & P. Frankl (Eds.), *The future of eco-labelling: Making environmental product information systems effective* (pp. 291–234). Sheffield: Greenleaf Publications.

Frater, J. (2009). Kala Raksha Vidhyalaya: Designing a sustainable future. *Dronah Magazine*, 43–52.

Frater, J. (2016). *Threads of identity.* Retrieved from https://threadsofidentity.wordpress.com/

Fraunhofer IZM (2005). *A guide for ecodesign tools* (2nd edition). Berlin: Franhofer IZM.

Fuad-Luke, A. (2009). *Design activism: Beautiful strangeness for a sustainable world.* London: Earthscan.

Fulgencio, H. (2012). *Collaborative innovation ensures innovation through pastiche.* Retrieved from www.academia.edu/11037990/Collaborative_Innovation_Ensues_Innovation_Through_Pastiche

Gallastegui, I. G. (2002). The use of eco-labels: A review of the literature. *European Environment,* 12(6): 316–331.

Gaur, M., & Gaur, H. (2004). Combating desertification: Building on traditional knowledge systems of the Thar desert communities. *Environmental Monitoring and Assessment,* 99(1): 89–103.

Gauziulusoy, A. I. (2015). A critical review of approaches available for design and innovation teams through the perspective of sustainability science and system innovation theories. *Journal of Cleaner Production,* 107: 336–377.

Ghoshal, S. (2005). Bad management theories are destroying good management practices. *Academy of Management Learning & Education,* 4(1): 75–91.

Golden, J. S. (Ed.) (2010, October 10). *An overview of ecolabels and sustainability certifications in the global marketplace* (Interim Report Document). Durham: Corporate Sustainability Initiative.

Gomez Castillo, L., Diehl, J. C. & Brezet, J. C. (2012, May 12). Design considerations for base of the pyramid (BOP) projects. *Cumulus conference,* Helsinki, pp. 24–26.

Good Weave (2014). *About GoodWeave.* Retrieved from www.goodweave.net/home.php

Gray, A. (1991). *Between the spice of life and the melting pot: Biodiversity conservation and its impact on indigenous peoples* (IWGIA Document no. 70.). Copenhagen: IWGIA.

Greenhalgh, P. (1997a). The history of craft. In P. Dormer (Ed.), *The culture of craft* (pp. 20–52). Manchester: Manchester University Press.

Greenhalgh, P. (1997b). The progress of Captain Ludd. In P. Dormer (Ed.), *The culture of craft* (pp. 104–115). Manchester: Manchester University Press.

Greenlees, R. (2013). New routes to sustainability: Strategies for realizing craft's potential. *Making Futures Journal,* 3: 23–30.

Guadalupe, J. (2012, June). *Restitution and empowerment through handicrafts: Bobbin lace.* Paper presented at 1st EJTHR International Conference on Destination Branding and Authenticity, Santiago de Compostela.

Guest, D. (1991, September 17). The hunt is on for the Renaissance Manof computing. *The Independent* (London).

Guinée, J. B. (2016). Life cycle sustainability assessment: What is it and what are its challenges? In R. Clift & A. Druckman (Eds.), *Taking stock of industrial ecology* (pp. 24–58). Cham: Springer.

Guinée, J. B., Heijungs, R., Huppes, G., Zamagni, A., Masoni, P., Buonamici, R., Ekvall, T., & Rydberg, T. (2011). Life cycle assessment: Past, present and future. *Environmental Science and Technology,* 45(1): 90–96.

Gupta, A. (2009). *India's hidden hotbeds of innovation* [Video file]. TedIndia2009. Retrieved from www.ted.com/talks/anil_gupta_india_s_hidden_hotbeds_of_invention?language=en

Hall, T. (n.d.). *The challenges of certification for fair trade crafts.* Retrieved from http://fairworldproject.org/voices-of-fair-trade/the-challenges-of-certification-for-fair-trade-crafts/

Hallberg, K. (1999). *Small and medium scale enterprises: A framework for intervention* (Small Enterprise Unit Private Sector Development Department, International Finance Corporation, Discussion Paper 40). Washington, DC: The World Bank.

Halme, M. (2015). *Co-creating innovations for sustainable development* [video]. Retrieved from www.youtube.com/watch?v=eMgtsHb4c04

Hankinson, M., & Breytenbach, A. (2012, May). *Barriers that impact on the implementation of sustainable design.* Paper presented at Cumulus, Helsinki.

Haq, M. (1999). *Reflections on human development* (2nd edition). Oxford: Oxford University Press.

Harding, G. (1968). The tragedy of the commons. *Science*, 62: 1243–1248.

Hargadon, A. (2002). Brokering knowledge: Linking learning and innovation. *Research in Organizational Behavior*, 24: 41–85.

Harris, S. (2007). Green tick™: An example of sustainability certification of goods and services. *Management of Environmental Quality*, 18(2): 167–178.

Harte, M. J. (1995). Ecology, sustainability and environment as capital. *Ecological Economics*, 15(2): 157–164.

Hawken, P., Lovins, A., & Lovins, L. H. (1999). *Natural capitalism: Creating the next industrial revolution.* Boston: Little, Brown.

Hawkes, J. (2001). *The fourth pillar of sustainability: Culture's essential role in public planning.* Champaign, IL: Common Ground Publishing.

Hayn, D., & Eberle, U. (2006). Kommunikation für eine Ernährungswende. In U. Simshäuser (Ed.), *Ernährungswende: Eine Herausforderung für Politik, Unternehmen und Gesellschaft* (pp. 168–182). München: Oekom-Verl.

Heinberg, R. (2010). What is sustainability? In R. Heinberg & D. Lerch (Eds.), *The post carbon reader: Managing the 21st century's sustainability crises* (pp. 25–30). Healdsburg, CA: Watershed Media.

Hendriks, C., Vogtländer, J. G., & Jansses, G. M. T. (2006). The eco-costs/value ration: A tool to determine the long-term strategy of de-linking economy and environmental ecology. *International Journal of Ecodynamics*, 1(2): 136–148.

Herbert, S. (1969). *The sciences of the artificial.* Cambridge: MIT Press.

Hes, D. (2005). *Facilitating 'green' building: Turning observation into practice* (PhD Dissertation). Melbourne: RMIT University.

Heslop, T. A. (1997). How strange the change from major to minor: Hierarchies and medieval art. In P. Dormer (Ed.), *Theculture of craft* (pp. 53–66). Manchester: Manchester University Press.

Hickel, J. (2015, August 8). *The problem with saving the world.* Retrieved from www.jacobinmag.com/2015/08/global-poverty-climate-change-sdgs/

Hickey, G. (1997). Craft within a consuming society. In P. Dormer (Ed.), *Theculture of craft* (pp. 83–100). Manchester: Manchester University Press.

Hicks, J. R. (1946). *Value and capital* (2nd edition). Oxford: Clarendon Press.

Hill, R. (1997). Writing about the crafts. In P. Dormer (Ed.), *Theculture of craft* (pp. 188–189). Manchester: Manchester University Press.

Hnatow, M. (2009). *Aid to artisans: Building profitable craft businesses* (Notes from the Field No. 4). Washington, DC: Business Growth Initiative Project.

Hockenstein, J. B., Stavins, R. N., & Whitehead, B. W. (1997). Crafting the next generation of market-based environmental tools. *Environment*, 39(4): 12–20.

Hofstede, G., Hofstede, G. J., & Minkov, M. (2010). *Cultures and organizations: Software of the mind* (3rd edition). New York: McGraw-Hill Professional.

Holling, C. S. (1986). The resilience of terrestrial ecosystems: Local surprise and global change. In W. C. Clark & R. E. Munn (Eds.), *Sustainable development of the biosphere* (pp. 292–317). Cambridge: Cambridge University Press.

House of Commons Environmental Audit Committee (2009). *Environmental labelling* (Second Report of Session 2008–09). London: House of Commons Environmental Audit Committee.

Howes, M., Wortley, L., Potts, R., Dedekorkut-Howes, A., Serrao-Neumann, S., Davidson, J., Smith, T., & Nunn, P. (2017). Environmental sustainability: A case of policy implementation failure? *Sustainability*, 9(2): 165.

Humbert, M. (2007). *Technology and workforce: Comparison between the information revolution and the industrial revolution* (School of Information, Report Number: Info 2010). California: University of California.

Hunkeler, D., Lichtenvort, K., & Rebitzer, G. (Eds.) (2008). *Environmental life cycle costing.* Florida: SETAC & CRC Press.

Huulgaard, R. D. (2015). *Ecodesign: A study of the ecodesign directive and ecodesign practices at Grundfos, Bang & Olufsen and Danfoss Power Electronics* (PhD Dissertation). Aalborg: Aalborg University.

IDEO (2009). **Human centered design toolkit**. Retrieved from www.ideo.com/work/human-centered-design-toolkit

IEFE &ICEM CEEM (1998). *Project for the promotion and the diffusion of the EU ecolabel in Italy and the Benelux: Final report.* Retrieved from http://ec.europa.eu/environment/emas/pdf/other/eversummary.pdf

Iftikar, A. (2012). *DecentWorkCheck: Analysing De-Jure Labour Market Institutions from Worker Rights Perspective, Wage Indicator Foundation.* Retrieved from www.wageindicator.org/documents/ decentworkcheck/Decentworkcheck-Methodology-IftikharAhmad-2012.pdf

Ihatsu, A. (2002). *Making sense of contemporary American craft* (Publications in Education No. 73). Savonlinna: University of Joensuu.

INBAR (n.d.). *From research to development: INBAR's strategy 2015–2030.* Retrieved from www.inbar.int/mission-strategy

Industrial (2018). *Merriam-webster.com.* Retrieved from www.merriam-webster.com/dictionary/industrial

Industry Council for Electronic Equipment Recycling (1993). *ICER guidelines, design for recycling: General principles.* London: ICER.

Intellect (n.d.). *Craft research.* Retrieved from www.intellectbooks.co.uk/journals/view-Journal,id=172/

Intellectual Property India (n.d.). *Geographical indications registry.* Retrieved from http://ipindia.nic.in/girindia/

International Council of Societies of Industrial Design (2015). *Definition of industrial design.* Retrieved from www.icsid.org/about/about/articles31.htm

International Labour Organization (1998). *International declaration on fundamental principles and rights at work and its follow-up* (adopted by the International Labour Conference at its Eighty-sixth Session). Geneva: ILO.

International Labour Organization (2016). *Conventions and recommendations.* Retrieved from www.ilo.org/global/standards/introduction-to-international-labour-standards/conventions-and-recommendations/lang-en/index.htm

International Labour Organization (2017). *Conventions.* Retrieved From www.ilo.org/dyn/normlex/en/f?p=1000:12000:::NO:::

International Labour Organization (2017b). *Article I. C100 – Equal Remuneration Convention, 1951 (No. 100).* Retrieved from http://www.ilo.org/dyn/normlex/en/f?p=NORML EXPUB:12100:0::NO::P12100_ILO_CODE:C100

International Trade Center Communications (2013). *Handmade in Luang Prabang Label boosts handicraft businesses.* Retrieved from www.intracen.org/news/%E2%80%98Handmade-in-Luang-Prabang%E2%80%98-label-boosts-handicraft-businesses/

ISO (n.d.). *Online browsing platform.* Retrieved from www.iso.org/iso/country_codes/iso_3166_code_lists/country_names_and_code_elements.htm

Jackson, M. (2003). *Systems thinking: Creative holism for managers.* Chichester: John Wiley & Sons, Ltd.

Jackson, T. (2009). *Prosperity without Growth: Economics for a Finite Planet.* London: Earthscan.

Jaitley, J. (2001). *Vi vakarm 'schildren: Stories of India's craftspeople.* New Delhi: Institute of Social Sciences.

Jaitley, J. (2005). *Crafts as industry: Creative industries: A symposium on culture based development strategies* (Seminar 553). Retrieved from www.india-seminar.com/2005/553/553%20jaya%20jaitly.htm

Jequier, N., & Blanc, C. (1983). A few definitions of technology. In M. Carr (Ed.), *Thereader: Theory and practice in appropriate technology.* London: Intermediate Technology Publications.

Jin, S. (2015). *Sustainability in a pressure cooker: Platforms for multi-cultural exploration in Vietnam* (PhD Thesis). Delft: Delft University of Technology.

Jin, S., Crul, M., & Brezet, H. (2011). Designers as change agents in emerging economies: An insider-outsider approach to collaborative product development with Vietnamese SMEs: Diversity and unity. In F. F. Roozenburg, L. L. Chen, & P. J. Stappers (Eds.), *Proceedings of IASDR 2011: The 4th world conference on design research.* Delft: IASDR.

Johnson, P. (n.d.). *North south project: A new model of viable design and craft collaborations in the developing world.* Retrieved from http://pattyjohnson.ca/gallery/north-south-project/

John Todd Ecological Design (2018). *Omega center for sustainable living eco machine.* Retrieved from www.toddecological.com/data/uploads/casestudies/jtedcasestudy_omega.pdf

Joore, P., & Brezet, H. (2015). A multilevel design model: The mutual relationship between product-service system development and societal change processes. *Journal of Cleaner Production,* 97: 92–105.

Jordan, A., Wurzel, R., & Zito, A. (2005). The rise of 'new' policy instruments, in comparative perspective: Has governance eclipsed government? *Political Studies,* 53(3): 477–496.

Jørgensen, A., Le Bocq, A., Nazurkina, L., & Hauschild, M. (2008). Methodologies for social life cycle assessment. *International Journal of Life Cycle Assessment,* 13(2): 96–103.

Jørgensen, U. (2012). Mapping and navigating transitions in the multi-level perspective compared with arenas of development. *Research Policy,* 41(6): 996–1010.

Julier, G. (2013). *The culture of design* (3rd edition). London: Sage Publications.

Kang, M., & Guerin, D. (2009). The state of environmentally sustainable interior design practice. *American Journal of Environmental Sciences,* 5(2): 179–186.

Kang, M., Kang, J. H., & Barnes, B. (2008). Interior design characteristics influencing sustainable energy awareness and application. *International Journal of Spatial Design & Research,* 8(10): 17–28.

Karnani, A. (2007). The mirage of marketing to the bottom of the pyramid: How the private sector can help alleviate poverty. *California Management Review,* 4: 90e111.

Keolian, G. A., & Menerey, D. (1993). *Life cycle design guidance manual: Environmental requirements and the product system.* Michigan: United States Environmental Protection Agency.

Keskin, D., Diehl, J. C., & Molenaar, N. (2013). Innovation process of new ventures driven by sustainability. *Journal of Cleaner Production*, 45: 50–60.

Khan, N. (n.d.). *Strategy for revival and sustenance of artisanship: A critical parameter for conservation*. Retrieved from www.academia.edu/12954876/Strategy_for_the_Revival_and_Sustenance_of_Artisanship_A_Critical_Parameter_for_Conservation

Klöpffer, W. (2008). Life cycle sustainability assessment of products. *International Journal of Life Cycle Assessment*, 13(2): 89–95.

Klugman, J. (2010). *The real wealth of nations: Pathways to human development* (Human Development Report 2010). New York: United Nations Development Programme.

Kodapully, J. (n.d.a). *Learning from the Potter: Story of attempting revival of pottery at a traditional potter's community in Kerala*. Retrieved from www.academia.edu/8369457/Learning_from_the_potter-_Story_of_attempting_revival_of_pottery_at_a_-traditional_potters_community_in_Kerala

Kodapully, J. (n.d.b). *Product design to process design exploring/proposing a method for working with communities with traditional craft skills*. Retrieved from www.academia.edu/8369671/Product_design_to_Process_design_exploring_proposing_a_method_for_working_with_communities_with_traditional_craft_skills

Komiyama, H., & Takeuchi, K. (2006). Sustainability science: Building a new discipline. *Sustainability Science*, 1(1): 1–6.

Koning, J. (2001, November 22–23). *Social sustainability in a globalizing world: Context, theory and methodologyexplored*, Tilburg University, The Netherlands, paper prepared for the UNESCO/MOST Meeting, The Hague, Netherlands.

Kouhia, A. (2012). Categorizing the meanings of craft: A multi-perspectival framework for eight interrelated meaning categories. *Techne Series A*, 19(1): 25–40.

Küçüksayraç, E. (2015). Design for sustainability in companies: Strategies, drivers and needs of Turkey's best performing businesses. *Journal of Cleaner Production*, 106: 455–465.

Kumar, S., Kumar, N., & Saxena, V. (2016, January–March). Millennium Development Goals (MDGs) to Sustainable Development Goals (SDGs): Addressing unfinished agenda and Strengthening sustainable development and partnership. *Indian Journalof Community Medicine*, 41(1): 1–4.

Kumar, V., & Christodoulopoulou, A. (2014, January). Sustainability and branding: An integrated perspective. *Industrial Marketing Management*, 43(1): 6–15.

Larkin, J. H., & Simon, H. (1987). Why a diagram is (sometimes) worth ten thousand words. *Cognitive Science*, 11(1): 65–100.

Latouche, S. (2010). Degrowth. *Journal of Cleaner Production*, 18, 519–522.

Laurell, M. (2014). Sustainability of supply chains and sustainable public procurement: A pre study. The Swedish Environmental Management Council. *UN Environment Programme*. Retrieved from www.unep.org/10yfp/Portals/50150/downloads/Final_report_Sustainability_of_supply_chains_SPP_140630_aug19.pdf

Lea, D. (1984). One earth: William Morris's vision. In *William Morris today* (Exhibition Catalogue, pp. 54–56). London: The Institute of Contemporary Arts and ICA.

Le Blanc, D., Liu, W., O'Connor, D., & Zubcevic, I. (2012). *Issue 1: Development cooperation in the light of sustainable development and the SDGs: Preliminary exploration of the issues* (Rio+20 Working Papers). New York: United Nations Division for Sustainable Development (UNDESA).

Lehmann, A., Russi, D., Bala, A., Finkbeiner, M., & Fullana-i-Palmer, P. (2011). Integration of social aspects in decision support, based on life cycle thinking. *Sustainability*, 2011(3): 562–577.

Lélé, S. M. (1991). Sustainable development: A critical review. *World Development*, 19: 607–621.

Levin, M. (1993). Creating networks for rural economic development in Norway. *Human Relations*, 46(2):193–218.

Liebl, M., & Roy, T. (2000). *Handmade in India: Preliminary analysis of crafts producers and crafts production in India: Issues, initiatives, interventions* (A report prepared for the Policy Sciences Center, Inc. CT and World Bank). Washington, DC: World Bank.

Life Cycle Initiative (n.d.). *Methodological sheets of sub-categories of impact for a social LCA*. Retrieved from www.estis.net/sites/lcinit/default.asp?site=lcinit&page_id=EDA1E98F-412F-4F51-B407-3A7E006E1B83

Lloyd, C. (2008). *What on earth happened . . . in brief*. London: Bloomsbury.

Lobovikov, M., Paudel, S., Piazza, M., Ren, H., & Wu, J. (2007). *World bamboo resources: A thematic study prepared in the framework of the global forest resources assessment 2005* (Non-Wood Products 18). Rome: Food and Agriculture Organization.

Lockton, D. (2013). *Design with intent: A design pattern toolkit for environmental and social behaviour change* (PhD Thesis). London: School of Engineering and Design, Brunel University.

Lofthouse, V. A. (2004). Investigation into the role of core industrial designers in ecodesign projects. *Design Studies*, 25(2): 215–227. http://doi.org/10.1016/j.destud.2003.10.007

Lofthouse, V. A. (2006). Ecodesign tools for designers: Defining the requirements. *Journal of Cleaner Production*, 14(15–16): 1386–1395.

Lofthouse, V. A. (2017). Preparing the way for mainstream sustainable product design. *Form Akademisk – Forskningstidsskrift for Design Og Designdidaktikk*, 10(2).

Lofthouse, V. A., & Prendeville, S. (2018). Human-centred design of products and services for the circular economy: A review. *The Design Journal*, 21(4): 451–476

Lofthouse, V. A., & Stevenson, N. (2013, August 26–30). *Is the industrial designer's changing role improving their opportunities for responsible design practices?* Paper presented at the 5th International Congress of International Association of Societies of Design Research, IASDR 2013: Consilience and Innovation in Design, Tokyo, Japan.

Lohas Group (n.d). *Lohas market sectors*. Retrieved from www.lohas.com/about

Lønnea, I. A., & Skjold, E. (2016, June 27–30). *Design as a driver for understanding sustainability and creating value in the Fur Industry*. Proceedings of DRS 16, 3, Brighton, UK.

Lovins, A. B., Lovins, H. L., & Hawken, P. (1999, May–June). A road map for natural capitalism. *Harvard Business Review*.

Lumsden, F. (2014, March 20). *Cradle to cradle: 4 success stories from counter tops to fabrics*. Retrieved from www.greenbiz.com/blog/2014/03/20/4-cradle-cradle-certified-product-breakthroughs

Lyon, S. (2006). Evaluating fair trade consumption: Politics, defetishization and producer participation. *International Journal of Consumer Studies*, 30(5): 452–464.

Mabogunje, A. L. (2002). Poverty and environmental degradation: Challenges within the global economy. *Environment*, 44(1): 10–18.

Mäler, K.-G. (1990). International environmental problems. *Oxford Review of Economic Policy*, 6(1): 80–108.

Mann, S. (2011). *Sustainable lens: A visual guide*. Dunedin: NewSplash Studio.

Marchand, T. (2011). Craft-work as problem solving. *Making Futures Journal*, 3: 35–38.

Mate, K. J. (2006, November). *Champions, conformists, and challengers: Attitudes of interior designers as expressions of sustainability through materials selection*. Paper presented at the Design Research Society IADE International Conference, Lisbon.

Mathews, F. (2011). Towards a deeper philosophy of biomimicry. *Organization & Environment*, 24(4): 364e387. http://dx.doi.org/10.1177/1086026611425689

Maxwell, D., Sheate, W., & van der Vorst, R. (2003, October). *Sustainable innovation in product and service development.* Paper presented at Towards Sustainable Product Design 8, Stockholm.

Mazijn, B., Doom, R., Peeters, H., Spillemaeckers, S., Vanhoutte, G., Taverniers, L., Lavrysen, L., van Braeckel, D., & Duque Rivera, J. (2004). *Ecological, social and economic aspects of integrated product policy: Integrated product assessment and the development of the label 'sustainable development'* (Final report). Brussels: Belgian Science Policy.

Mazurek, J. (2002). Government-sponsored voluntary programs for firms: An initial survey. In T. Deitz & P. C. Stern (Eds.), *New tools for environmental protection: Education, information, and voluntary measures* (pp. 219–234). Washington, DC: National Academy Press.

McKenzie, S. (2004). Social sustainability: towards some definitions: Hawke Research Institute, University of South Australia Magill

McKeown, R. (2002). *Education for sustainable development toolkit version 2.* Retrieved from http://esdtoolkit.org/esd_toolkit_v2.pdf

McKinley, W., Latham, S., & Braun, M. (2014). Organizational decline and innovation: Turnarounds and downward spirals. *Academy of Management Review*, 39: 88–110.

McManus, P. (1996). Contested terrains: Politics, stories and discourses of sustainability. *Environmental Politics*, 5(1): 48–73.

Mead, M., & Metraux, R. (Eds.) (1953). *The study of culture at a distance.* Chicago: University of Chicago Press.

Merriam, S. B. (1998). *Qualitative research and case study applications in education.* San Francisco: Jossey-Bass.

Metcalf, B. (1997). Craft and art, culture and biology. In P. Dormer (Ed.), *Theculture of craft* (pp. 67–82). Manchester: Manchester University Press.

Mil-Homens Loureio, J. M. (2011). *Labeling schemes or labeling scams? Auditors' perspectives on ISO 14001 certification* (PhD Dissertation). Blacksburg: Virginia Polytechnic Institute and State University.

Moon, B. K. (2014). *Report on the UN's development agenda beyond 2015.* Geneva: United Nations.

Moon, J. A. (2004). *A handbook of reflective and experiential learning: Theory and practice.* New York: Routledge-Falmer.

Morable, L. (2000). *Using active learning techniques: Teal compendium.* Texas: Richland College.

Morelli, N. (2003, April). *Design for social responsibility and market oriented design: Convergences and divergences.* Paper presented at the Common Techne, the design wisdom, Barcelona.

Morelli, N. (2006, November). *Industrialization and social innovation: Design in a new context.* Paper presented at the Design Research Society, International Conference, Lisbon.

Moreno, Y. J., Santagata, W., & Tabassum, A. (2004, June). *Material cultural heritage, cultural diversity, and sustainable development.* Paper presented at ACEI, 13th International Conference on Cultural Economics, Chicago.

Moreno, Y. J., Santagata, W., & Tabassum, A. (2005). *Material cultural heritage, cultural diversity, and sustainable development* (EBLA Working Paper No. 07/2005). Turin: Economics of Culture, Institutions and Creativity (EBLA).

Moser, C. (1989). Gender planning in the third world: Meeting practical and strategic gender needs. *World Development*, 17(11): 1799–1825.

Munasinghe, M. (1992, June). *Environmental economics and sustainable development*. Paper presented at the UN Earth Summit, Rio de Janeirio.

Munasinghe, M. (1993). *The East Asian miracle* (Policy Research Report). Washington, DC: World Bank.

Munasinghe, M. (2009). *Sustainable development in practice: Sustainomics methodology and applications*. Cambridge: Cambridge University Press.

Munasinghe, M. (2010). *Making development more sustainable: Sustainomics framework and practical applications*. Colombo: Munasinghe Institute for Development (MIND).

Munasinghe, M., & Shearer, W. (Eds.) (1995). *Defining and measuring sustainability: The biogeophysical foundation*. Washington, DC: The United Nations University and the World Bank.

Murray, K. (2010). Outsourcing the hand: An analysis of craft: Design collaborations across the global divide. *Design + Craft Enquiry*, 2: 1–23.

Na, Y. (2011). Repositioning contemporary crafts by crafts-consumers' values: Roles of crafts and craftspeople for sustainable crafts. *Making Futures Journal*, 2: 157–167.

Narain, S. (2012). Rio + 20: Why it failed? *The Huffington Post*. Retrieved from www.huffingtonpost.com/sunita-narain/rio20-why-it-failed_b_1648399.html

Nash, J., & Ehrenfeld, J. (1997). Codes of environmental management practice: Assessing their potential as a tool for change. *Annual Reviews Energy and Environment*, 22(5): 487–535.

Naylor, G. (1980). *The arts and crafts movement: A study of its sources, deals and influence on design theory*. London: Studio Vista.

New Zealand Ministry for Culture and Heritage (2006). *Cultural well-being and local government Report 1: Definitions and contexts of cultural well-being*. Retrieved from www.mch.govt.nz/files/report1.pdf

Nkechinyere, V. A. (2010). *Environmental sustainability and sustainable growth: A global outlook* (Master's Thesis). Philadelphia: University of Pennsylvania.

North, D. (1990). *Institutions, institutional change and the economic performance*. Cambridge: Cambridge University Press.

Nugraha, A. (2010, June). *Transforming tradition for sustainability through 'TCUSM' tool*. Paper presented at the InSEA European Congress on 'Sustainable Art Education', University of Lapland, Rovaniemi.

Nurse, K. (2006). *Culture as the fourth pillar of sustainable development* (Report prepared for Commonwealth Secretariat). London: Commonwealth Secretariat.

O'Connor, M. (2007). The four spheres framework for sustainability. *Ecological Complexity*, 3(2006): 285–292.

Oksannen, M. (2007). Species extinction and collective responsibility. In Z. Davran & S. Voss (Eds.),*The proceedings of the twenty-first world congress of philosophy. Vol. 3: Human rights* (pp. 179–183). Ankara: Philosophical Society of Turkey.

Oosterlaken, I. (2008). *Product innovation for human development: A capability approach to designing for the bottom of the pyramid* (Internal Report for the 3TU Centre for Ethics and Technology). Eindhoven,

O'Rafferty, S., & O'Connor, F. (2010). Regional perspectives on capacity building for ecodesign: Insights from Wales. In J. Sarkis, J. Cordeiro, & D. V. Brust (Eds.), *Facilitating sustainable innovation through collaboration* (pp. 1–16). London: Springer.

Overy, R. (2007). *Complete history of the world*. London: Times Books.

Panchal, J. A., & Ranjan, M. P. (1993). *Feasibility report on the proposed institute of crafts.* Ahmedabad: National Institute of Design.

Papanek, V. (1971). *Design for the real world: Human ecology and social change.* New York: Pantheon Books.

Papanek, V. (1995). *The green imperative: Ecology and ethics in design and architecture.* London: Thames and Hudson Ltd.

Pape, J., Rau, H., Fahy, F., & Davies, A. (2011). Developing policies and instruments for sustainable household consumption: Irish experiences and futures. *Journal of Consumer Policy,* 34: 25–42.

Partridge, E. (2005, September 28–30). *Social sustainability: A useful theoretical framework.* Paper presented at Australasian Dunedin, New Zealand.

Perez, V. M. (2016). *Facilitating sustainability of a product's lifecycle impact in the early stages of product development* (Doctoral thesis). Northumbria University: Newcastle.

Peters, A. (1997). The status of craft. In P. Dormer (Ed.), *The culture of craft* (pp. 17–20). Manchester: Manchester University Press.

Peterson, G., Allen, C. R., & Holling, C. S. (1998). Ecological resilience, biodiversity, and scale. *Ecosystems,*1(1): 6–18.

Pezzey, J. C. V., & Toman, M. A. (2002). *The economics of sustainability: A review of journal articles* (Discussion Paper 02–03). Washington, DC: Resources for the Future.

Pimm,S. L. (1984). The complexity and stability of ecosystems. *Nature,* 307(5949): 321–326.

Pizzirani, S., McLaren, S. J., & Seadon, J. K. (2014). Is there a place for culture in life cycle sustainability assessment? *International Journal of Life Cycle Assessment,* 19(6): 1316–1330.

Plomp, T. (2009). Educational design research: An introduction. In T. Plomp & N. Nieveen (Eds.), *Educational design research: Illustrative cases* (pp. 9–50). Enschede: SLO.

Plymouth College of Art (n.d.). *Making futures: The crafts in the context of emerging global sustainability agendas.* Retrieved from http://makingfutures.plymouthart.ac.uk/

Potts, J., van der Meer, J., & Daitchman, J. (2010). *The state of sustainability initiatives review 2010: Sustainability and transparency* (SSI Review 2010). Winnepeg: International Institute for Sustainable Development & International Institute for Environment and Development.

Prahalad, C. K. (2004). *The fortune of the bottom of the pyramid.* Upper Saddle River, N J: Wharton School Publishing Upper Saddle River.

Prahalad, C. K., & Hart, S. L. (2002). The fortune at the bottom of the pyramid. *Strategy + Business,* 26(1): 54–67.

Putnam, R. (1995). Tuning in, tuning out: The strange disappearance of social capital in America. *Political Science and Politics,* 28(4): 664–683.

PwC. (n.d.). *Sustainability: Moving from compliance to leadership.* Retrieved from www.pwc.com/us/en/technology-forecast/2011/issue4/features/feature-sustainability-as-normal-business.jhtml

Rangan, V. K., Quelch, J. A., Herrero, G., & Barton, B. (2007). *Business solutions for the global poor: Creating social and economic value.* San Francisco: Jossey-Bass.

Ranjan, M. P. (1995, June). *Green design and bamboo handicrafts: A scenario for research and action in the Asian Region.* Paper presented at the International Bamboo Workshop, Bali.

Ranjan, M. P. (2009). *Katlamara multiplied: Seeds of design in Tripura.* Retrieved from http://design-for-india.blogspot.com/2009/05/katlamara-multiplied-seeds-of-design-in.html

Ranjan, M. P. (n.d.). *Design for India.* Retrieved from http://design-for-india.blogspot.in/

Rao, S. S. (2006). Indigenous knowledge organization: An Indian scenario. *International Journal of Information Management*, 26(2006): 224–233.

Rawls, R. (1971). *A theory of justice as fairness.* Cambridge: Harvard University Press.

Reap, J., Baumeister, D., & Bras, B. (2005). *Holism, biomimicry and sustainable engineering.* ASME 2005 International Mechanical Engineering Congress and Exposition (IMECE2005) ASME (pp. 423–431).

Rees, H. (1997). Patterns of making: Thinking and making in industrial design. In P. Dormer (Ed.), *The culture of craft* (pp. 116–136). Manchester: Manchester University Press.

Reijnders, L. (2008). Are emissions or wastes consisting of biological nutrients good or healthy? *Journal of Cleaner Production*, 16(10): 1138–1141.

Rennings, K. (2000). Redefining innovation: Eco-innovation research and the contribution from ecological economics. *Ecological Economics*, 32(2): 319–332.

Repetto, R. (1985, October). *Natural resource accounting in a resource-based economy: An Indonesian case study.* Paper presented at 3rd Environmental Accounting Workshop, Paris.

Reubens, R. (2005). *Final status report: INBAR-GTZ project.* New Delhi: International Network for Bamboo and Rattan.

Reubens, R. (2010a). Bamboo canopy: Creating new reference-points for the craft of the Kotwalia community in India through sustainability. *Craft Research*, 1: 11–38.

Reubens, R. (2010b). *Bamboo in sustainable contemporary design* (INBAR Working Paper 60). Beijing: International Network for Bamboo and Rattan.

Reubens, R. (2010c). *Diagnostic study report for development of bamboo craft cluster at Vyara, Songadh, Utchal and Valod blocks of Tapi district.* Ahmedabad: National Bank for Agricultural and Rural Development.

Reubens, R. (2013a). Holistic sustainability through design innovation: The Rhizome approach. *The Journal of Design Strategies: Designing for Billions*, 6(1): 67–75.

Reubens, R. (2013b). *Achieving, assessing and communicating sustainability: A manual for the Vietnamese handicraft sector.* Vienna: United Nations Industrial Development Organization.

Reubens, R. (2016a). Towards holistic sustainability design: The Rhizome approach. In P. Sparke & F. Fisher (Eds.), *The Routledge companion to design studies* (pp. 409–420). London: Routledge.

Reubens, R. (2016b, March 16). *Rhizome approach* [Video file]. Retrieved from www.youtube.com/watch?v=B3_RVr2J7ts

Reubens, R. (2016c). *To craft, by design, for sustainability: Towards holistic sustainability design for developing country enterprises.* PhD thesis, Faculty of Industrial Design Engineering, Design for Sustainability Program. Delft: Delft Universiy of Technology.

REWEGroup (n.d.). *Pro-planet: The Rewe Group navigation system for more sustainable products and services.* Retrieved March 5, 2012, from www.proplanetlabel.com/Download/1203HandbProPlanet_engl_Web_A4h.pdf.

Rhodes, S. (2011). *Beyond 'nourishing the soul of a nation': Craft in the context of South Africa.* Making Futures: The Crafts as Change Maker in Sustainably Aware Cultures, 2. ISSN 2042-1664.

Risatti, H. (2007). *A theory of craft: Function and aesthetic expression.* Chapel Hill: University of North Carolina Press.

Risz, Y., Cammarata, C., Wellise, C., & Swibel, M. (2018, April 30–May 2). *Show me the money: Societal LCC or optimizing for societal and business transactions.* 25th CIPF Life Cycle Engineering (LCE) Conference, Copenhagen, Denmark.

Robinson, J. (2004). Squaring the circle? Some thoughts on the idea of sustainable development. *Ecological Economics*, 48: 369–384.

Robson, C. (2011). *Real world research: A resource for social-scientists and practitioner-researchers* (3rd edition). Oxford: Blackwell Publishing.

Roddick, A. (2001). *Globalization: Take it personally*. London: Harper Collins Publishers Ltd.

Roduner, D. (2007). *Donor Interventions in value chain development* (Working Paper). Berne: Swiss Agency for Development and Cooperation.

Rostow, W. W. (1960). *The stages of economic growth: A non-communist manifesto*. London: Cambridge University Press.

Rothermund, D. (1992). *India in the great depression, 1929–1939*. New Delhi: Manohar Publications.

Roy, T. (1999). *Traditional industry in the economy of colonial India*. Cambridge: Cambridge University Press.

Roy, T. (2001). 'Outline of a history of labour in traditional industry in India' Issues 2001–2015 of NLI research studies series, Writing labour history series, V. V. Giri National Labour Institute: Noida.

Rubik, E. F., & Frankl, E. P. (Eds.) (2005). *The future of eco-labeling*. Sheffield: Greenleaf Publishing.

Runnalls, C. (2007). *Choreographing community sustainability: The importance of cultural planning to community viability*. Vancouver: Centre of Expertise on Culture and Communities.

Ryan, C. (2003). Learning from a decade (or so) of eco-design experience, part I. *Journal of Industrial Ecology*, 7(2): 10–12.

Salmon, E. (2000). Kincentric ecology: Indigenous perceptions of the human-nature relationship. *Ecological Applications*, 10(5): 1327–1332.

Sarkar, A. N. (2013). Promoting eco-innovations to leverage sustainable development of eco-industry and green growth. *European Journal of Sustainable Development*, 2(1): 171–224.

Sarkis, J., & Zhu, Q. (2017). Environmental sustainability and production: Taking the road less travelled. *International Journal of Production Research*, 56(1–2): 743–759.

Saroyan, A., & Amundsen, C. (Eds.) (2004). *Rethinking teaching in higher education: From a course design workshop to a faculty development framework*. Sterling, Virginia: Stylus Publishing, LLC.

Satyanand, S., & Singh, K. (1995). *India's artisans: A status report*. New Delhi: Society for Rural, Urban and Tribal Initiatives. (p. ii).

Saunders, B. W. (1971). Facilities design: A problem of systems analysis. *International Journal of Production Research*, 9(1): 3–10.

Scheer, D., & Rubik, F. (2005). Environmental product information schemes: An overview. In F. Rubik & P. Frankl (Eds.), *The future of eco-labelling: Making environmental product labelling systems effective* (pp. 46–88). Sheffield: Green Leaf.

Schmidheiny, S. (1992). *Changing course: A global business perspective on development and the environment*. Cambridge: MIT Press.

Schumacher, E. F. (1973). *Small is beautiful: Economics as if people mattered*. London: Blond and Briggs Ltd.

Schwartz, M. (n.d.). *Best practices in experiential learning*. Retrieved from www.ryerson.ca/content/dam/lt/resources/handouts/ExperientialLearningReport.pdf

Scrase, T. (2003). Precarious production: Globalisation and artisan labour in the third world. *Third World Quarterly*, 24(3): 449–461.

Secondo, J. (2002). Poor materials imaginatively applied: New approaches to furniture. In P. Greenhalgh (Ed.), *The persistence of craft* (pp. 117–127). London: A & C Black (Publishers) Ltd.

Sen, A. K. (1980). Equality of what? In S. M. McMurrin (Ed.), *The Tanner lectures on human values* (Vol. 1, pp. 195–220). Salt Lake City: University of Utah Press.

Sen, A. K. (1999). *Development as freedom.* Oxford: Oxford University Press.

Seuring, S., & Muller, M. (2008). From a literature review to a conceptual framework for sustainable supply chain management. *Journal of Cleaner Production,* 16(15): 1699–1710.

Sharma, K. (2007). *National policies for natural resource management marginalization of poor rural women.* Retrieved from www.cwds.ac.in/OCPaper/NaturalResourcesManagement KumudSharma

Shedroff, N. (2009). *Design is the problem: The future of design must be sustainable.* Brooklyn, NY: Rosenfeld Media.

Sheldon, R., & Arens, E. (1932). *Consumer engineering: A new technique for prosperity.* New York: Harper and Brothers.

Shenton, A. K. (2004). Strategies for ensuring trustworthiness in qualitative research projects. *Education for Information,* 22(2): 63–75.

Sherwin, C., & Evans, S. (2000, August). *Ecodesign innovation: Is 'early' always the 'best'?* Paper presented at IEEE Xplore, San Francisco.

Shiva, V. (2005). *Earth democracy.* Cambridge: South End Press.

The Sigma Project (n.d.). *The Sigma guidelines: Putting sustainable development into practice: A guide for organizations.* Retrieved from www.projectsigma.co.uk/Guidelines/SigmaGuidelines.pdf

Silverman, D. (2000). *Doing qualitative research: A practical handbook.* London: Sage Publications.

Simanis, E., & Hart, S. (2008). *Base of the pyramid protocol* (2nd edition). Ithaca, NY: Cornell University.

Sinclair, D. (1997). Self-regulation versus command and control? Beyond false dichotomies. *Law & Policy,* 19(4): 529–560.

Sire, J. W. (1976). *The universe next door: A basic worldview catalogue.* Leicester: IVP.

Sixth College (n.d.). *Icebreakers, team building activities, and energizers.* Retrieved from https://sixth.ucsd.edu/_files/_home/student-life/icebreakers-teambuilding-activities-energizers.pdf

Smink, C. K. (2002). *Modernisation of environmental regulations: End-of-life vehicle regulations in the Netherlands and Denmark* (PhD Dissertation). Aalborg: Aalborg University, Department of Development and Planning.

Smith, C. (2007). *Design for the other 90%.* New York: Cooper-Hewitt, National Design Museum.

Smith, D., & Kochhar, R. (2004). *The Dhokra artisans of Bankura and Dariapur, West Bengal: A case study and knowledge archive of technological change in progress.* London: Arts and Humanities Research Board.

Snodgrass, D., & Biggs, D. (1996). *Industrialization and the small firm: Patterns and policies.* San Francisco: International Center for Economic Growth.

Social Compliance Initiative (BSCI) (2015). *Business social compliance initiative code of conduct.* Retrieved from www.standardsmap.org/review.aspx?standards=5

Society for Rural, Urban and Tribal Initiatives (1995). *India's artisans: A status report.* New Delhi: Excellent Printing House.

Sridhar, K. (2011). The emissions trading scheme: An analysis on its economic instruments and methods to reduce greenhouse gas emissions. *International Journal of Business Excellence,* 4(1): 1–14.

Stahel, W., McDonough, W., & Braungart, M. (2002). *Cradle to cradle: Remaking the way we make things.* New York: North Point Press.

Stake, R. E. (1994). Case studies. In N. K. Denzin & Y. S. Lincoln (Eds.), *Handbook of qualitative research* (pp. 236–247). Thousand Oaks: Sage.

Stanners, D., Bosch. P., Dom, A., Gabrielsen, P., Gee, D., Martin, J., Rickard, L., & Weber, J. L. (2007). Frameworks for environmental assessment and indicators at the EEA. In T. Hak, B. Moldan, & L. Dahl (Eds.), *Sustainability indicators* (pp. 127–144). Washington, DC: Island Press.

Stappers, P. J. (2007). Doing design as part of doing research. In R. Michel (Ed.) *Design research now: Essays and selected projects* (pp. 81–97). Basel: Birkhauser Verlag.

Stavins, R. N., Wagner, A. F., & Wagner, G. (2003). Interpreting sustainability in economic terms: Dynamic efficiency plus intergenerational equity. *Economics Letters*, 79(2003): 339–343.

Stevenson, N. (2013). *A better world by design? An investigation into industrial design consultants undertaking responsible design within their commercial remits.* Loughborough: Loughborough University.

Stevenson, N., Lilley, D., Lofthouse, V. A., & Cheyne, A. (2011). The complexity of responsible design: Key factors affecting industrial design consultants addressing the greater needs of society. In *Sustainable innovation 11: 'State of the art' in sustainable innovation and design, 16th international conference* (pp. 178–188). Farnham, Surrey: The Center for Sustainable Design:.

Stewart, L. (2010) *Eco labels 101: Green certifications explained!* Retrieved from https://inhabitat.com/demystifying-eco-labels/

Stiglitz, J. (2002). Globalization and its discontents. *Economic Notes*, 32(1): 123–142.

Storacker, A., Wever, R., Dewulf, K., & Blankenburg, D. (2013, December 4–8). *Sustainability in the front-end of innovation at design agencies.* 8th International Symposium on Environmentally Conscious Design and Inverse Manufacturing, Proceedings. Jeju Island, Korea.

Strand, R. (2011). Toward sustainable sustainability learning: Lessons from a U.S. MBA study abroad program in Scandinavia. *Journal of Strategic Innovation and Sustainability*, 7(2): 41–63.

Streeten, P. P., Burki, S. J., Haq, M., Hicks, N., & Stewart, F. (1981). *First things first, meeting basic human needs in developing countries.* New York: Oxford University Press.

Sustain (2007). *Discussion paper from Sustain: Pictorial representations for sustainability scoring.* Retrieved March 17, 2011, from www.sustainweb.org/pdf/sustainability_labelling_flowers.pdf

Sustainable Brands (2017, January 5). *Study: Effectively marketing sustainable goods could represent $1T market opportunity.* Retrieved from www.sustainablebrands.com/news_and_views/stakeholder_trends_insights/sustainable_brands/study_effectively_marketing_sustainabl

Sustainable Business Associates (n.d.). *National Moroccan handicraft label.* Retrieved from www.sba-int.ch/1315-National_Moroccan_Handicraft_Label

Sustainable Development Commission (2008). *Green, healthy and fair: A review of government´s role in supporting sustainable supermarket food.* London: Sustainable Development Commission.

Sustainable Development Research Institute (1998). *Social capital formation and institutions for sustainability.* Vancouver: SDRI.

Sutton, P. (2004). *Living well within our environment: A perspective on environmental sustainability* (A paper for the Victorian Commissioner for Environmental Sustainability). Retrieved from www.green-innovations.asn.au/A-Perspective-on-Environmental-Sustainability.pdf

Swedish Design Industry (2004). *Design maturity in Swedish companies.* Stockholm: Swedish Industrial Design Foundation and the Association of Swedish Engineering Industry.

Tapscott, D., & Williams, A. D. (2006). *Wikinomics: How mass collaboration changes everything.* New York: Portfolio.

Taylor-Hough, D. (2011). *Frugal living for dummies.* New Jersey: John Wiley and Sons.

Technology Innovation Hub (n.d.). *An attempt to define collaborative innovation: Thoughts from fieldwork.* Retrieved from www.ict4dc.org/blog/andrea-jim%C3%A9nez-cisneros/attempt-define-collaborative-innovation-thoughts-fieldwork

Teisl, M. F., & Roe, B. (2005). Evaluating the factors that impact the effectiveness of eco-labelling programs. In S. Karup & C. Russel (Eds.), *New horizons in environmental economics: Environment, information and consumer behavior* (pp. 65–90). Cheltenham: Elgar.

Teufel, J., Rubik, F., Scholl, G., Stratmann, B., Graulich, K., & Manhart, A. (2009). *Untersuchung zur möglichen Ausgestaltung und Marktimplementierung eines Nachhaltigkeitslabels zur Verbraucherinformation. Endbericht.* Freiburg: *Federal Office for Agriculture and Food.*

Thorpe, A. (2007). *The designer's atlas of sustainability.* London: Island Press.

Thorpe, A. (a.b.thorpe@open.ak.uk) (2010), *Craft Research Paper*, Email to Rebecca Reubens (rreubens@gmail.com), 7th May 2010.

Toffler, A. (1980). *The third wave.* New York: Bantam Books.

Tonkinwise, C. (2015, September 24). *Keynote address.* Lecture presented at Making Futures 4 in Mount Edgcumbe House, Plymouth.

Truffer, B., Markard, J., & Wustenhagen, R. (2001). Eco-labeling of electricity: Strategies and tradeoffs in the definition of environmental standards. *Energy Policy,* 29(11): 885–897.

United Nations (n.d.) *About the Sustainable Development Goals.* Retrieved from https://www.un.org/sustainabledevelopment/sustainable-development-goals/

United Nations (2015, August 12). *Draft outcome of the United Nations Summit for the adoption of the post-2015 development agenda.* Retrieved from www.un.org/ga/search/view_doc.asp?symbol=A/69/L.85&Lang=E

United Nations (n.d.). *The Rio conventions.* Retrieved from www.cbd.int/rio/

United Nations Conference on Sustainable Development (2012). *The future we want* (Outcome Document of the United Nations Conference on Sustainable Development). Retrieved from www.uncsd2012.org/thefuturewewant.html

United Nations Conference on Trade and Development (2008). *The challenge of assessing the creative economy: Towards informed policy making* (Creative Economy Report 2008). Geneva: UNCTD.

United Nations Industrial Development Organization (2002). *Creative industries and micro & small scale enterprise development: A contribution to poverty alleviation* (Project XP/RAS/05/002). Vienna: UNIDO.

United Nations Development Program (2004). *Cultural liberty in today's diverse world* (Human Development Report 2004). New York: UNDP.

United Nations Development Programme (UNDP), & United Nations Educational, Scientific and Cultural Organization (UNESCO) (2013). *Creative economy report 2013: Widening local development pathways.* Paris: UNDP & UNESCO. Retrieved from www.unesco.org/culture/pdf/creative-economy-report-2013.pdf

United Nations Economic and Social Council Economic Commission for Africa (2013). *Industrialization for an emerging Africa.* Issues Paper, Sixth Joint Annual Meetings of the ECA Conference of African Ministers of Finance, Planning and Economic Development and AU Conference of Ministers of Economy and Finance. E/ECA/CM/46/2 AU/CAMEF/MIN/2(VIII). Abidjan: African Union Commission.

United Nations Educational, Scientific and Cultural Programme (1995). *Ourcreative diversity* (Report of the World Commission on Culture and Development). Paris: UNESCO.

United Nations Educational, Scientific and Cultural Organization (UNESCO) (2002). *Universal declaration on cultural diversity* (Cultural Diversity Series No. 1: A Document for the World Summit on Sustainable Development). Paris: UNESCO.

United Nations Educational, Scientific and Cultural Organization (UNESCO) (2005). *Background documents: Elements of a policy framework* (Document Developed at the Asia-Pacific Creative Communities Symposium, Promoting the Cultural Industries for Local Socio-Economic Development: A Strategy for the 21st Century). Bangkok: UNESCO.

United Nations Educational, Scientific and Cultural Programme (2009). *UNESCO culture for development indicators*. Retrieved from http://en.unesco.org/creativity/sites/creativity/files/brochurecdis_web_only_eng_0.pdf

United Nations Environment Programme (2005). *Selection, design and implementation of economic instruments in the solid waste management sector in Kenya: The case of plastic bags.* Retrieved from www.unep.ch/etb/publications/EconInst/Kenya.pdf

United Nations Environmental Program (2009). *Guidelines for social life cycle assessment of products*. UNEP-SETAC Life-Cycle Initiative. Paris: UNEP.

United Nations Environmental Programme (UNEP) (2006). *Design for sustainability: A practical approach for developing countries*. Paris: UNEP.

United Nations Industrial Development Organization (2013). *Sustaining employment growth: The role of manufacturing and structural change overview* (Industrial Development Report 2013). Vienna: UNIDO.

United Nations Sustainable Development (1992). *Agenda 21*. Retrieved from https://sustainabledevelopment.un.org/content/documents/Agenda21.pdf

United States Congress, Office of Technology Assessment (1992). *Green products by design: Choices for a cleaner environment (OTA-E-541)*. Washington, DC: United States Government Printing Office.

Unsustainable (2016). *OxfordDictionaries.com*. Retrieved from www.oxforddictionaries.com/definition/english/unsustainable

Unsustainability (2019). *wordnik.com*. Retrieved from https://www.wordnik.com/words/unsustainability

Valdivia, S., Ugaya, C. M. L., Hildenbrand, J., Traverso, M., Mazijn, B., & Sonnemann, G. (2013). A UNEP/SETAC approach towards a life cycle sustainability assessment: Our contribution to Rio+20. *The International Journal of Life Cycle Assessment*, 18(9): 1673–1685.

Valencia, A., Mugge, R., Schoormans, J. P. L., & Schifferstein, N. J. (2015). The design of smart product-service systems (PSSs): An exploration of design characteristics. *International Journal of Design*, 1(1). Retrieved from www.ijdesign.org/index.php/IJDesign/article/view/1740/677

Vallance, S., Perkins, H. C., & Dixon, J. E. (2011). What is social sustainability? A clarification of concepts. *Geoforum*, 43: 248–342.

Valtonen, A. (2005, May). *Six decades: And six different roles for the industrial designer*. Paper presented at the Nordic Design Research Conference, Copenhagen.

Van Boeijen, A., & Daalhuizen J. (2013). *Delft design guide*. Amsterdam: BIS Publishers.

Van Boeijen, S., Jaap, D., & van der Schoor, R. (2014). *Delft design guide: Design strategies and methods*. Amsterdam: BIS Publishers.

Van den Akker, J. (1999). Principles and methods of development research. In J. van den Akker, R. Branch, K. Gustafson, N. Nieveen, & T. Plomp (Eds.), *Design approaches and tools in education and training* (pp. 1–15). Dordrecht: Kluwer Academic Publishers.

Van den Akker, J., Gravemeijer, K., McKenney, S., & Nieveen, N. (Eds.) (2006). *Educational design research*. London: Routledge.

Van der Lugt, P. (2007). *Dutch design meets bamboo*. Einhoven: (Z)oo Producties.

Van der Lugt, P. (2008). *Design interventions for simulating bamboo's commercialization: 'Dutch design meets bamboo' as a replicable model* (PhD Thesis). Delft: Delft University of Technology.

Van der Lugt, P. (2017). *Booming Bamboo*. Naarden, the Netherlands: Materia.

Van der Lugt, P., & Otten, G. (2010). *Bamboo product commercialization for the West: A state-of-the-art analysis of bottlenecks and opportunities* (INBAR Technical Report 29). Beijing: International Network for Bamboo and Rattan.

Van Hemel, C. (1998). *Ecodesign empirically explored: Design for environment in Dutch small and medium sized enterprises* (PhD Thesis). Delft: Delft University of Technology.

Van Hemel, C., & Cramer, J. (2002). Barriers and stimuli for ecodesign in SMEs. *Journal of Cleaner Production*, 10(5): 439–453.

Van Maanen, J. (1983). The fact and fiction in organizational ethnography. In J. Van Maanen (Ed.), *Qualitative methodology* (pp. 37–55). Beverly Hills: Sage.

VDI (1993). *Konstruieren recyclinggerechter technischer produckte (Designing technical products for ease of recycling)*. VDI-Richtlinien (VDI Standards), VDI 2243-Gesselschaft Entwicklung Konstruktion Vertrieb.

Veillard, P. (2014). *Gender and fair trade handicrafts: The impact of fair trade handicrafts on women's empowerment in India and Bangladesh*. Wavre: OXFAM.

Venable, J. R. (2009, June). *Identifying and addressing stakeholder interests in design research: An analysis using critical system heuristics*. Paper presented at the IFIP WG 8.2 Working Conference on the Role of IS in Leveraging the Intelligence and Creativity of SMEs. Guimaraes.

Vencatachellum, I. (2006). Foreword. In Craft Revival Trust (Ed.), *Designers meet artisans* (pp. v–vi). New Delhi: Grass Root Publications Pvt. Ltd.

Vezzoli, C. A., & Manzini, E. (2008). *Design for environmental sustainability*. London: Springer Science & Business Media.

Victor, P. A. (2008). *Managing without growth: Slower by design, not disaster, advances inecological economics*. Cheltenham, UK & Northampton, MA: Edward Elgar.

Vietcraft Excellence (2015). *Vietcraft excellence*. Retrieved from http://vietcraftexcellence.org/

Vogtländer, J. (2011). *Life cycle assessment and carbon sequestration: Bamboo products of MOSO Internaltional* (LCA Report). Delft: TU Delft.

Volstad, N. L. (2008, August 21–23). *Biomimicry: A useful tool for the industrial designer: Shedding light on nature as a source of inspiration in industrial design*. NordDesign 2008, Estonia.

Waage, S. A. (2005). Re-considering product design: A practical 'road-map' for integration of sustainability issues. *Journal of Cleaner Production*, 15(2007): 638–649.

Wahl, D. C., &Baxter, S. (2008). 'The designer' S role in facilitating sustainable solutions. *Design Issues*, 24.

Walker, J. (1989). *Design history and the history of design*. Winchester: Pluto Press.

Walker, S. (1998). Experiments in sustainable product design. *The Journal of Sustainable Product Design*, 7(1): 41–50.

Walker, S. (2011). *The spirit of design: Objects, environment and meaning*. London: Earthscan.

Weinberg, G. M. (2001). *An introduction to general systemsthinking* (25th Anniversary edition). New York: Dorset House Publishing Company Inc.

Wenger, E. (1998). *Communities of practice: Learning, meaning, and identity.* Cambridge: Cambridge University Press.

Wever, R., van Kuijk, J., & Boks, C. (2008). User-centered design for sustainable behavior. *International Journal of Sustainable Engineering,* 1(1): 9–20.

Wever, R., & Vogtländer, J. (2015). Design for the value of sustainability. In J. van den Hoven, I. van de Poel, & P. Vermaas (Eds.), *Handbook of ethics, values and technological design* (pp. 513–549). Netherlands: Springer.

White, C., Stewart, E., Howes, T., & Adams, B. (2008). *Aligned for sustainable design: An A-B-C-D approach to making better products.* Business for Social Responsibility and Ideo. Retrieved from www.bsr.org/reports/BSR_Sustainable_Design_Report_0508.pdf

Whitely, N. (1993). *Design for society.* London: Reaktion Books Ltd.

Willard, B. (2002). *The sustainability advantage: Seven business case benefits of a triple bottom line.* Gabriola Island: New Society Publishers.

Williams, A. (2007). *Comparative study of cut roses for the British market produced in Kenya and the Netherlands* (Précis Report for World Flowers). Bedfordshire: Cranfield University.

Williamson, D., & Lynch-Wood, G. (2012). Ecological modernisation and the regulation of firms. *Environmental Politics,* 21: 941–959.

Winsemius, P. (1986). *Gast in eigen huis: Beschouwingen over milieumanagement.* Alphen aan den Rijn: Samsom H.D. Tjeenk Willink.

Working Group on Culture of United Cities and Local Governments (UCLG) (2006). *Working group on culture: Activities 2006.* Working Group on Culture 31 January 2006–Circular 1. Barcelona: UCLG.

World Economic Forum (2015, 16 September). *10 facts about the sustainable development goals.* Retrieved from www.weforum.org/agenda/2015/09/10-things-to-know-about-the-sustainable-development-goals/

Wurdinger, S. D. (2005). *Using experiential learning in the classroom.* Lanham: Scarecrow Education.

Yes Paper (n.d.). *Yes paper.* Retrieved from www.yes-paper.com/index.php?yespaper=yespaper-yes-light&ch_nav_eb2=yespaper-yes-light

Yin, R. K. (1994). *Case study research: Design and methods* (Applied Social Research Methods Series, Vol. 5., 2nd edition). Thousand Oaks: Sage.

Yong, L. (2013). Foreword. In *Sustaining employment growth: The role of manufacturing and structural change overview* (Industrial Development Report 2013). Vienna: UNIDO.

Yoon, E., & Tello, S. (2009). Drivers of sustainable innovation: Exploratory views and corporate strategies. *Seoul Journal of Business,* 15: 2.

Zils, M. (2014). *Moving toward a circular economy.* Retrieved from www.mckinsey.com/insights/manufacturing/moving_toward_a_circular_economy

Index